Branded!

WILEY & SAS BUSINESS SERIES

The Wiley & SAS Business Series presents books that help senior-level managers with their critical management decisions.

Titles in the Wiley & SAS Business Series include:

For more information on any of the above titles, please visit www.wiley.com.

Branded!

How Retailers Engage Consumers with Social Media and Mobility

Bernie Brennan
Lori Schafer

WILEY
John Wiley & Sons, Inc.

Published by John Wiley & Sons, Inc., Hoboken, New Jersey.

Published simultaneously in Canada.

For general information on our other products and services or for technical support, please contact our Customer Care Department within the United States at (800) 762-2974, outside the United States at (317) 572-3993 or fax (317) 572-4002.

Wiley also publishes its books in a variety of electronic formats. Some content that appears in print may not be available in electronic books. For more information about Wiley products, visit our web site at www.wiley.com.

Library of Congress Cataloging-in-Publication Data:

Brennan, Bernie.
    Branded! : how retailers engage consumers with social media and mobility / Bernie Brennan, Lori Schafer.
        p. cm. – (Wiley and SAS business series)
    Includes index.
        ISBN 978-0-470-76867-9 (hardback); ISBN 978-0-470-93173-8 (ebk); ISBN 978-0-470-93175-2 (ebk); ISBN 978-0-470-93176-9 (ebk)
1. Internet marketing. 2. Social media–Economic aspects. 3. Branding (Marketing) 4. Online social networks. 5. Telemarketing. I. Schafer, Lori. II. Title.
    HF5415.1265.B744 2010
    658.8'72–dc22

                                                                    2010029406

Printed in the United States of America
10 9 8 7 6 5 4 3 2 1

Contents

Chapter 7   Macy's: Shooting for the Stars! 119

Chapter 8   1-800-Flowers.com: "Build a Relationship First—Do Business Second" 147

Chapter 9   JCPenney: Digital Transformation 167

Chapter 10   Pizza Hut: Creating the Perfect Pizza—Digitally 189

Foreword

I first met Lori Schafer at the SAS Institute 2010 Executive Global Forum in Seattle, Washington, where I was presenting a session on social media. Talking with Lori briefly afterward, I knew right away that I wanted to contribute to this book: Business is my passion, and my vision for the next generation of consumers—my nine-year-old son and his peers in particular—is that their retail experiences be driven less by interruptive advertisements and more by the wealth of information available through shared, or *social*, media, delivered to them wherever they are.

When Lori introduced me to Bernie Brennan, I knew that this book was the real deal: Bernie's retail expertise speaks for itself. Together, the two have produced an insightful and practical book for retailers or anyone engaging with customers interested in social media and its application to their business. The retailer stories are well chosen and well researched: While you may have heard anecdotes related to some of them regarding their use of these new digital channels, the *detail* in these reviews and the analysis that accompanies them will provide you with a new level of understanding of how the combination of social media and mobility is driving brands like Starbucks, Zappos, Wet Seal, Macy's, 1-800-Flowers.com, JCPenney, Pizza Hut, and Best Buy. Best of all, you'll see how you can tap the knowledge that these brands have amassed around social media and mobility and adopt them in your own business.

Through social media, consumers are sharing their own stories and experiences: In technical terms, they are creating content to inform other consumers, competing for attention—and winning—

alongside your advertising programs. Consumers also are collaborating, working together to sort out the best products and services, the best deals, and the best places to buy. As a retailer, your antennae should be fully extended: The combination of social media and mobility truly represents a significant shift in how the retail experience plays out. *Branded!* will show you why—at a level of detail and with a sense of business maturity that translate directly into practices potentially beneficial to your own organization.

Branded! takes an in-depth, retailer-specific approach: Not only does the book tell you who is doing what, but it also tells you why and how, showing the early successes in this technology-driven media form. Learn how Starbucks is combining loyalty and payment without physical cards or cash. (Answer: Mobile.) Discover how Best Buy crowd-sources near-instantaneous answers to consumers' technology questions. (Answer: Twitter-based Twelpforce.) And, how Wet Seal is increasing its per-transaction, *in-store* sales. (Answer: Connecting with Facebook and selling outfits, rather than items.) Find out how Pizza Hut is discovering—ahead of its competitors—what its customers *really* want on their pizzas and then giving it to them. (Answer: Comprehensive social-analytics and a mobile-friendly, social-media program.) Learn, too, how Zappos has come out of nowhere to be one of the best-known online brands. (Answer: Customer delight and branding its culture through social media with one third of its employees on Twitter.)

Beyond these detailed retailer accounts, *Branded!* takes you into the new world of social-media and mobile-driven retail. A world where connected consumers are making decisions about the goods and services they buy for their families using the iPhone, Android, and similar next-generation smart phones with built-in GPS and bar code scanners. Forty years ago, Walmart founder Sam Walton said to his associates, "When you have a question, go to the store. The customer has the answer." Sam could not have been more prescient: Whether comparing competing brands of bottled water or fresh bread, today's savvy shopper can scan the product's UPC code and obtain—instantly and inside your store—the manufacturer's carbon footprint, investment practices, and a summary of its corporate responsibility efforts, along with ratings, reviews, and a map to a nearby competitor where the identical item is available for less. Having that information right in the palm of the consumer's hands changes her retail experience. In the process, it also changes yours, and at the heart of *Branded!* are best practices and analytical techniques you can apply—today—to put yourself back on an even footing with your customers.

You owe it to yourself, to your colleagues, and to your stakeholders to read this book. You'll be glad you did.

Dave Evans

Author of *Social Media Marketing: An Hour a Day* and the forthcoming *Social Media: The Next Generation of Business Engagement*, and

Co-founder, Digital Voodoo

Preface

As co-authors, we begin this preface first from our individual perspectives of how and why we partnered on writing this book. The powerful intersection of retail, social media, and mobility offers new and unique opportunities for retailers to engage with their customers. Our backgrounds in both retail and technology gave us the courage to embark upon this writing journey—a significant effort with a simple purpose. Our primary intent is to stimulate your mind on how to effectively use these new channels to better communicate with your customers as the retail industry moves even faster into the digital era.

Lori Schafer ...

In one form or another, I've spent the past 25 years of my career focusing on the intersection of retailing, consumers, and technology. At heart, I'll always be an entrepreneur who loves the retail and consumer-goods industries, and the strategic impact of innovative technology in continually reshaping their future.

I first met Bernie Brennan in 1999, when I was CEO of Marketmax, a retail software company. Bernie is a well-known retail executive with focus, deep knowledge, and experience. In our first meeting, I described my company and explained the value of its products. As a former retail CEO, he immediately grasped the business application, value, and financial metrics for everything I told him about the company and its software solutions. He knew retail; I knew technology. It seemed like a perfect match. Shortly thereafter, Bernie became an investor in the company, and he ultimately became managing director, working closely with me until the company was acquired by

SAS Institute in 2003. Our relationship was initially challenging, given our diverse backgrounds, styles, and personalities, but over the years we formed a deep mutual respect and ultimately a strong friendship based on our appreciation of the ways in which our two worlds of retail and technology intersect.

In 2008, I had the opportunity to hear Don Tapscott, author of *Wikinomics*, speak about how organizations can harness "mass collaboration" to spur innovation and success. He mentioned new terms such as "prosumers," "the Net Generation," "crowd sourcing," and the "wiki workplace." At the time, the concepts seemed foreign to me, but they made enough sense that I devoured *Wikinomics* over the following weekend and began taking a personal interest in learning these new principles. Social networks such as MySpace and Facebook were gaining momentum with Gen X and Gen Y consumers, but they were not being used widely by my middle-aged friends and business associates. Nevertheless, I was intrigued by this whole other cyberspace world and believed these new forms of communication somehow would change business forever. I found myself studying Web 2.0, Second Life, and a variety of social sites, and I began signing up for blogs and RSS feeds, both being new terms in my vocabulary.

I had my day job, a busy career, a busy life—none of it having to do with social media—but I found myself drawn to reading any article I could find on the topic. I also bought an iPhone and started familiarizing myself with apps. For the past several years, mobile shopping had had mixed reviews in retail. User interfaces weren't friendly and Internet access was painfully slow, but, with wider use of broadband and the introduction of the iPhone, that all changed. As had been the case with social media, I became excited about the potential of mobile applications for retailers and began learning as much as I could absorb. I began addressing the potential business applications of social media and mobility with retailers and industry colleagues, but at the time I received more perplexed looks than any validation that these worlds someday might connect.

As 2009 unfolded, I found myself ordering any business book published on social media or mobility and continuing to read every article I discovered. My home office had stacks of news printouts describing how retailers and consumer goods companies were using these new technologies. I began talking about these new channels with business colleagues over meals and sketching on napkins how the Internet, retail, social media, and mobility were going to converge in a way that would forever change the industry.

Over time, I had been talking off and on to Bernie Brennan about my strong interest in these areas. I figured that if Bernie believed these new channels of social media and mobility had significant implications for the retail industry—and better yet, if he'd be willing to partner with me in writing a book on the subject—then the idea had merit. For several months, we batted the idea back and forth, and by late 2009 we had educated ourselves to the point that we both were convinced of how strongly these new channels would affect retail. At that juncture, we decided to write the book.

Bernie Brennan ...

Lori and I met in the early dot-com era. I had spent a number of years in the retail industry, many of them as a CEO, and had become intrigued with retail technology and the role of the Internet. I had invested in an online startup that needed a merchandise-planning system, when the CEO of my company introduced me to Lori, who was CEO of Marketmax, a retail-merchandise analytics company. In her typical entrepreneurial style, she pursued my interest in becoming an investor in her company. Lori was always looking forward to the next technology on the horizon.

Although both of us had strong points of view, we succeeded in working collaboratively to build breakthrough merchandising technology for the retail industry. The business did very well, securing major retailers in both the United States and Europe. Marketmax eventually was sold to SAS Institute, and the acquisition was beneficial to both companies, forming the roots for the larger software company's entrée into retail software solutions. Having continued to invest in retail-related technology businesses, I was aware of new technological developments. In late 2008, Lori called me and described Don Tapscott's presentation. She sensed the validity of his comments and said that she wanted to learn more about this whole new way for people to engage digitally.

Recognizing that I needed to learn more about social media and mobility, I began to research the potential from a retailing viewpoint. The breakthrough for me came when I became a fan of retail Facebook sites and studied how various retailers were using this medium. Imagine my surprise when I subsequently saw my picture on the Wet Seal Facebook page. It occurred to me that although I did not fit its demographic, I was learning about all types of companies. At this point, I realized that some important customer-engagement opportunities that had not existed previously in the retail industry were now available. While retailers have always talked about better serving customers, here was a real opportunity to truly engage with them. I quickly realized that writing this book could help other executives in the retail industry focus on this opportunity. My one caveat was that the use of social media and mobility had to be a seamless extension of a retailer's strategy.

In late 2009, Mark Millstein of Retail Connections invited me to speak at his annual February conference. I suggested to him the possibility of my discussing—from a CEO's perspective—the value of social media and mobility to a retailer. I constructed a scoreboard, listing retailers and ratings that showed where they ranked, both qualitatively and quantitatively, in their use of these new channels. In every case, the leaders were strengthening their cultures and strategies, as well as leveraging their brand equity. The title of my speech, "Branding," supported this evaluation. Ultimately, "Branding" became the prototype for the title of this book.

* * *

By late 2009, social-media and mobile applications were beginning to emerge in retail, but still only among early adopters. We were somewhat concerned that we might be premature in writing a book about these topics: Was the retail industry really ready to learn about the potential impact of social media and mobility on shaping its future? We drew up an outline, and over the course of the next few months, we began doing even more extensive research. In early 2010, we began to solicit market feedback on the idea of writing the book. Retailers, including some early adopters, responded positively, but most were still trying to understand the possible value of these two new channels to their businesses. We also spoke with several executives from the National Retail Federation who believed the industry needed this kind of book to help retailers recognize early successes and understand the opportunities represented by these new channels of engagement.

Over the next couple of months, the news around social media and mobility suddenly began to accelerate. We had been reviewing several articles per week, but suddenly we were seeing dozens per day, and our outline quickly became obsolete. Throughout 2010, the rapid rate of change in both of these new channels had been unlike anything we'd ever seen. Because our subject represents an ever-moving, morphing, and accelerating target, writing this book has been extraordinarily challenging.

BRANDED! FROM IDEA TO INK

While there are now numerous "how-to" books on social-media marketing, none focus on retailers and the importance of first understanding their strategies and cultures and then discovering how to harness social media and mobility to strengthen their brand equity. We also emphasize the additional communication leverage these new channels provide for retailers. By including market-leading quick service restaurants, we confirmed how store-only retailers can become successful cross-channel retailers through customer engagement in social media and mobility.

Having researched our subject and interviewed numerous retailers, we selected those we felt have been most successful to date in executing social-media and mobility programs. We also wanted a cross-section representing different retail segments. Each chapter begins with an introduction, followed by a detailed overview of social-media and mobility retail applications. The thrust of the book is our interviews and the extensive research we conducted on eight diverse retailers that have led the way in applying these new communication channels to their businesses. A variety of illustrations is included to help convey key concepts. These chapters are followed by a brief discussion of the analytical software that has emerged to help monitor, analyze, and quantify the value of these new customer data. Our conclusion urges retailers to seize this unprecedented digital opportunity to engage with customers.

Because *Branded!* is all about engaging customers and consumers—and because we use the words "consumer" and "customer" throughout—we believe that it's important to explain the distinction between these two often-interchanged terms. Here is our view of the definitions and context in which we use these terms:

Customer. We define "customer" as a person who regularly patronizes a retail establishment, purchasing from and establishing a relationship with that retailer.

Consumer. We define "consumer" as one who purchases goods and services, but does not yet have a relationship with the retailer that we are reviewing. A consumer who is not buying from a particular retailer in an industry segment is a potential customer.

While we've had an energizing journey, writing *Branded!* has not been devoid of obstacles. Writing about a subject that is on a meteoric rise, changing daily and involving new terminology and enormous amounts of new information, proved challenging when it came to assembling the relevant information. This reality led us to write separate chapters defining social-media and mobility retail applications and then doing in-depth reviews of each of the retailers' strategies and uses of these new channels. Second, as co-authors, we come from differing points of view, and while we sometimes found it difficult to reach a consensus, we believe that our different perspectives ultimately have produced a better book.

Third, we chose to research and tell the stories of eight retail companies, none of which we are affiliated with, so we know we could never portray them as fully as could someone on the inside. Finally, we are businesspeople with deep convictions about our subject matter, but we are not professional writers. We both love our work in retail and retail technology, and we wrote this book believing that the ideas contained therein could help educate companies, better prepare them for the future, and ultimately improve the retail industry. The benefit to you, our readers, is that you know you are getting our combined perspectives unfiltered.

ACKNOWLEDGMENTS

While our names appear on the cover, we want to express our heart-felt appreciation to the individuals who made this book possible. We're grateful to all the retailers that shared with us their strategies, cultures, and digital journeys in the new worlds of social media and mobility. The leaders that we profiled and interviewed include Jim and Chris McCann of 1-800-Flowers.com; Seth Lasser, Vincent Raguseo, Kevin Ranford, and Yanique Woodall, also of 1-800-Flowers.com; Brian Dunn, Barry Judge, and John Thompson of Best Buy; Myron (Mike) Ullman and Mike Boylson of JCPenney; Terry Lundgren and Peter Sachse of Macy's; Chris Fuller, Armando Garza, and Brian Niccol of Pizza Hut; Howard Schultz, Chris Bruzzo, and Matthew Guiste of Starbucks; Ed Thomas and Jon Kubo of Wet Seal; David Novak of Yum! Brands; and Tony Hsieh and Aaron Magness of Zappos.

The individuals within each of these retail companies who orchestrated, organized, and quietly made things happen behind the scenes also deserve our gratitude; they include Kathy Gladkowsky of 1-800-Flowers.com; Gail Anderson, Wendy Franta, and Lisa Hawks of Best Buy; Kristin Hays and Michelle Miller of JCPenney; Sherrill Cresdee of Macy's; Laura Baker, Nancy Kent, Christina McPherson, and Heidi Peiper of Starbucks; Alyssa Montes of Wet Seal; and Virginia Ferguson and Ben Golden of Yum! Brands.

Key staff members in several trade organizations were also especially helpful in providing their time, knowledge, perspectives, and research. They include John Walls, David Diggs, Kate Kingberger, Athena Polydorou, Robert Roche and Jeff Simmons of CTIA—The Wireless Association® and Scott Silverman of National Retail Federation's Digital Division, Shop.org.

Our gratitude also goes to Dave Evans, author of *Social Media Marketing: An Hour a Day* and the forthcoming *Social Media: The Next Generation of Business Engagement*, and co-founder of Digital Voodoo. Dave wrote the Foreword to this book. Despite being in the midst of writing his second book and traveling internationally to consult with major corporations on social media, he was most gracious with his time.

Several individuals reviewed our manuscript. First, a special thanks to Karen Becker, who devoted many hours—often on weekends and at other odd times, with little notice and short deadlines—to proofreading, editing, and providing improvements to each of the chapters. Our sincere appreciation also goes to Laura Brumley, Sandy DeFelice, Stacey Hamilton, and Diana McHenry of SAS Institute, who volunteered their time to edit and improve countless drafts. Every one of their comments was helpful, and we've incorporated nearly all of them.

An added mention of thanks to Stacey Hamilton for her continual coaching and project management, which was much needed and appreciated. Kathy Council, Shelly Goodin, and Shelley Sessoms of SAS Publishing also deserve recognition for their persuasiveness in finally getting us to make the time to write this book. Mark Chaves and Dave Thomas of SAS were also gracious with their time in educating us about social-media analytics. Sheck Cho of John Wiley & Sons was always there with advice and a willingness to maneuver around our crazy schedules.

Finally, we want to thank our entire families for their patience and understanding and also highlight Tamie Brennan and Bob Schafer for their insights, support, and balance as we dedicated hundreds of hours over the past several months to making this book a reality.

Bernie Brennan
Lori Schafer
October 2010

CHAPTER **1**

Introduction:
Bringing Your
Store to
Your Customers

You need to go where your customers are spending their time. Instead of expecting your customers to come to your store, you must now bring your store directly to them. In today's world, consumers are technologically savvy and skeptical of mass marketing, and enjoy personalized treatment. Successful retailers not only must better understand customer preferences and differentiate their stores from those of their competition, but also must engage with customers where they already spend a lot of time: blogging, texting, friending, tweeting, and surfing.

We are living in one of the most exciting times in retailing history, thanks to continuous technology innovation, supported by the World Wide Web and open-source networks. Those retailers who embrace this breakthrough technology can gain market acceptance and potentially leap-frog longstanding incumbent competition. The transition from locked rooms and long-term plans to an open, transparent, fast-paced, and more creative world also is being embraced by leading businesses. Recognizing how critical these new technology-based channels are to their success, leading-edge retailers have adopted a

1

proactive culture, unleashing the untapped talent within their organizations and focusing on engaging with customers by using social media and mobility.

YOUR CUSTOMERS ARE SPEAKING. ARE YOU LISTENING?

Consumers today are more discerning and value-conscious than ever before. They blog about product reviews and customer service, instantly compare prices from mobile phones in store aisles, become fans of favorite brands on Facebook, show off purchases on YouTube, and provide accolades—or vent complaints—to friends and the masses on Twitter.

We view social media and mobility as revolutionary extensions of the current retail channels—stores, e-commerce, catalogs, and call centers. Although a number of retailers are successful marketers, they now face a new paradigm. For the first time, customers are in charge, and they use these new channels to continually communicate their views of a retailer's quality, products, and services. Retailers who seize this opportunity are now in a position to virtually listen to customers, engage with them, support their needs, and enjoy the benefits of extending their brand. Those who don't, will be left at the gate.

There are many promising ways a retailer can benefit from embracing social media and mobility: by improving brand awareness, listening to customer sentiments, creating incentives to drive cross-channel traffic and purchases, building content-focused communities to improve loyalty, enticing fans to try new products, understanding assortment preferences, and improving customer service. That said, these new digital channels alone will not solve all the problems of an underperforming business. Social-media and mobile channels significantly *amplify* a company's culture, strategy, and customer service. The emphasis here is on the word *amplify*! The retailer that excels as a brand has all the elements of its business—from merchandise assortment to service—integrated into its culture and strategy. Its opportunities magnified by social media and mobility, this retailer can further enhance its market position.

In many ways, these new digital channels level the playing field, allowing a retailer, regardless of size or segment, to bring its brand to millions of consumers and engage with them personally. Innovative retail concepts can now enable a company to rapidly gain market share in the digital world first—for far less money and in far less time than it would take to build stores. If retailers eventually choose to build stores, they'll have market acceptance from the day of their grand opening.

RETAIL 2.0

More than a decade ago, the dot-com phenomenon shocked everyone. Both digital evangelists and doubters made valid points. After much pain in the financial and investment markets and the inevitable burst bubble, the power of the Web is now rapidly unfolding, and individuals and groups are voicing their opinions and interacting digitally in a manner never before imagined.

The Web has become a powerful channel of information, communication, community, and commerce. Nearly 2 billion people access the World Wide Web, with 239 million users in the United States alone (making up 77.4% of the nation's population). The Web has opened up an entirely new world of communication, first for entrepreneurs and technologists, then for all businesses. By changing the landscape of how consumers interact with educators, government, retailers, information service providers, and all other consumer-oriented businesses, it has bred an entirely new opportunity for interaction and commerce.

Web retail commerce had its impetus from Web-only retailers. Amazon, the undisputed Web-only retail leader, played a significant role in proving the viability of e-commerce. The company started selling books online in 1994 and has grown to sales of almost $25 billion in 2009. Also in 2009, Amazon acquired Zappos, another highly successful Web-only retailer. At the same time, cross-channel retailers are gaining momentum, not only in ecommerce sales, but in utilizing a digital strategy to reach all consumer channels. 1-800-Flowers.com, Best Buy, JCPenney, and Macy's are among the market leaders in cross-channel retailing.

Now on the heels of the Web explosion comes enormous growth in social media and mobility. The increase in the use of these new consumer channels represents an unprecedented rate of change. Much like the diverse views of the Web in its early years, people hold conflicting views toward social media and mobility. Early adopters are leading the charge, while skeptics wonder if it's a passing fad. When we consider the massive growth in accessing these communication channels and leveraging the Web's success, retailers must recognize that they can either embrace this enormous opportunity or let it pass them by.

Consider the fact that the leading social-media Web sites have a compelling number of users. As of July 2010, Facebook had over 487 million[1] users, Twitter had over 105 million registered[2] users, YouTube served up over 32 billion videos/month in the United States alone,[3] and MySpace had over 119 million [4] users. Mobile phone users currently number 4.6 billion[5] worldwide, with 286 million[6] in the United States, and these figures are growing dramatically. The use of smart phones, which allow consumers to enjoy the benefits of the Web and social media in the palm of their hands, is growing even more dramatically, exceeding 180 million[7] users worldwide and nearly 50 million[8] users in the United States. Millions of smart phone users are now communicating, viewing, gathering, playing games, learning, and purchasing on their mobile devices.

Although most retailers were not early adopters of selling and marketing on the Web, they do not have that luxury when it comes to social media and mobility. These new communication channels are here to stay, and consumers have already staked their positions. For retailers, the present is a time to either leverage this opportunity or give up brand- and market-share growth. The upside of embracing social media and mobility is so compelling that once retailers unlock the mystery of these new communication channels to strategically engage customers, they almost certainly will succeed.

Now anyone can communicate and state his or her views on any available digital platform. The current public parity of information and opinion has never before existed; this paradigm resembles the introduction of the Web. In this case, however, the doubters will have far less time to catch up. Retailers and marketers must be aware that customers are talking about them, and in this mode of communication, they offer opinions on everything imaginable. Just ask United Airlines about the now famous YouTube video entitled "United Breaks

Guitars"[9] or talk to Continental Airlines about the "tarmac tweets" detailing their notorious Rochester, Minnesota, flight delay on August 7–8, 2009.[10] What is said about a brand is broadcast widely and memorialized forever in a tweet, a text message, or a blog post. We all know that even the best companies make mistakes. The key is that smart companies listen to their customers and interact with them in a caring, problem-solving manner that inspires loyalty.

At the same time, with our many combined years of experience in retail, technology, and direct marketing, we also understand that taking advantage of these massive market changes is not easy. Retailers need to carefully evaluate how these new channels best fit into their overall digital strategy. Both social media and mobility are effective vehicles for extending a company's culture and overall strategy. If these channels are viewed as extensions of the brand and as an integral part of the total business, they will be successful, and—more important—they will add to the success of a retailer's overall growth and market share.

RETAIL LEADERS

This book resulted from our extensive exploration and analysis of social media and mobility and their relationship to key elements of a retailer's business. We focused on elements that we believed needed to be in place for a company to succeed in using social media and mobility. These factors led us to develop the theme for the book: how a company's culture and strategy, communicated through the new channels of social media and mobility, leverage brand equity.

Our approach is relatively simple: to define social media and mobility, show their application to a retailer's business, and provide examples of successful retailers that are early adopters. We confirmed that a retailer's understanding and rate of adoption of social media and mobility do not necessarily follow a particular size or retail segment.

As part of the research process, we interviewed retail, e-commerce, technology, marketing, and trade organization executives, ultimately choosing to focus on a core group of eight retailers—of varying sizes and from different sectors—that embrace these new technologies. Specifically, we studied some of the most productive retailers, those that were taking a leading position in the lightning-fast, continually evolving worlds of social media and mobility.

Our research included a careful study of how individual retailers rank in numbers of fans and followers in various social-media networks versus the comparable numbers for their relevant competition. We also focused on the breadth and depth of their social-media penetration, as well as the importance of actual content. As we discovered, when it comes to social media, individual and community customer engagements can be more important than promotions and incentives. Both are important, but understanding objectives and achievements is absolutely crucial to the individual retailer's execution of a strategy.

The eight retailers that we selected have been highly successful in utilizing social media and/or mobility. Equally important, we recognize that success begins with a company's culture and strategy, so we focused on retailers that have these firmly in place and are reflecting them in their use of social media and mobility.

Starbucks

Starbucks has grown from a few stores in Seattle to the world's largest international coffee company with a rapidly emerging consumer-products division. Starbucks is not only about retail growth; it has attained its financial success by focusing on all elements of the business. The company is committed to product integrity, treating its partners (employees) and customers with respect, and meeting its social responsibilities to the neighborhoods it serves, as well as supporting worldwide needs. Although Starbucks was highly successful before many of the rapidly growing digital innovations emerged, it has seized the opportunity to create social engagement through technology: With more fans than any other brand on Facebook, Starbucks clearly utilizes social media and mobility very effectively.

Zappos

Zappos, one of the great successes of Internet retailing, grew to over $1 billion in gross merchandise sales before being acquired by Amazon, the world's Number-One Internet retailer. The company's success shows that opportunities exist for new retailers who can offer compelling reasons for customers to shop their stores. Today Zappos is the Number-One seller of shoes online, and it has added a number of apparel and accessory categories. Its passion for customer satisfaction and service is legendary, and it is extending its customer experience through leadership in social media. Zappos' culture is contagious: Its 500 tweeting employees have already amassed nearly 2 million followers. That's engagement!

Wet Seal

Wet Seal targets 13- to 19-year-old girls with trendy value-priced apparel and accessories. Known as a fast-fashion retailer, the company identifies and buys the newest trends, ships quickly to stores, limits quantities, then repeats the cycle. The business strategy focuses on a continuing flow of new merchandise at affordable prices. Wet Seal was well ahead of the curve in developing its digital "Fashion Community" before the explosive popularity of Smart Phones and social networks, but it has since added interfaces to both the iPhone and Facebook. The company's applications engage teens by allowing them to view, assemble, rate, and purchase peer-generated outfits. Using this valuable customer data in its design and buying decisions, Wet Seal has already announced the next generation of compelling social-media applications for use by its customers.

Macy's

The iconic Macy's brand now has a national platform but remains sensitive to the local focus of department stores. The company's key strategy, My Macy's, is all about tailoring merchandise specific to the local climate and customer demographics. Macy's has elevated its position in the digital world, with Macy's.com as the hub, facilitating customer interaction across all consumer channels, including a focus on social media and mobility. The company's ability to understand customers' preferences and requirements has positioned it to enjoy significant growth and brand equity. Macy's Inc. also owns Bloomingdale's, a luxury department store chain with an international fashion reputation; it, too, now interacts and engages digitally with its loyal customer base, in the same personal and caring manner that exists in-store.

1-800-Flowers.com

Flowers and gifts are all about relationships—and that is how the McCann brothers have built 1-800-Flowers.com. Starting with one flower shop, it is now the largest flower and gift retailer in the United States, with an unaided brand awareness of 90%. The strategic decisions that contributed to its significant growth all began with relationships. The culture that is based on working together to make the company better permeates the entire 1-800-Flowers.com team. The company has a comprehensive cross-channel platform with presence and growth opportunities in all retail channels: stores, Web, catalogs, and call centers. Because of its culture, structure, and technology base, 1-800-Flowers.com has growth opportunity in many businesses and channels.

JCPenney

As an American retailer for over a century, JCPenney is known for being reliable, having fashion-forward, good quality merchandise, and moderate prices. With close to $18 billion in sales, JCPenney has developed an innovative merchandise strategy focusing on private brands and brand exclusives. This is a major step for the company as it positions itself to become "America's shopping destination for discovering great styles at compelling prices."[11] JCPenney's addition of Sephora shops in more than 230 of its stores further supports its strategy, and the company's decision to close its "big book" catalog and redeploy investment in its digital platform provides the opportunity to fully leverage cross-channel retailing. With a CEO driving innovation and a significant focus on social media and mobility, JCPenney's digital transformation is well under way.

Pizza Hut

Pizza Hut was named a 2009 top-ten franchise by *Entrepreneur* magazine, a designation that attests to the company's focus on people: its employees, franchisees, and customers. The world's Number-One pizza chain, Pizza Hut began over 50 years ago, and it continues to seek new and innovative ways to connect with its customers. It competes not only in the pizza market, but also in the entire casual food market. A member of the Yum! Brands portfolio, Pizza Hut has a passion for "Customer Mania"; once we learned about its active "Tweetologist" and "Twintern" programs and had experienced the award-winning Pizza Hut "Killer App" on our iPhones, we were eager to learn more about the company. We found a number of ways in which Pizza Hut engages with its customers and delivers on its promise of quality food, attractive prices, and excellent customer service.

Best Buy

The leading consumer electronics retailer in the United States, Best Buy also is growing internationally. This $50 billion electronics specialty chain has built its business by being selective with the national brands it chooses to sell and by featuring the support of the "blue shirts," its enthusiastic and well-trained store teams. Best Buy's leadership position in cross-channel retailing is extraordinary; its strategic thrust is to make the BestBuy.com Web site the hub for all customer interaction. Seventy percent of Best Buy customers access the site to view items before going into the store for pickup or purchase. This strategy, focused on accessibility, localization, and personalization, is made possible by the company's digital leadership, including its early and effective customer engagement in social media and mobility.

YOUR WORLD IS CHANGING—ARE YOU?

Before we explore these innovative retailers and their use of social media and mobility, we will first provide an overview and discuss the significant impact of these new channels on the overall retail industry. With the communication benefits these channels provide, they also are producing mountains of data that must be mined to turn insights into action. And so we appropriately conclude the book with a chapter on the white-hot market for social-media analytics and how these tools allow retailers to listen, learn, react, and engage with their customers on their terms. Retail, as we know it, is about to become more personal, more local, and more transparent, and will change dramatically—forever. Let's begin our digital journey!

NOTES

1. www.checkfacebook.com/ (accessed July 21, 2010).
2. "Twitter Has 105 Million Registered Users," Mashable/Social Media, Adam Ostrow, April 2010, available at http://mashable.com/2010/04/14/twitter-registered-users/ (accessed June 21, 2010).
3. "What Is the Speed of Social Media?" Jeffbulla's Blog, April 15, 2010, available at http://jeffbullas.com/2010/04/15/what-is-the-speed-of-social-media/ (accessed June 16, 2010).
4. "MySpace Readies Site Overhaul to Rekindle Growth," Reuters, March 2010, available at www.reuters.com/article/idustre6290I220100310 (accessed June 16, 2010).
5. "UN: 4.6b Mobile Phone Subscriptions Worldwide," China Daily, February 15, 2010, available at www2.chinadaily.com.cn/world/2010/02/15/content_9470888.htm (accessed June 21, 2010).
6. "Wireless in the U.S.: A Snapshot," June 11, 2010, CTIA The Wireless Association®.
7. "Number of Smartphone Users to Quadruple Exceeding 1 Billion Worldwide by 2015," Connections™ Industry Insights Blog, March 23, 2010, available at http://connectionsconference.blogspot.com/2010/03/number-of-smartphone-users-to-quadruple.html (accessed June 21, 2010).
8. "Wireless in the U.S.: A Snapshot," June 11, 2010, CTIA—The Wireless Association.
9. "United Breaks Guitars," YouTube, www.youtube.com/watch?v=5YGc4zOqozo (accessed June 15, 2010).
10. Shannon Buggs, "Transportation Secretary Wants Answers on Tarmac Delay," Houston Chronicle (Chron Business), www.chron.com/disp/story.mpl/business/6567936.html, August, 11, 2009 (accessed June 15, 2010).
11. J.C.Penney Company, Inc. Summary Annual Report 2009, http://media.corporate-ir.net/media_files/irol/70/70528/2009IAR/2009IAR/images/JC_Penney-AR2009.pdf (accessed June 15, 2010).

CHAPTER **2**

Social Media

N ot a day goes by that a story about social media isn't headlined in traditional print media such as the *New York Times*, the *Wall Street Journal*, or *USA Today*. During the past 12 months, the growth of social media has been astounding, with Facebook, YouTube, Twitter, and other social sites continuing to gather new users at triple-digit rates. New applications and new uses continue to emerge, for example, Google Buzz and location-based social gaming sites such as Foursquare, Brightkite, and Gowalla. Consider that in 2003, none of these social-media sites even existed and today Facebook has far more users than the entire population of the United States. At the same time, hardware continues to rapidly improve, making it faster and easier for users to view information anytime, anywhere, using devices such as GPS-based smart phones and the Apple iPad. In a matter of a few short years, the speed of change will devastate, invigorate, and create industries that we never before could have imagined.

The speed of change and growth in social media and its transformation of the Web have and will continue to revolutionize marketing, shopping, socializing, publishing, gaming, and music. Let's take a look at a few recent statistics:

- Forty-eight percent of Americans currently have personal profile pages on Facebook, MySpace, LinkedIn, or other social-networking Web sites, and this figure has doubled since 2008.[1]

- As of July 2010, Facebook had more than 487 million users and is expected to surpass 500 million users in a matter of months. If Facebook were a country, it would be the third largest in the world.[2]

- With 125.5 million users in the United States alone, over 40% of the U.S. population has Facebook pages. Facebook gained more than 4.4 million active users in April 2010 and accelerated on that in May 2010 with 7.8 million new users to reach 125 million.[3]

- Since the summer of 2009, Twitter has been growing at a rate of more than 1000%, with similar growth in the previous year.[4]

- Twitter's more than 105 million users create more than 50 million tweets a day.[5]

- MySpace serves more than 119 million members, with 57 million in the United States alone.[6]

- LinkedIn boasts more than 60 million users.[7]

- YouTube now carries more than 32.4 billion videos per month from the United States alone.[8]

- The number of blogs is estimated to be more than 200 million.[9]

Social-media usage over the past couple of years has grown at a frenzied pace, proliferating so fast that it's nearly impossible to keep statistics current. In fact, we recognize that by the time this book is published, many of the statistics cited will be obsolete. But rather than focus on absolute statistics, we describe the general trends and major aspects of social media that retailers should evaluate when building their communication strategies.

When we first decided to write this book in the fall of 2009, many retailers wondered whether the social-media phenomenon was just a passing fad and therefore were questioning the necessity of becoming involved with it. At the time, although a few retailers had a Facebook or YouTube presence, social-media initiatives were delegated to an outside media agency or an internal marketing department. Retailers hadn't yet realized how powerful these tools are in engaging with customers. Over the past year, however, social media has gone mainstream, and its longevity and viability are now widely understood.

DEFINITIONS

Since this book focuses on retailers' use of social media and mobility, we first define our use of the terms "social media," "Web 2.0," and "social network."

Web 2.0 is appropriately named because it represents the second generation of the World Wide Web, where content is user-generated, interactive, and dynamic. According to Dictionary.com, Web 2.0 is "the second generation of the World Wide Web in which content is user-generated and dynamic."[10] Examples include social-networking sites like Facebook, Twitter and other Web-based communities, hosted services like Google Docs, Web applications like Gmail, video-sharing sites (YouTube), wikis (Wikipedia), blogs, and mashups.

Social media is electronic media for social interaction. It makes use of Web 2.0 highly scalable and accessible publishing techniques to transform and broadcast media monologues into social-media dialogues.[11] Social media supports the democratization of knowledge and information and allows general users to go from being content consumers to content producers. Examples of public social-media Web sites include Facebook, Twitter, MySpace, Flickr, Foursquare, LinkedIn, YouTube, Yelp, Digg, Second Life, Tumblr, and Stylehive, among many others. Social media also includes message boards, online discussion forums, and private or "white label" social-media sites such as homegrown sites and those produced by companies like Yammer, often used by companies for internal behind-the-firewall social communication.

According to Dictionary.com, a computer-based **social network** is "a website where one connects with those sharing personal or professional interests, place of origin, education at a particular school, etc. The sites typically allow users to create a 'profile' describing themselves and to exchange public or private messages and list other users or groups they are connected to in some way."[12] A social network is not necessarily computer-based, although more often than not, when people refer to social networking, they mean social-networking sites on the Internet, where people interact.

While the terms "social media" and "social network" often are used interchangeably, one can argue that social-networking Web sites are a subset of social media. In other words, not all forms of social media are social networks. Social-media Web sites that are also social networks are those with the primary purpose of connecting people with common interests, such as Facebook, LinkedIn, MySpace, and Twitter.

Even YouTube, which began as a video-sharing site, incorporates aspects of social networking, since it offers users a personal profile page—which YouTube calls a "channel page"—and enables "friending." Flickr, a photo-sharing site, also is considered a social network as it enables communities to form around a topic. However, wikis, blogs, and social-bookmarking sites are considered social media, but not social networks. Throughout this book, we will refer to all social networks as "social media."

WHY MAKE SOCIAL MEDIA ANOTHER RETAIL CHANNEL?

So why should retail executives embrace social media as a critical new communications channel? "Retailers who aren't engaging customers through social media could be missing the boat," says Mike Gatti, executive director for the Retail Advertising and Marketing Association (RAMA), National Retail Federations Marketing Division.[13] Discussing a recent study about the propensity of social-media usage among U.S. "moms," Gatti continues, "Twitter, Facebook, and blogs are becoming increasingly popular with moms as they search for coupons or deals and keep in touch with loved ones. The Web provides efficient, convenient ways for brands to stay in front of their most loyal shoppers and [to] attract new ones." The popular comment, "People are talking about your brands every day [on social media], so you need to listen and become part of that conversation," certainly has received plenty of airtime in the past year.

Consider the following statistics:

■ According to a recent study conducted by ForeSee Results, "The Key to Driving Retail Success with Social Media: Focus on Facebook," of all online shoppers, 56% use Facebook and 22% use YouTube regularly. Of these online shoppers who use social media regularly, 81% use Facebook and 31% use YouTube (see Exhibit 2.1). Equally important, 82% of respondents interact with 1–10 retailers or brands (see Exhibit 2.2). These numbers

Exhibit 2.1 ForeSee Study: Number of Online Shoppers Using Popular Social-Media Sites

All Online Shoppers		Shoppers Who Use Social Sites	
Which of the following websites do you use regularly? (Please select all that apply.)		Which of the following websites do you use regularly? (Please select all that apply.)	
Social Site	% Using Each Site	Social Site	% Using Each Site
Facebook	56%	Facebook	81%
I don't use social sites	31%	YouTube	31%
YouTube	22%	MySpace	22%
MySpace	15%	Twitter	16%
Twitter	11%	Linkedin	12%
Linkedin	8%	Flickr	7%
Flickr	5%	Other social website (please specify):	3%
Other social websites (please specify):	2%	Yelp	2%
Yelp	2%		

Source: "The Key to Driving Retail Success with Social Media: Focus on Facebook," ForeSee Results, Kevin Ertell, February 9, 2010, available at https://community.atg.com/.../ForeSeeResults_Retail%20Success_Social%20MediaUS_2010.pdf (accessed June 16, 2010).

Exhibit 2.2 ForeSee Study: Number of Retailers or Brands with Which Social-Media Users Interact

If you do use social media sites, approximately how many retailers or brands do you interact with (follow/friend/fan of)?	
	% of respondents
1 to 5	61%
6 to 10	21%
11 to 20	10%
More than 20	8%

Source: "The Key to Driving Retail Success with Social Media: Focus on Facebook," ForeSee Results, Kevin Ertell, February 9, 2010, available at https:// community.atg.com/.../ForeSeeResults_Retail%20Success_Social%20 MediaUS_2010.pdf (accessed June 16, 2010).

strongly attest to both customer loyalty and interest in social engagement with retailers. Shoppers are *choosing* to proactively engage in relationships with retailers on social sites.[14]

■ Customers interact with retailers on social-media sites primarily to learn about products and promotions.[15]

■ Nearly one fifth of social-media users interact with 11 or more retailers (see Exhibit 2.2).[16]

■ Those who interact with a retailer on a social-media site are more satisfied, more committed to the brand, and more likely to make future purchases from that company than those who don't. Research shows that when retailers provide rewarding social-media experiences, customers become even more satisfied and loyal.[17]

Consumers want to connect with retailers via social media to learn about company information, products, and promotions. According to the June 9, 2010, article in *eMarketer*, "Coupons Drive Sales on Social Media," "the brands that have enjoyed the most success using social media to drive consumers toward purchases follow one of two paths: Either they offer coupons or discounts, or they position themselves in front of consumers during sales or other special events."[18] While consumers are always interested in discounts and special events, there is a danger to the retailer in overusing social media as a traditional promotional vehicle. Social media should first be used to build relationships which require a balance of relevant information about its company, brand and culture.

In addition to recognizing the positive momentum social media can provide, retailers also need to be listening defensively to ensure that they are aware of potentially damaging chatter while they can still do something about it.

DEMOGRAPHICS—NOT JUST KIDS!

While a larger percentage of younger people use social media, its use is growing most rapidly among older age groups. According to the recent Edison Research/Arbitron study "Twitter Usage In America: 2010," the percentage of U.S. consumers who have a profile page on at least one social-network site ranges from 13% for the 65-and-over age group, to 78% for those ages 12 to17.[19] Over half of U.S. consumers ages 35 to 44 and over one-third of the age group 45 to 54 have a profile page on at least one social-network site. Even more impressive is the rate of year-over-year growth in social-media usage in all age categories, with double-digit growth rates for people ages 12 to 54 and triple-digit growth rates for those over age 55 (see Exhibit 2.3).

For a retailer, the opportunity to directly engage with its customers and leverage its brand's message is amplified by the size, growth rate, and level of engagement of the global social-media audience. Users of social networks are highly active, with 50% of them accessing these sites at least once per day and 82% accessing them at least once per week (see Exhibit 2.4).

POPULAR SOCIAL-MEDIA WEB SITES

Retailers are beginning to use a variety of social media, embedding on their Web sites such Web 2.0 tools as customer ratings, reviews, and blogs, and they are developing a brand presence on some of the most popular Web sites, such as Facebook, Twitter, YouTube, Flickr, and

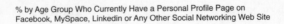

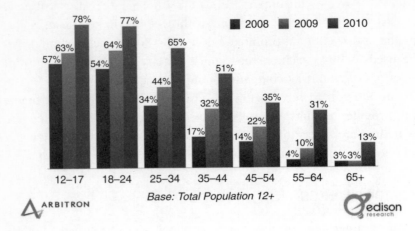

Exhibit 2.3 Year-over-Year Social-Media Growth
Source: "Twitter Usage In America: 2010," The Edison Research/Arbitron Internet and
Multimedia Study, Tom Webster—Vice President, Strategy and Marketing, Edison
Research, available at www.google.com/search?hl=en&rlz=1R2_____en&q
=twitter+usage+in+america+2010&aq=0&aqi=g2&aql=&oq=twitter+usage+in+ameri&gs_
rfai=&emsg=NCSR&ei=6b8aTJ-XlZOQ8gSx4aCGCQ (accessed June 16, 2010).

Foursquare. They are even building their own social networks where
appropriate. Each of these social-media sites has a different following
and a different means of communication. Facebook, for example, is
well suited to bringing the store to the customer. The ability of retailers
to set up their own pages, with multiple "tabs" from which they can
interact with consumers, provides the deepest functionality and allows
the deepest level of engagement. Twitter is well suited for providing
customer service, building a following around a culture, and tweeting
about special events. YouTube provides a venue for sharing videos and
bringing to life a company's culture, community outreach programs,
training and other "how-to" videos, promotions, and commercials.

Not all social-media sites are appropriate for all retailers. Although
we can't possibly discuss every social-media Web site, the following
section provides a brief overview of the most popular ones used by
retailers for consumer engagement.

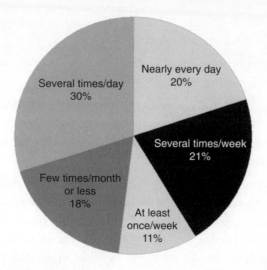

Exhibit 2.4 All Social-Network Users
Source: "Twitter Usage In America: 2010," The Edison Research/Arbitron Internet and Multimedia Study, Tom Webster—Vice President, Strategy and Marketing, Edison Research, available at www.google.com/search?hl=en&rlz=1R2____en&q=twitter+usage+in+america+2010&aq=0&aqi=g2&aql=&oq=twitter+usage+in+ameri&gs_rfai=&emsg=NCSR&ei=6b8aTJ-XIZOQ8gSx4aCGCQ (accessed June 16, 2010).

Facebook

Engaging in social media is not just about having a Facebook (www.facebook.com) page. But, for a retailer just getting started using social media, and with 40% of the U.S. population already on Facebook, it is often a good place to begin.[20] At present, Facebook is the largest and most influential social network and allows demographic data to be easily segmented for targeted research and promotions. As a result, retailers who want to engage with consumers have a big reach on Facebook. A few relevant statistics about Facebook:

- More than 250,000 external Web sites have integrated with Facebook, and more than 100 million users engage with Facebook on external Web sites every month.[21]
- More than 100 million active users currently access Facebook through their mobile devices.[22]

- Since the beginning of 2009, the number of advertisers on Facebook has quadrupled.[23]

- According to Google, Facebook is "the World's Most Popular Site," surpassing Yahoo.[24]

- The ForeSee study previously referenced concluded that more than half of the consumers who shop online use Facebook, and of those online shoppers who engage in social media, more than 80% use Facebook.[25]

- According to the RAMA survey previously mentioned, seven out of ten social-media users between the ages of 18 and 34 regularly use Facebook more than other similar sites such as MySpace, Twitter, and Classmates. Facebook remains the favorite social-media site for those 18 to 34 years old, 35 to 54, and even 55 and older.[26]

- Facebook is used regularly by 70.6% of female social-media users, as compared with 61% of males.[27]

- Sixty-one percent of Facebook users are age 26 and older.[28]

Facebook is not just for Gen X and Gen Y. Usage by older age groups is rapidly accelerating. A detailed age breakdown of the 125.5 million U.S. Facebook users is shown in Exhibit 2.5.

Since the summer of 2009, we have seen a surge in the number of retailers with Facebook pages; a year ago, retailers' use of the site was experimental. Although the majority of retailers are still using Facebook for communicating promotions, the more effective use—as all of our retail examples in future chapters indicate—is to build loyal relationships with "fans" by engaging them on a variety of topics that leverage a retailer's strategy and exude its culture. This strategy also enables retailers to attract more fans and therefore potentially more customers. In regard to its base of Facebook followers, Starbucks far surpasses any other retailer and any other consumer brand. (A look at how Starbucks has engaged consumers is detailed in Chapter 4.)

While it is the most popular social-media site, retailers are still only beginning to use Facebook. As of June 2010, 699 worldwide retailers had registered Facebook pages, although only 212 of them

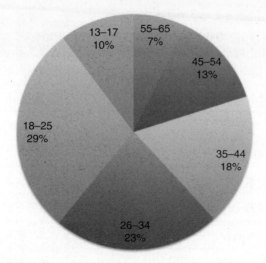

Exhibit 2.5 U.S. Facebook Users by Age
Source: www.insidefacebook.com, 6/1/2010, www.insidefacebook.com/2010/01/04/december-data-on-facebook%E2%80%99s-us-growth-by-age-and-gender-beyond-100-million/.

had more than 10,000 fans. Internet Retailer's *Top 500 Guide* (Internet 500) mentions that of the Top 500 Internet retailers (in terms of sales volume), 371 have Facebook pages in 2010 as compared with 284 in 2009.[29] The top retail Facebook sites (in terms of number of fans) are shown in Exhibit 2.6.

Social Web sites have become amplifiers for businesses, and Facebook is an especially effective one. The interconnectivity of its members, along with their ability to voice their opinions and share product/brand preferences and purchasing decisions, provides retailers with an important opportunity to connect with their customers.

Twitter

Twitter (www.twitter.com) is another social-media Web site among brands. Providing users with an opportunity to engage in "microblogging," Twitter is considered the most transparent of the social networks. It enables its users to send and read messages known as

Exhibit 2.6 Top Retailers on Facebook: June 2010

Name	Fans
Starbucks	12,074,884
Kohl's	1,781,443
Target	1,584,617
Walmart	1,568,859
Best Buy	1,183,918
JCPenney	925,560
Hot Topic	877,858
7-ELEVEN	635,116
Toys "R" Us	628,688
Levi's	527,523
Macy's	496,700

Source: InsideFacebook. Insidefacebook.com, Top Pages for Retailers (accessed August 9, 2010). Note: Fashion brands and retailers are categorized separately and not included in this list.

tweets, which are text-based posts of up to 140 characters, displayed on the author's profile page and delivered to the author's subscribers, known as "followers." The idea is that users build a following around their particular subjects of interest. While an option exists to protect who can follow you, most users do not use this functionality, and transparency is expected. Somewhat like the old-fashioned chain letter, Tweets can be "retweeted" by followers, except that with Twitter, a message can go out to millions of users in a matter of minutes.

With more than 105 million registered users worldwide[30]—17 million in the United States alone—Twitter has a much smaller reach than Facebook, but retailers can leverage it to build strong customer loyalty. Twitter also has a different demographic profile and is used differently than Facebook, so retailers first need to understand whether

Twitter fits their strategy by listening before engaging. Although some retailers use Twitter to communicate promotions, such campaigns have to be done carefully, because the user base customarily frowns on the use of the network to overtly sell something. Twitter is an excellent channel for providing customer service and for covering live events, as well as for communicating a culture. Some retailers, such as Best Buy, Starbucks, and Zappos (see Chapters 11, 4, and 5, respectively), have excelled at building customer loyalty through Twitter.

The Edison/Arbitron study mentioned previously provides some relevant statistics:[31]

- Awareness of Twitter has exploded recently with the percentage of Americans who are familiar with Twitter surging from 5% in 2008 to 87% in 2010.

- Twitter is a natural "companion medium" to other media channels—in particular, to live TV.

- Although Americans are equally aware of Twitter and Facebook, Twitter trails Facebook significantly in usage: Only 7% of Americans (17 million persons) actively use Twitter; however, growth rates of Twitter exceed 1000%. In 2009, 2% of Americans used Twitter and in 2008, the percentage was far less than 1%.

- Twitter demographics are skewed toward well-educated, higher income households whose members are "very frequent" short message service (SMS) users and who access the Internet from multiple locations. (SMS allows "short" text communication of up to 160 characters across mobile phones.)

- Nearly two-thirds of active Twitter users access social-networking sites using a mobile phone.

- Twitter users split between habitual "Tweeters" and those who access occasionally. The majority of Twitter users are "lurkers," passively following and reading the updates of others without contributing updates of their own, but they are listening, reading, and clicking.

- As compared with social networkers in general, Twitter users are far more likely to follow brands and companies, and

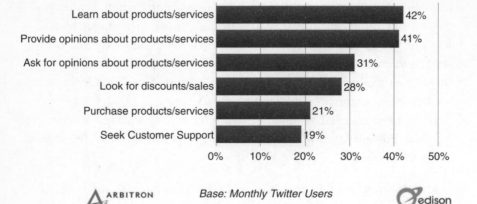

% Using Twitter to...

Learn about products/services	42%
Provide opinions about products/services	41%
Ask for opinions about products/services	31%
Look for discounts/sales	28%
Purchase products/services	21%
Seek Customer Support	19%

ARBITRON   *Base: Monthly Twitter Users*   edison research

Copyright 2010, Edison Research/Arbitron Inc.

Exhibit 2.7 Twitter Users Frequently Exchange Information About Products and Services
Source: "Twitter Usage In America: 2010," The Edison Research/Arbitron Internet and Multimedia Study, Tom Webster—Vice President, Strategy and Marketing, Edison Research, available at www.google.com/search?hl=en&rlz=1R2____en&q=twitter+ usage+in+america+2010&aq=0&aqi=g2&aql=&oq=twitter+usage+in+ameri&gs_ rfai=&emsg=NCSR&ei=6b8aTJ-XlZOQ8gSx4aCGCQ (accessed June 16, 2010).

frequently exchange information about products and services (see Exhibit 2.7).

■ Of active Twitter users, 51% follow companies, brands, or products on social networks and frequently exchange information about those products.

■ Twitter appears to be functioning as more of a broadcast medium compared with Facebook and many other social-networking sites and services.

■ Marketing and business uses for Twitter far exceed similar usage for social-networking Web sites in general.

With 71% of Twitter users in the United States older than 25 years of age, Twitter has shifted from being a tool used mainly by youth to one used predominantly by older age groups, which makes it a strong channel for brands to use in communicating with consumers of all age groups. Exhibit 2.8 shows the breakdown of Twitter users by age group.

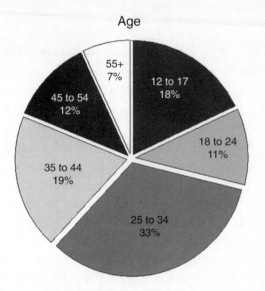

Age

Exhibit 2.8 Twitter Usage by Age Group. U.S. Statistics
Source: "Twitter Usage In America: 2010," The Edison Research/Arbitron Internet and
Multimedia Study, Tom Webster—Vice President, Strategy and Marketing, Edison
Research, available at www.google.com/search?hl=en&rlz=1R2_____en&q
=twitter+usage+in+america+2010&aq=0&aqi=g2&aql=&oq=twitter+usage+in+ameri&gs_
rfai=&emsg=NCSR&ei=6b8aTJ-XlZOQ8gSx4aCGCQ (accessed June 16, 2010).

Twitter does not publish specific data about the number of its
users. Per the *Internet Retailer*, of the top 500 Internet retailers in 2010,
254 have a Twitter account as compared with 102 retailers in 2009.[32]
One December 2009 study by *Retail eCommerce* showed that of the top
100 retailers with an e-commerce presence, 92 are on Twitter, but a
large number of them are not yet very active. Surprisingly, many
major retail chains still have only a few thousand followers, and
many more are not yet using Twitter. Companies like Zappos (whose
CEO alone has 1.72 million followers and who also has 500 employees
tweeting for the company), Whole Foods (with 1.79 million), and
Starbucks (with just under one million) have the most followers
and also have been successful in messaging their culture and building
their brand on Twitter. Some of these companies have multiple
accounts—one for the main brand, one for customer service, and often
several for employees who tweet on behalf of the company. Best Buy
also has been highly successful with its Twitter-based Twelpforce
online help desk.

MySpace

While it was once the leader in Internet social networking, since 2008 MySpace (www.myspace.com) has been diminishing in popularity and growth. In March 2010 Reuters reported that "MySpace had 119.6 million unique visitors worldwide in January 2010, down 7.4% year-over-year (though up from its November low of 108.1 million), according to comScore."[33] Although these are still impressive numbers, growth clearly is decelerating. Whereas Facebook's and Twitter's demographics have shifted to an older age group over the past couple of years, the MySpace demographic has gotten younger and the site now focuses on music and entertainment. "MySpace saw its user composition shift toward younger audience segments in 2009, with people age 24 and younger now comprising 44.4% of the site's audience, up more than 7 percentage points from the previous year. Facebook's audience, by contrast, was evenly split between those younger and [those] older than 35 years of age."[34]

Retailers with brands targeted at the MySpace demographic should consider participating. The 2010 Internet 500 shows 146 of the top 500 Internet retailers as having a MySpace page as compared with 143 retailers in 2009.[35] Because of the narrow focus of its demographics and overall declining growth, this book does not specifically cover retailer usage of MySpace .

Social Gaming

We could not describe Facebook or MySpace adequately without briefly mentioning the social-gaming phenomenon. While each of these games has a different theme, the strategies are similar. Users take on an identity, perform various tasks to collect points, and compete against other users in cyberspace. After accruing a certain number of points, a user is "leveled up" to a higher status, where he or she can accumulate points faster. Most important, using Facebook as an example, the games give "bragging rights" to the user by automatically informing his or her friends of each new achievement.

Social gaming is one of the most popular activities on Facebook and MySpace, where games such as FarmVille, Birthday Cards, Texas

HoldEm Poker, Café World, Treasure Isle, Mafia Wars, and Petville each boast more than 20 million players per month.[36] With more than 82 million monthly active users, equating to just over 1% of the world's population, FarmVille is by far the most popular.[37] Although one could assume that most social gamers are Gen Y youth, in actuality the average age of female Facebook casual gamers is 48. In fact, 46% of all casual gamers in the United States are over the age of 50.[38]

On the surface, these games may not seem to apply to retailers' businesses, but in fact they can represent a branding opportunity. In most games, if users want to increase their number of points, in addition to earning them the old-fashioned way, they have the option of purchasing more points for cash, as well as through surveys or purchases from a real-world brand. Retailers can advertise on the gaming sites; in fact, gaming companies such as Zynga, the maker of FarmVille, Mafia Wars, and YoVille, are highly lucrative businesses. According to a March 2010 *TechCrunch* article entitled "Zynga Rolls Out Pre-Paid Game Cards At Major Retailers," Zynga is now selling prepaid game cards at several major U.S. retailers, "including 7-Eleven, Best Buy, GameStop, and Target. Gift certificates to spend money on Zynga games, FarmVille, Mafia Wars, and YoVille, will be sold at more than 12,800 stores."[39]

Future retail applications pertinent to these social games could soon become a way of building customer loyalty. Why not tie real-world incentives to fantasy gaming? Wet Seal, a fast-fashion apparel retailer, has figured out how to apply social gaming to its business in a unique and innovative way—by dressing the game's avatar in Wet Seal fashions and tying real-world store visits and purchases to points and performance in the make-believe world.

YouTube

YouTube (www.youtube.com) is a video-sharing Web site on which users can upload, share, and view videos. YouTube was created in February 2005 and sold to Google in November 2006 for $1.65 billion. Users—either an individual or a company—can create a YouTube "channel" that functions like a home page on a Web site. Other users can subscribe to the channel and receive updates. The channel shows the account name, account type, public videos uploaded, and any user information that has been entered. YouTube channels also display favorite videos from other users, as well as activity streams, comments, number of subscribers, and other social-networking features.

Of the top 500 Internet retailers in 2010, 269 had official YouTube channels as compared with 207 in 2009.[40] Searching on a retailer such as Macy's will yield tens of thousands of videos, many of which are not part of the Macy's channel, which means they were posted by other users, not by the department store chain. It is beneficial for a retailer to create and maintain a YouTube channel if it has a series of videos that help define its culture, strategy, brand, and products for consumers. Retailers discussed in this book (e.g., Starbucks, Best Buy, Macy's, JCPenney, and Zappos) all have impressive YouTube channels. Videos from the official channel give the consumer a feel for both the brand and the culture.

Flickr

Flickr (www.flickr.com) is a popular Web site on which consumers can share personal photographs, and bloggers can host images that they embed in blogs and social media. As of October 2009, Flickr claimed "to host more than 4 billion images."[41]

Photos are another good way to depict a company's brand and its culture. Regardless of whether a retailer sponsors its own group on Flickr, it ought to "listen" to what is being said about its brands—and see what photos are being posted—because Flickr is growing in popularity. While Flickr is not yet commonplace among retailers, several of the companies we studied do sponsor groups on the site, have amassed quite a following, and thus have enabled group members to share photos about the brand. Starbucks, for example, has sponsored its own group and provides a moderator for the group's discussion threads.

Google Buzz

Google Buzz (buzz.google.com), or simply Buzz, launched in February 2010, is a social-media tool from Google, which integrates into Google's

Gmail email program. Users can share—either publicly or privately with a group of friends—links, photos, videos, messages, and comments organized in "conversations" and visible in the user's Gmail inbox. Buzz is viewed by industry analysts as Google's competitive product to social-networking Web sites like Facebook and Twitter.

It is too early to tell whether Google Buzz will have a significant impact on retail brands. Given the size and popularity of Google and Gmail, however, Buzz deserves mention here—even though we have not yet encountered any retailers making serious use of Google Buzz in their communication efforts.

Private Social Media

Private social-media sites are those that are owned specifically by a brand for a specific purpose. Unlike public sites like Facebook and Twitter, private social sites can be tailored by the retailer for specific purposes. More compelling and personalized content can be offered, benefiting the consumer. Furthermore, the retailer owns and controls the key asset: the valuable consumer data contained within. These private social networks can be developed by the retailer or by one of several companies that specialize in developing private social networks.

These private social sites are typically accessible from retailers' Web sites. Two companies explored in this book, Starbucks and Wet Seal, have built highly successful private social networks. To engage customers in feedback about its products and services, Starbucks created "My Starbucks Idea," and Wet Seal did the same with its popular Fashion Community. Both Starbucks and Wet Seal have established strong followings on private social sites that are tailored to their specific businesses. Standard devices such as Facebook Connect, Twitter API, and OpenSocial can connect the data from these networks with more public social-media sites when appropriate.

Blogs

A blog (short for "Web log") is a type of Web site or Web page on which individuals called "bloggers" provide a stream of remarks or observations about a particular topic. Blogs often combine text, images, videos, and links to other media related to their topics and reflect the personality of their authors. Typically blogs also allow readers to leave comments in an interactive format.

Retailers are using blogs to engage consumers in several ways:

- Creating their own blogs to educate consumers about their brand(s), strategy, and culture. Companies like Zappos, Best Buy, and 1-800-Flowers.com have all added company-sponsored blogs to their social-media communication channels.

- Tapping into the comments of other bloggers who can help promote and spread the word about their company's brand. For example, the so-called mommy bloggers write blogs about homemaking, family, and parenting. Some of these bloggers have large followings and a lot of influence. Retailers of household items and children's merchandise would benefit from associating with these types of bloggers. Companies like 1-800-Flowers.com, JCPenney, and Macy's have figured out how to tap into this network and engage the bloggers in new item introductions and large promotional events so that the bloggers themselves are spreading the word.

Location-Based Social Media

Location-based social media, where users share their locations through GPS, mobile email, or text, most likely will become the next generation of usage. As smart phones proliferate, these sites will gain momentum. A user can add comments about a restaurant or retail outlets he is visiting, or just find out if anyone she knows happens to be nearby and wants to meet for a cup of coffee.

Examples of increasingly popular location-based social-media sites that retailers should understand include Foursquare, Gowalla, Loopt, Brightkite, Citysense, iPling, GyPSii, Plazes, and Whrrl. Recently Facebook also has added a location-based capability. Most of these sites combine aspects of social media, social gaming, and mobility. They allow users to earn points for "checking in" at a certain location and to receive status "badges" after accomplishing certain goals like visiting a location multiple times. Foursquare, for example, awards a "mayor" badge to the player who frequents a particular location most often. Since each location can have only one mayor, the idea is to become mayor of multiple locations.

Retailers are beginning to take advantage of these sites by offering promotions and other incentives to people who visit their establishments and play these location-based social games and who visit their establishments. These applications have the potential to build strong loyalty for a particular retail outlet. To date, restaurants and local retailers appear to be more active in promoting themselves on these sites; however, some national chains also are beginning to test the concept. For example, Starbucks is exploring this possibility with developers such as Foursquare and Brightkite.

WHERE TO FOCUS

Literally hundreds of popular social-media sites already exist, and more are popping up every month. At this early stage, it is impossible to predict which of these sites ultimately will have staying power. For now, it's probably safe to say that at a minimum, retailers should consider a presence on the most popular sites, which most observers now identify as Facebook, Twitter, and YouTube.

In the following chapters, we examine eight retailers that have developed successful social-media channels by using a combination of the tactics outlined above. Although not meant to be a comprehensive list of successful retailers, these companies represent retailers from different sectors and use social media in a variety of ways. Retailers must keep in mind that like everything else in technology, these specific tools themselves will continue to migrate and evolve, so today's most popular sites may not be tomorrow's favorites.

That possibility aside, Web 2.0 and social media have fundamentally transformed the ways in which individuals and societal groups become actively involved in transparent dialogue about a variety of topics, including retailers and their products. And that fundamental transformation is undeniably here to stay.

TODAY'S RETAILER ENGAGEMENT

This leads us to the important question of how far along the retail industry is in the adoption and implementation of social media. Typical of major initiatives, these vary widely on the part of individual retailers. We will review companies that have taken a leadership position in social media, discussing the relationship of the overall business strategy to the execution of social media and mobility. There is a second category of retailers that are experimenting with these new channels; some will be successful, and others will not, based upon leadership commitment. A third category is in the "wait and see" mode, and we believe this is not a good place to be given the lightning fast pace of social media. A better-informed customer is already there making purchasing decisions, so it's essential that retailers be there as well to engage them.

We discussed retailers' progress with social media and mobility with Shop.org's Managing Director, Scott Silverman (Shop.org, a division of the National Retail Federation [NRF], is the world's leading membership community for digital retail). Silverman states that "progress has been made as retailers have begun to see the importance of this new world of social media and mobility, but they aren't yet actively participating at an executive level on a broad-scale basis".[42] He emphasizes the critical need for these new channels to be supported at the leadership level, even though a number of retail executives haven't yet been sufficiently exposed to them to understand how to best weave these communication channels into their company's strategy.

To support retailers, NRF is working hard to educate its executive members. At the January 2010 NRF board of directors' meeting, a social-media expert gave an hour-long presentation to many of the nation's most senior retail executives. Silverman said "For retailers just getting started with social media, we recommend this sort of peer engagement as well as attendance at other digital media events. In 2010, NRF also conducted its first conference focused on these new areas. Its Retail Innovations and Technology conference was a sell-out success, with more than 600 industry executives attending."

We also reviewed the enormous challenge of large traditional retailers making this transition. Silverman cited Mike Ullman, chairman and CEO of JCPenney as someone who has embraced social media and mobility as part of his larger digital strategy. He added Terry Lundgren, chairman, president and CEO of Macy's as "being clearly focused on engaging customers through these new digital channels and the My Macy's localization strategy."

Because social media produces massive volumes of conversational data, we discussed the need for sophisticated analytics for monitoring and measurement. Silverman said "There aren't any solid metrics for measurement. It's too new. Right now it comes down to 'gut feel', in terms of knowing that you're active enough." We too, see the critical need for metrics and analytical measurement tools to assess the results of and plan the appropriate use of social media. Sophisticated analytics software and services are coming to market as we will discuss in a later chapter. Meanwhile, those retailers that are now engaging customers are getting smarter every day and making better decisions.

As you read though the individual company chapters, the leadership roles of the CEO's and their senior management teams are evident. Also important is leaderships' empowerment of talented staff members to effectively execute customer engagement never before experienced in retail.

NOTES

1. "Twitter Usage In America: 2010," The Edison Research/Arbitron Internet and Multimedia Study, Tom Webster—Vice President, Strategy and Marketing, Edison Research, available at www.google.com/#hl=en&rlz=1R2____en&q=twitter+usage+in+america+2010&aq=0&aqi=g2&aql=&oq=twitter+usage+in+ameri&gs_rfai=&fp=c08633561c63305 (accessed June 16, 2010).
2. Available at www.checkfacebook.com/ (accessed June 16, 2010).
3. Ibid.
4. "What Is the Speed of Social Media?" Jeffbulla's Blog, April 15, 2010, available at http://jeffbullas.com/2010/04/15/what-is-the-speed-of-social-media/ (accessed June 16, 2010).
5. Ibid.
6. Ibid.

7. Ibid.

8. Ibid.

9. Ibid.

10. Dictionary.com, Web 2.0, available at http://dictionary.reference.com/browse/web+2.0 (accessed June 21, 2010).

11. "What Is Social Media?" Pro PR, Exploring Social Media and Public Relations, April 8, 2008, available at http://propr.ca/2008/what-is-social-media/ (accessed June 21, 2010).

12. Dictionary.com, Social Network, available at http://dictionary.reference.com/browse/social+network?o=100074 (accessed June 21, 2010).

13. "Moms Use Facebook, Twitter, Blogs More than Average Adults, According to RAMA Research," National Retail Federation Press Release September 16, 2009 re: "All About Moms: A RAMA/BIGresearch Initiative," available at www.nrf.com/modules.php?name=News&op=viewlive&sp_id=786 (accessed June 16, 2010).

14. "The Key to Driving Retail Success with Social Media: Focus on Facebook," ForeSee Results, Kevin Ertell, February 9, 2010, available at https://community.atg.com/.../ForeSeeResults_Retail%20Success_Social%20MediaUS_2010.pdf (accessed June 16, 2010).

15. Ibid.

16. Ibid.

17. Ibid.

18. "Coupons Drive Sales on Social Media," *eMarketer*, June 9, 2009, available at www.adweek.com/aw/content_display/news/digital/e3i81776746af8563534ea58a78ac0050f2?imw=Y(accessedJune16,2010).

19. "Twitter Usage In America: 2010," The Edison Research/Arbitron Internet and Multimedia Study, Tom Webster—Vice President, Strategy and Marketing, Edison Research, available at www.google.com/search?hl=en&rlz=1R2_____en&q=twitter+usage+in+america+2010&aq=0&aqi=g2&aql=&oq=twitter+usage+in+ameri&gs_rfai=&emsg=NCSR&ei=6b8aTJ-XIZOQ8gSx4aCGCQ (accessed June 16, 2010).

20. www.checkfacebook.com (accessed June 16, 2010).

21. www.facebook.com/press/info.php?statistics (accessed June 16, 2010).

22. Ibid.

23. "Facebook's May 2010 US Traffic by Age and Sex: Younger Users Lead Growth," InsideFacebook, Eric Eldon, June 3, 2010, available at www.insidefacebook.com/2010/06/03/facebook%E2%80%99s-may-2010-us-traffic-by-age-and-sex-younger-users-lead-growth/ (accessed June 16, 2010).

24. Ibid.

25. "The Key to Driving Retail Success with Social Media: Focus on Facebook," ForeSee Results, Kevin Ertell, February 9, 2010, available at https://community.atg.com/.../ForeSeeResults_Retail%20Success_Social%20MediaUS_2010.pdf (accessed June 16, 2010).

26. "Social Media: An Inside Look at the People Who Use It," RAMA (Retail Advertising & Marketing Association) of the National Retail Federation®, December 2009, available at nrf.com/modules.php?name=D ocuments&op=viewlive&sp_id=4503 (accessed June 16, 2010).

27. Ibid.

28. www.insidefacebook.com (accessed June 16, 2010).

29. *Internet Retailer 2010 Edition Top 500 Guide*® and *Internet Retailer 2009 Edition Top 500 Guide*, Social Media section. Published by Internet Retailer, available at http://www.internetretailer.com/top500/.

30. "Twitter Has 105 Million Registered Users," Mashable/Social Media, Adam Ostrow, April 2010, available at http://mashable.com/2010/04/14/ twitter-registered-users/ (accessed June 21, 2010).

31. "Twitter Usage In America: 2010," The Edison Research/Arbitron Internet and Multimedia Study, Tom Webster—Vice President, Strategy and Marketing, Edison Research, available at www.google.com/#hl=en&rlz= 1R2___en&q=twitter+usage+in+america+2010&aq=0&aqi=g2&aql=&oq=t witter+usage+in+ameri&gs_rfai=&fp=c08633561c63305 (accessed June 16, 2010).

32. *Internet Retailer 2010 Edition Top 500 Guide* and *Internet Retailer 2009 Edition Top 500 Guide*, Social Media section.

33. "MySpace Readies Site Overhaul to Rekindle Growth," Reuters, March 2010, available at www.reuters.com/article/idustre6290I220100310 (accessed June 16, 2010).

34. "MySpace Demographic Gets Younger, Facebook Grows Older," Web Analytics World, Menoj Jasra, February 10, 2010, available at www.webanalyticsworld.net/2010/02/myspace-demographic-gets-younger.html (accessed June 16, 2010).

35. *Internet Retailer 2010 Edition Top 500 Guide* and *Internet Retailer 2009 Edition Top 500 Guide*, Social Media section.

36. "Top 25 Facebook Games for May 2010," Inside Social Games, www.insidesocialgames.com/2010/05/03/top-25-facebook-games-for-may-2010 (accessed June 7, 2010).

37. "What's Behind FarmVille's 80+ Million User Count?," Joost Schuur, March 27, 2010, available at http://joostschuur.com/2010/03/27/ farmville-user-count/ (accessed July 21, 2010).

38. "A Collection of Social Network Stats for 2010," Web Strategy Blog, Jeremiah Owyang, January 19, 2009, available at www.webstrategist.com/ blog/2010/01/19/a-collection-of-social-network-stats-for-2010/ (accessed June 16, 2010).

39. "Zynga Rolls Out Pre-Paid Game Cards At Major Retailers," TechCrunch, Leena Rao, March 25, 2010, available at http://techcrunch.com/2010/ 03/25/zynga-rolls-out-pre-paid-game-cards-at-major-retailers/ (accessed June 16, 2010).

40. *Internet Retailer 2010 Edition Top 500 Guide* and *Internet Retailer 2009 Edition Top 500 Guide*, Social Media section.

41. "4,000,000,000," Flickr Blog, October 12, 2009, available at http://blog.flickr.net/en/2009/10/12/4000000000/ (accessed June 16, 2010).

42. Interview with Scott Silverman, conducted at NRF Headquarters, Washington, DC, April 23, 2010. All subsequent quotes from Silverman are from this interview.

CHAPTER **3**

Mobility

t is impossible to go anywhere today—to work, a restaurant, a store, a sporting event, or the airport—without hearing or observing someone on a mobile phone. The human need to connect is ubiquitous, and the numbers are astounding: There are now nearly 300 million mobile devices in the United States.[1] Talking on mobile devices represents only a small portion of consumer activities; users are texting, playing games, checking the weather and sports scores, researching and purchasing products and increasingly using social media. Mobile usage has expanded so far beyond the traditional phone that to many, these devices have become indispensable.

Listen to a mobile phone ring in an airport and watch everyone in the crowd grab for their own phones—or try to get someone out the door if they have misplaced their mobile device. We have been living in the information age for a long time, but now information is instantly accessible and interactive. Offering a powerful channel for leveraging data, content, and communication, mobility offers progressive retailers the opportunity to implement solutions never before anticipated. In fact, we believe that the premise of our book, stated in the subtitle *How Retailers Engage Consumers with Social Media and Mobility*, is already happening, showing the many ways that mobility has become vital to successful consumer engagement.

Although mobile phones have been in people's hands for many years, with browser access and now smart phones, the mobile phone is now one of the most important technological phenomena of all time. It would be impossible to discuss the uses and applications of mobile devices without looking at their tremendous growth. Statistics are important not only because of the numbers of consumers using these devices, but also because of their reasons for use. In the United States, there were approximately 86 million mobile devices in 1999, and that number grew to 286 million by the end of 2009, an increase of 200 million in only 10 years (see Exhibit 3.1).[2]

With 91% of Americans now owning mobile phones, the market is approaching saturation, which inevitably brings innovation. As John Walls, Vice-President of Public Affairs of CTIA—The Wireless

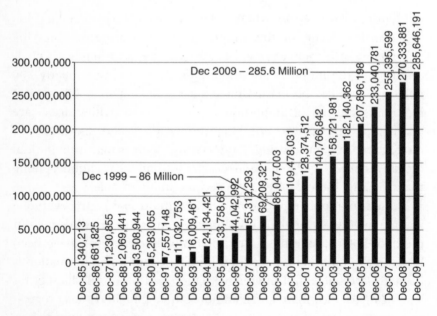

Exhibit 3.1 U.S. Mobile Phone Growth
Source: Reprinted by permission of CTIA—The Wireless Association.

Association®, says, "Extraordinary competition in the wireless industry has created tremendous communications opportunities. Just look at what's happened with smart phones and applications in a relatively short period of time. The devices are sophisticated, applications are wide-ranging and together, they are revolutionizing one of the most basic human functions: how we communicate with one another."[3] No longer just about voice, phones are now used more for data communication. According to CTIA, for the year ended December 31, 2009, statistics show a movement toward additional enhancements, including short message service (SMS), Web access, and smart phones:[4]

- Growth in wireless connectivity went from 86 million in 1999 to 286 million in 2009, representing a 10-year increase of 200 million.
- Ninety-one percent of Americans now have mobile devices.
- Over 90% of consumers have a choice of four or more wireless providers.
- Wireless consumers can choose from more than 630 different wireless devices.
- More than 87% of devices reported on carriers' networks were Web- and SMS-capable.
- More than 94% of devices reported on carriers' networks were data-capable.
- Almost 50 million smart phones and wireless-enabled PDAs were reported active on carriers' networks.

In summarizing the overall opportunity, Walls said, "I think wireless is creating a 'Gutenberg'-type experience that could benefit every human being on the planet. It doesn't matter who or where you are, the technology and cutting-edge devices such as today's smart phones are dramatically changing lives for the better."

DEFINITIONS

The mobile phone market comprises two major types of phones: feature phones and smart phones. Companies can communicate to consumers on their mobile devices through software applications that run on a mobile browser, a messaging service (SMS or MMS) or directly on the mobile device (mobile applications). Because we will reference these terms in subsequent sections, we will first provide definitions.

A **smart phone** is a wireless mobile device that offers more advanced computing ability in addition to making telephone calls. A smart phone adds features such as the ability to access the Internet and send and receive email, a camera, an address book, and many other applications. Smart phones run complete operating software and provide a platform for application (app) developers. "According to a study by comScore, in 2010, over 45 million people in the United States owned Smartphones, and it is the fastest growing segment of the mobile phone market."[5]

A **feature phone** is a term used to describe a low-end mobile phone that has less computing ability than a smart phone. Feature phones sometimes are referred to as "dumb phones," as they don't have all the computing power or connectivity of a smart phone. Feature phones have proprietary operating systems (firmware) and have limited applications, if any. Feature phones represent over 70% of the mobile phones in the United States.[6]

A **mobile browser** is an Internet browser which runs on a mobile phone. "Mobile browsers are optimized so as to display Internet content most effectively for small screens on portable devices."[7] Mobile browser software must be efficient due to the low memory capacity and bandwidth of wireless handheld devices. Retailers often want to make their Web sites available to consumers through mobile devices. Mobile phones with a browser can access these Web sites; however, the user experience is often unsatisfactory because of the mobile device's small screen size, slow speed, and keyboard. Therefore applications designed specifically for a mobile browser provide a much better user experience.

A **mobile messaging service** can take on two forms: **short message service (SMS)** and **multimedia message service (MMS)**. **SMS** describes the transmission of short text messages to and from a mobile phone, fax machine and/or IP address. Messages must be no longer than 160 alpha-numeric characters and contain no images or graphics.[8] SMS is a feature available with practically all modern mobile phones that allow users to send and receive short text messages. **MMS** is a descendant of SMS and extends text messaging to include longer text, graphics, photos, audio clips, video clips, or any combination of the above, within certain size limits.[9] While not as user-friendly or sophisticated as mobile applications, message-based applications work on nearly all mobile phones and therefore are the most widely used applications. Retailers can use SMS or MMS applications for marketing campaigns and ordering and tracking delivery of products. For example, Best Buy offers text alerts for product information, weekly specials and nearest store locations. 1-800-Flowers.com is engaged in SMS messaging campaigns and growing its SMS Mobile Club.

A **mobile application (or app)** is software that can run on a mobile device such as a cell phone and/or PDA (personal digital assistant) that will allow the device to perform specific tasks that are typically restricted to PCs. PDAs and smartphones, such as the Blackberry, iPhone, and Android-based devices, are all capable of downloading and using apps.[10] As smart phone usage continues to grow, mobile apps are an effective way for retailers to directly communicate with customers. Apps offer quick response time and are typically graphically oriented, friendly and easy to learn and use. They can be tailored to exploit specific categories, products, services and events. We explore many detailed examples of retailer mobile applications in the following chapters such as Macy's iShop described as "Your favorite store now fits in your pocket," and Pizza Hut's "killer app," which among other features, allows customers to visually create and then order customized pizzas.

SMART PHONES CHANGE IT ALL

The number of people using smart phones is increasing rapidly. The Nielsen Company predicts that the current proportion of approximately 70% feature phones to 30% smart phones will change significantly,

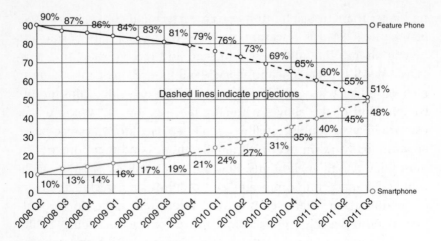

Exhibit 3.2 Smart Phones Overtake Feature Phones in the United States by 2011
Source: Used with permission of The Nielsen Company. Roger Entner, "Smart Phones to Overtake Feature Phones in U.S. by 2011," Nielsenwire, available at http:// blog.nielsen.com/nielsenwire/consumer/smartphones-to-overtake-feature-phones-in-u-s-by-2011/ (accessed March 26, 2010).

with smart phones overtaking feature phones by the end of 2011 (see Exhibit 3.2).

Smart Phones Offer Retailers Engagement with Consumers

Given the projected increase in the use of smart phones and the significant opportunity that this increased usage offers, retailers should be developing and implementing mobile Web sites and applications. Some facts that should motivate retailers to capitalize on the growth in smart phones are:

- The average smart phone user generates 10 times the amount of traffic generated by the average non-smart phone user.[11]
- iPhones can generate as much traffic as 30 basic feature phones.[12]
- 35% of smart phone owners browse the Internet on their phones at least daily, versus only 4% of feature phone owners.[13]
- 61% of smart phone owners send or receive SMS daily, versus 32% of feature phone owners.[14]

- 30.8% of smart phone users have accessed social networks using their mobile browsers, as compared with 6.8% of feature phone users.[15]

- 80% of smart phone users have accessed mobile media on their mobile devices, versus 26% of non-smart phone users.[16]

- 70% of smart phone users have accessed email on their mobile devices, versus 12% of non-smart phone users.[17]

- Data traffic for an iPhone user is almost 14 times that of a non-iPhone user.[18]

Smart Phone Users Post Triple-Digit Growth in App and Browser Access

Smart phone users are driving growth in browser usage (up 111% in the past year) and also in application access (up 112%). While the growth in application usage on smart phones continues to dominate the spotlight in the mobile market, feature phone users still constitute nearly half of all users accessing mobile browsers and apps (see Exhibit 3.3).[19]

Exhibit 3.3 Smart Phone vs. Feature Phone Growth in Apps and Browsers

3-Month Average Ending April 2010 vs. 3-Month Average Ending April 2009 Total U.S. Age 13+							
Browser	April 2009	April 2010	% Change	Application	April 2009	April 2010	% Change
Total Mobile Market	55,503	72,872	31	Total Mobile Market	54,414	69,639	28
Smart Phone	17,785	37,577	111	Smart Phone	18,126	38,413	112
Feature Phone	37,718	35,295	−6	Feature Phone	36,288	31,226	−14

Source: "Social Networking Ranks as Fastest-Growing Mobile Content Category," comScore, June 2, 2010, available at www.comscore.com/Press_Events/Press_Releases/2010/6/Social_Networking_Ranks_as_Fastest-Growing_Mobile_Content_Category.

INTERSECTION OF SOCIAL MEDIA AND MOBILITY

The recent growth of smart phones, led by the innovative iPhone and quickly followed by Android-based phones, has created consumer opportunities never before envisioned. Concurrent with the growth in mobility, a new and transparent method of digital communication—social media—captivated the market. Having examined the astounding numbers associated with social-media growth, we believe that the intersection of social media and mobility will profoundly affect worldwide communication. In the United States, mobile social networks are projected to include 56.2 million participants by 2013, representing 45% of the Internet user population.[20] Improvements in mobile engagement for social networking have been fueled by the success of the smart phone.

Mobile Social-Networking App Audience More Than Triples

For the three-month period ending April 2010 as compared with the same three-month period ending April 2009, social networking experienced the strongest growth in app access, increasing 240%, to 14.5 million users. This percentage represents an increase of 10 million users, year-over-year, during the same three-month period (see Exhibit 3.4).[21]

Mobile Browser Access of Facebook and Twitter Posts Triple-Digit Growth

For the three-month period ending January 2010, versus the comparable period ending January 2009, 25.1 million mobile subscribers accessed Facebook via their mobile browsers, up 112%. Twitter also experienced tremendous growth, with 4.7 million mobile users and a 347% increase (see Exhibit 3.5).[22]

RETAIL HAS BREAKTHROUGH OPPORTUNITY

The movement of retailers into social media and mobility is currently inconsistent. Nevertheless, progressive retailers are leading the way

Exhibit 3.4 Fastest-Growing Content Categories via Application Access

3-Month Average Ending April 2010 vs. 3-Month Average Ending April 2009 Total U.S. Age 13+			
Application Access Category	Total Audience (000)		
	April 2009	April 2010	% Change
Total Audience 13+ yrs old	232,000	234,000	1
Used application (except native games)	54,414	69,639	28
Social Networking	4,270	14,518	240
News	4,148	9,292	124
Sports Information	3,598	7,672	113
Bank Accounts	2,340	4,974	113
Weather	8,557	18,063	111
Movie Information	3,296	6,359	93
Maps	8,708	16,773	93
Online Retail	1,416	2,701	91
Photo or Video Sharing Service	3,131	5,950	90
Search	5,434	10,315	90

Source: "Social Networking Ranks as Fastest-Growing Mobile Content Category," comScore, June 2, 2010, available at www.comscore.com/Press_Events/Press_Releases/2010/6/Social_Networking_Ranks_as_Fastest-Growing_Mobile_Content_Category.

and demonstrating the opportunity to digitally connect with their customers. These early adopters are proving that this move to digital communication can represent a transformation in their business and gains in market share.

Retailers are in different stages of implementing social media and mobility strategies. The *Internet Retailer 2010 Edition Top 500 Guide*

Exhibit 3.5 Mobile Browser Access of Facebook, MySpace, and Twitter

Number of Mobile Subscribers Accessing Facebook, MySpace and Twitter via Mobile Browser 3-month average ending January 2010 vs. January 2009 Total U.S. Age 13+			
	Total Audience (000)		
	January 2009	January 2010	% Change
Facebook.com	11,874	25,137	112
MySpace.com	12,338	11,439	−7
Twitter.com	1,051	4,700	347

Source: "Facebook and Twitter Access via Mobile Browser Grows by Triple-Digits in the Past Year." www.comscore.com/Press_Events/Press_Releases/2010/3/Facebook_and_Twitter_Access_via_Mobile_Browser_Grows_by_Triple-Digits.

estimates that there are 150 U.S. retailers, 76 of them listed in the *Internet Retailer Top 500*, with nearly 200 mobile commerce sites and/or applications.[23] On any given day, nearly 60 million American consumers access the Web via mobile devices, and 32% of Americans— nearly one third of the population—have used a conventional mobile or smart phone to access the Internet.[24]

In 2009, total retail industry Internet sales in the United States were just under $135 billion,[25] which demonstrates a significant opportunity for retailers to build a sizable mobile commerce (m-commerce) business. Mobility, however, pertains to so much more than commerce; it's also about bringing the store to the customer, bringing the customer into the store, and, once the customer is in the store, bringing added knowledge to both the customer and the store associate.

Web 2.0 provides vast opportunities for cross-channel retailers to leverage digital channels—e-commerce, social media, and mobility— to reach customers wherever they are. The current challenge for retailers is that mobile sites and applications must be developed for various operating systems and hardware devices. Investments should therefore be selected based on market share.

Mobility represents a channel through which all proactive retailers can win. The digital platform finally enables retailers to execute strategies that they previously have attempted for years, with limited success. It opens up cross-channel opportunities that extend far beyond simply referencing e-commerce and stores. Take Starbucks and Pizza Hut: Neither has extensive Web commerce, but each has become a successful cross-channel business, thanks to the effective use of social media, direct Web marketing, and connecting through mobility. These two companies represent the ability to extend a brand in the digital world. No one simple, cross-channel approach exists, as each company's strategy should be based on its needs and business model.

APPLICATIONS FOR MOBILE LEADERSHIP

What follows are the most common mobile applications in use by retailers. Since every day brings new opportunities in today's dynamic digital world, this list is not all-encompassing.

Marketing and Advertising

Digital marketing and advertising are extensions of both equity marketing and promotional advertising. Customers are moving away from traditional media as the use of digital marketing and advertising is more flexible, personalized, and targeted. Mobile marketing and advertising applications include:

- **Mobile call-to-action.** Includes incentives offered to the customer to shop either online or in-store, including banner ads, time-sensitive coupons, and other promotional offers.
- **Mobile promotional pre-shopping.** Shoppers can check circulars, coupons, and other promotional offerings on their mobile devices at home, on the way to the store, or while shopping at the store. The customer has access to this information at all times, and if the retailer is satisfying the customer's purchasing needs, they both benefit. The retail circular is still important to retailers, so the creation of a "digital circular"

represents a major breakthrough. Best Buy, for example, offers customers the opportunity to "GET WEEKLY DEALS," which are sent to customers' phones. JCPenney offers its weekly promotional circular via mobile phone as well as apps for weekly deals. Macy's utilizes mobile print ads and allows customers tap-to-buy, e-commerce functionality.

- **Mobile interactive brand marketing.** Magazine advertising has always played an important role in presenting apparel and home-furnishings fashions, in addition to other higher-end categories. Bloomingdale's offers customers the opportunity to vote and comment on fashions that it features. JCPenney and Macy's invite interaction through iPads that is consistent with fashion buyers' habits. To initiate a customer relationship, they also afford consumers opt-in opportunities by offering appropriate incentives.

- **Location-based marketing.** As a new but rapidly evolving strategy, location-based marketing involves identifying, via GPS on a mobile device, the precise location of a customer in relation to the retailer's store, then enticing the customer to visit that store. Scott Silverman of Shop.org points out that Google and Facebook are both seeking to expand location-based marketing: "I think location-based mobile will be huge," he says. "I think about being out and needing to buy something like a vacuum cleaner bag. Imagine if retailers selling this item had sent a data feed to a search engine like Google, and I know it's in stock in this zip code, my phone could actually give me directions to the nearest store … that's really cool."

Cross-Channel Shopping

Mobile devices are being used to provide customers with important information to benefit their shopping experience, regardless of their shopping channel.

- **Mobile product research—ratings and reviews.** After a long period of experiencing retail store associates with little—and sometimes inaccurate—product information, consumers are using the Internet to educate themselves about products. They can receive detailed product information on the Web, along with customer ratings, reviews, and comments. Best Buy, a seller of technology-based merchandise, estimates that 70% of its customers go to its Web site to view items before going to the store for purchase or pickup. Now the company is putting this information directly in the customers' hands via their mobile devices. Other progressive retailers are offering this same information, relative to their merchandise offers, via mobile. While the days of *caveat emptor* ("Let the buyer beware") will never be over, retailers must now recognize that consumers are well informed—and anxious to share their shopping experiences with their friends via social media.

■ **Mobile commerce.** From 2008 to 2009, mobile shopping sales tripled, to reach $1.2 billion, and 2010 mobile shopping sales are estimated to grow to $2.4 billion, according to ABI Research.[26] While impressive, this trend represents a relatively small base. The opportunity to grow sales rapidly will materialize as consumers see the benefits of smart phone mobile shopping. In understanding products, doing comparison reviews, and taking advantage of promotions and other initiatives, consumers will use their mobile phones more extensively Amazon has emerged as the leader in mobile commerce with over $1 billion in sales during a 12-month period.

■ **Mobile customer loyalty.** Customer-loyalty programs are extremely important to retailers, as they entice their best, most loyal customers to shop their stores more often and buy more on the average store visit. In addition, these programs provide retailers with important information about their customers, thus enabling them to offer relevant incentives to loyal shoppers. Customers who participate in loyalty programs feel that they are special, and accordingly develop a stronger relationship with the retailer. The timing and relevance of loyalty-program promotion offers, such as earning points, represent a major factor in the success of these programs. Since most retailers have now created loyalty incentives, these programs, leveraged through digital channels, must be more meaningful and creative for the retailer to be successful. The mobile channel virtually has brought these programs to life for innovative retailers. Starbucks, for example—already a leader in customer loyalty—also has become a strong force in mobile-based customer loyalty through its Starbucks Card Mobile iPhone application.

- **Store locator.** A retailer's store-locator application makes use of a mobile phone's native GPS and mapping capabilities to allow customers to easily locate and navigate to its nearest physical store. Applications also can provide specific store information such as amenities, hours, and phone numbers.

- **Better educated store associates.** Now that retailers are better educating their customers, it's important to provide their store associates with the same information that customers are receiving. The opportunity to better prepare store associates is not related to time-pressured training sessions as much as it is to enabling them to have the relevant information on hand when talking to customers on the sales floor. If it was previously difficult for an uninformed customer to effectively engage with a store associate, just imagine the frustration of an informed customer encountering a poorly informed store associate. As Silverman points out, "The idea of a customer bringing a mobile device into the store makes it impossible for retailers to ignore. It's an impetus to better equip their sales associates. The relevance of the iPad in retail is for retailers to give them to their sales associates to research product and use them as sales tools. Recognizing how rapidly technology is moving, there will be more similar pad-type devices soon."

- **Mobile payment.** Mobile payment can take two forms: (1) store associates using mobile devices to bring the checkout process to the customer at point-of-purchase (e.g., Apple stores), or (2) consumers using mobile devices for payment and application of any electronic discounts such as coupons or other incentives. This concept is rapidly evolving. The companies that are testing consumer-based mobile payment include Starbucks with its Starbucks Card Mobile initiative.

Mobile Social Media

The 240% growth in 2009 in accessing mobile social media via applications, as well as the 111% growth in accessing social media via browsers, demonstrates the enormous future growth opportunities available. Consumers have a keen interest in using social media via mobile; of all the current mobile applications, social media represents the fastest growing sector. Browser-based access to Facebook increased 112%, and access to Twitter increased 347% in 2009.

Social networks are an extremely important source for a retailer's customers to hear from other customers about their opinions of products. This source of information and trust is important in all merchandise categories. For instance, consumers say that word-of-mouth is still the Number-One influence in their electronics (47.3%) and apparel (33.6%) purchases.[27]

Location-Based Social Networks/Social Gaming

As noted in the prior chapter on social media, Foursquare, Gowalla, Loopt, and several other location-based, social-networking sites are gaining rapid acceptance among consumers. These sites provide retailers with a unique opportunity for customer engagement. "I'm surprised retailers aren't using things like Foursquare more," says Silverman. "There's competitiveness in me that I like to be mayor! If I'm out and about, and I check in at a restaurant, and my favorite retailer is down the street, it would be great for that retailer to give me an incentive to stop by."

Future mobile-gaming growth opportunities also exist, based on the shifting balance between smart phones and feature phones. Smart phone subscribers are three times more likely (47.1%) than feature phone subscribers (15.7%) to play games on their devices at least once a month.[28] Gaming is the largest socially acceptable activity offered on Facebook. Retailers have opportunities both to advertise within existing games and to produce their own games as part of a strategy to attract customers. For instance, Wet Seal is introducing a game with an appeal similar to that of Zynga's FarmVille; it will tie directly into Wet Seal's merchandise, allowing customers both to have fun and to make purchases.

RETAIL MOBILE INNOVATORS

As we studied the market, looking for retailers with early successful strategies, we focused on companies that were already acknowledged leaders or were making major moves into the world of mobility. While these companies' mobile initiatives are reviewed in subsequent chapters, here are a few headlines regarding their progress:

- Starbucks Card Mobile and myStarbucks are acknowledged in the retail industry as leading consumer mobile applications.

- Best Buy, an industry leader in mobility, is helping mobile customers through "SHOP, LEARN & BUY," bringing its brand to customers' hands through their mobile devices.

- Macy's and Best Buy are the two retail companies that are testing ShopKick, a personalized mobile-based loyalty program.

- Pizza Hut's "Killer App," which allows customers to visually build their own pizzas and have them delivered, was selected by *Forbes* as "# 1 Mobile Application for 2009."

- 1-800-Flowers.com, a pioneer in mobile commerce, was awarded "App of the Year" in 2010 by *RIS* (Retail Information Systems) magazine for its smart phone application.

- Wet Seal's iRunway mobile app received the *RIS* magazine "Mobility Customer Engagement Award" in 2010.

- JCPenney is also one of Apple's Charter Partners on the new iPad application-based marketing program.

All these retailers are successful mobile leaders, as you will discover when you encounter all the strategies that they are leveraging through social media and mobility.

NOTES

1. "Wireless in the U.S.: A Snapshot," June 11, 2010, CTIA—The Wireless Association®.
2. Ibid.
3. Interview with John Walls, conducted at CTIA headquarters, April 23, 2010. All subsequent quotes from Walls are from this interview.
4. Ibid.

5. "45 million US Smartphone Users—comScore," AdMob Mobile Metrics, April 5, 2010, available at http://metrics.admob.com/2010/04/45-million-us-smartphone-users-comscore/ (accessed June 21, 2010).

6. Roger Entner, "Smart Phones to Overtake Feature Phones in U.S. by 2011," Nielsenwire, available at http://blog.nielsen.com/nielsenwire/consumer/smartphones-to-overtake-feature-phones-in-u-s-by-2011/ (accessed March 26, 2010).

7. wordIQ.com, available at www.wordiq.com/definition/Mobile_Browser (accessed July 20, 2010).

8. Webopedia.com, available at www.webopedia.com/TERM/S/short_message_service.html (accessed July 20, 2010).

9. phonescoop.com, available at www.phonescoop.com/glossary/term.php?gid=416 (accessed July 20, 2010).

10. eHow.com, available at www.ehow.com/facts_6001849_define-mobile-application.html (accessed July 20, 2010).

11. "Cisco Visual Networking Index: Global Mobile Data Traffic Forecast Update, 2009–2014, Cisco," February 9, 2010, available at www.cisco.com/en/US/solutions/collateral/ns341/ns525/ns537/ns705/ns827/white_paper_c11-520862.html (accessed June 21, 2010).

12. Ibid.

13. Seth Fowler, Julie A. Ask, with J. P. Gownder, "Engaging Smart Phone Users: Why Designing Strategies for High-End Mobile Devices Makes Sense," *Forrester Research*, January 19, 2010, available at www.forrester.com/rb/Research/engaging_smartphone_users/q/id/56086/t/2 (accessed June 21, 2010).

14. Ibid.

15. "Facebook and Twitter Access via Mobile Browser Grows by Triple-Digits in the Past Year," comScore, March 3, 2010, available at www.comscore.com/Press_Events/Press_Releases/2010/3/Facebook_and_Twitter_Access_via_Mobile_Browser_Grows_by_Triple-Digits?utm_source=feedburner&utm_medium=feed&utm_campaign=Feed%3A+comscore+%28comScore+Networks%29 (accessed June 21, 2010).

16. "How Alike Are Android and iPhone Users?" *eMarketer*, December 28, 2009, available at www.emarketer.com/Article.aspx?R=1007439 (accessed June 21, 2010).

17. Ibid.

18. "Mobile Internet Traffic: Analyzing Global Usage Trends," 2010 Informa UK Ltd., available at http://media2.telecoms.com/downloads/mobile-internet-traffic-trends.pdf (accessed July 14, 2010).

19. "Social Networking Ranks as Fastest-Growing Mobile Content Category," comScore, June 2, 2010, available at www.comscore.com/Press_Events/Press_Releases/2010/6/Social_Networking_Ranks_as_Fastest-Growing_Mobile_Content_Category (accessed June 21, 2010).

20. Dan Butcher, "Mobile Social Networkers in U.S. to Surpass 56M by 2013," *eMarketer*, November 16, 2009, available at www.mobilemarketer.com/cms/news/research/4648.html (accessed June 21, 2010).

21. "Social Networking Ranks as Fastest-Growing Mobile Content Category," comScore, June 2, 2010, available at www.comscore.com/Press_Events/Press_Releases/2010/6/Social_Networking_Ranks_as_Fastest-Growing_Mobile_Content_Category (accessed June 21, 2010).

22. "Facebook and Twitter Access via Mobile Browser Grows by Triple-Digits in the Past Year," comScore, March 3, 2010, available at www.comscore.com/Press_Events/Press_Releases/2010/3/Facebook_and_Twitter_Access_via_Mobile_Browser_Grows_by_Triple-Digits?utm_source=feedburner&utm_medium=feed&utm_campaign=Feed%3A+comscore+%28comScore+Networks%29 (accessed June 21, 2010).

23. *Internet Retailer 2010 Edition Top 500 Guide*, p. 62. Published by Internet Retailer, available at www.internetretailer.com/top500/.

24. Pew Research Center's Internet & American Life Project, as referenced in *Internet Retailer 2010 Edition Top 500 Guide*, p. 62.

25. *Internet Retailer 2010 Edition Top 500 Guide*, p. 22.

26. "Mobile Shopping in US Will Grow to $2.4 Billion This Year: ABI Research," *Mobile Commerce Daily*, February 17, 2010, available at www.mobilecommercedaily.com/mobile-shopping-in-us-will-grow-to-24-billion-this-year-abi-research/ (accessed June 15, 2010).

27. RAMA BIGresearch Study, The Retail Advertising & Marketing Association, a division of the National Retail Federation, December 2009.

28. Ibid.

4

Starbucks: It's the Experience![1]

W hen looking at which brands are using social media effectively, people are amazed by the success of Starbucks. The brand-specific name "Starbucks" is already mentioned more frequently online than the more generic word "coffee."[2]

Take a minute to think about your own Starbucks experience—your desire to stop there for your morning favorites, the always-friendly store visit—and you realize how you look forward to savoring your favorite beverage. Starbucks believes it is the "third place" that its customers make a part of their daily lives, between work and home. What is more social than a visit to your local Starbucks?

Let's start with a look back. When Starbucks began in 1971 as a single store in Seattle, Washington, specialty coffee was virtually unknown. Its founders, sharing their passion and expertise with customers, helped create a new market by offering exceptional quality coffee from around the world.

LEARNING—FORMULATING—INNOVATING

Starbucks' first step in the journey to becoming an international brand started in 1981 when Howard Schultz, currently chairman, president, and chief executive officer of Starbucks Coffee Company, walked into its flagship store in Seattle's Pike Place Market.[3] He was welcomed and invited into conversation with these connoisseurs who were meticulous in finding and roasting the highest quality coffee. Schultz immediately sensed the authenticity, open communication, and conviction of these entrepreneurs. After subsequent meetings with its owners, he began to think that if Starbucks could maintain its exceptional quality, integrity, and service, it could grow regionally, even possibly nationally. Impressed by its extraordinary coffee culture, Schultz, a native New Yorker, made the decision to move cross-country to Seattle. He joined Starbucks in 1982, as director of operations and marketing, when Starbucks had only four stores.

A year later, Schultz, in his quest to provide the best possible coffee experience, traveled to Italy, known for the social atmosphere of its coffee bars. The Italians understood the importance of quality coffee, its preparation, and the relationship of baristas and customers—all of which contributed to the ambience of their coffeehouses. Schultz imagined bringing this same sense of community and human interaction to coffee shops in America. In pursuit of his vision, he left Starbucks for a short period to open his Il Giornale coffeehouses. With the help of local investors, Schultz returned to purchase Starbucks in August 1987, becoming its chief executive officer.

Schultz's mission was to build a coffee company unlike any that existed in America, and one with a culture of respect and dignity. He focused on a commitment to his partners (employees), customers, stores, and neighborhoods. Schultz instituted comprehensive health coverage for eligible full- and part-time partners, among the first in the retail industry. He also offered partners equity in the company in the form of stock options, called *Bean Stock*. These two programs, which represented an investment in people, formed the foundation for Starbucks, a company that stands for its partners and community, while performing as a growing and profitable business.

In these early days, this experience was based on an almost sacred connection—an exceptional cup of coffee, the human connection with the barista, and the welcoming environment of the store. The number of stores grew from a handful to thousands, eventually with new stores opening every day, and with the partners' commitment that each one represents the mission of Starbucks. Today, many years and stores later, that same connection remains, a testimony to Schultz and all of the partners of Starbucks.

As Starbucks grew, so did its suite of products—now extending beyond the four walls of the stores. Customers were interacting with the brand outside of the store environment, starting with bottled Frappuccino in 1996, and eventually extending to a global multibillion dollar business in ready-to-drink beverages, packaged coffee, and super-premium ice cream. Starbucks was able to reach into these channels because of the brand equity and trust it had built with the many customers who frequented its stores.

At the same time, there was a seismic shift in the technology world and the way in which consumers gained access to information. Customer conversations about the brand were beginning to occur in the digital world on Web sites, blogs, and eventually social-media channels. These conversations were happening, and Starbucks was not yet actively participating.

TRANSFORMING STARBUCKS FOR THE FUTURE

In January 2008, Starbucks was at a crossroads. Same-store sales had declined, and for the first time, store traffic had slowed. Chairman since 2000, Schultz resumed the role of president and chief executive officer. Faced with these challenges and an unprecedented global recession, he led a complete transformation of the company, bringing Starbucks to sustainable, profitable growth.[4]

At the heart of the transformation was reigniting the emotional attachment customers had to the brand, what Schultz termed "touching the customer." A key component of that strategy was to actively engage customers in the digital world—extending authentic human connections beyond the coffeehouse.

As Chris Bruzzo, Starbucks vice president, Brand, Content & Online, tells it, Starbucks' journey into social media began against this backdrop. He describes an early 2008 meeting during which Schultz said "We have a mandate for change—we can't hear our customers anymore."[5] Bruzzo was given the challenge of figuring out how to give those customers who frequented Starbucks stores a voice and a place for conversation with Starbucks online.

"We didn't build a social-media marketing strategy—it was more about [creating] a social strategy. It's about hanging out with our customers online," says Bruzzo. Starbucks wants to be where its customers are, but in a way that's relevant and adds value to their experience. It may sound easy, but in reality it's extraordinarily difficult to replicate the social conversations that take place in a coffee shop and bring them to life online. Bruzzo and his team needed to figure out how to provide compelling, engaging, and emotionally appealing social content that would allow Starbucks to further build its relationship with its customers. It was a difficult challenge, but Bruzzo understood that to do this effectively, Starbucks needed to create a digital coffee shop—an online community that allowed customers to speak their minds to one another and to Starbucks partners, just as they do in the stores.

MY STARBUCKS IDEA IS BORN

Bruzzo didn't have much time. He was given just 60 days to open up Starbucks first online community. Figuring out what the conversation should be about, the team looked at its key insights about Starbucks customers. The observation that bubbled to the top was that customers love to share their ideas. "When we say we work at Starbucks, people are excited, because they always have a list of ideas that they want to share with us." What better way to engage its customers in conversation, at a time when the company was rebuilding its deep relationship with them, than to listen to their ideas about how to make Starbucks a better place? *My Starbucks Idea* (mystarbucksidea.com) was born.

The online community *My Starbucks Idea* encourages people to join in and share their ideas about how to create the perfect Starbucks experience (see Exhibit 4.1). Because Starbucks wanted to listen to its customers identify the ideas that mattered to them most, it invited them into *My Starbucks Idea* to discuss what was most important to them and help shape the future of Starbucks. Like a great cup of

my STARBUCKS IDEA

FAQ

GOT AN IDEA?   VIEW IDEAS   IDEAS IN ACTION

Hi there, [Sign In] to make a comment.

Share 🔲 🔲 🔲
Follow us on twitter

Ideas so far

[Search Ideas]

PRODUCT IDEAS

21,639   Coffee & Espresso Drinks
610   Frappuccino® Beverages
6,651   Tea & Other Drinks
9,690   Food
4,452   Merchandise & Music
6,156   Starbucks Card
6,605   Other Product Ideas

EXPERIENCE IDEAS

5,292   Ordering, Payment, & Pick-Up
9,035   Atmosphere & Locations
7,611   Other Experience Ideas

INVOLVEMENT IDEAS

2,888   Building Community
6,104   Social Responsibility
4,208   Other Involvement Ideas
299   Outside USA

SHARE. VOTE. DISCUSS. SEE.

You know better than anyone else what you want from Starbucks. So tell us. What's your Starbucks Idea? Revolutionary or simple – we want to hear it. Share your ideas, tell us what you think of other people's ideas and join the discussion. We're here, and we're ready to make ideas happen. Let's get started.

Most Recent Ideas

1 Hour(s) Ago   Sell Reusable Lids
2 Hour(s) Ago   Prevent the drip
3 Hour(s) Ago   coffee's from around the world
5 Hour(s) Ago   CHANGE IT BACK
12 Hour(s) Ago   "the usual"... automatically served!
13 Hour(s) Ago   I just had to share this
15 Hour(s) Ago   Ridiculously Expensive Custom Mug with Benefits
16 Hour(s) Ago   Please bring the recycled glassware back!!!
17 Hour(s) Ago   A new hot cocoa!
18 Hour(s) Ago   Green tea with mixed berry

Exhibit 4.1 *My Starbucks Idea* Home Page
Source: Reprinted with permission of Starbucks.

coffee, the ideas started pouring in, tens of thousands of ideas in the first few months. Some ideas were big, some were small, but all of them mattered to customers. Starbucks needed to show its customers that it was willing not only to listen, but also to engage in conversation and be responsive to their feedback.

Customers started sharing ideas about Starbucks drinks and its menu offerings, its customer-loyalty program, ways of improving the stores' atmosphere and ambience, recycling, and Starbucks community involvement. To listen, respond to, and help prioritize these ideas, Starbucks set up a dedicated team of "Idea Partners," not a marketing team but a group of Starbucks partners who are experts in their respective fields. That team has grown to approximately 40 Idea Partners, whose expertise ranges from coffee, to store operations, to community programs. The Idea Partners are responsible for reading all the ideas and comments, and then gathering the most popular and most innovative ones for consideration.

How It Works

Customers can share in the conversation by joining *My Starbucks Idea* through the Starbucks Web site or by going directly to mystarbucksidea. com. Participants can then post ideas and comments to the community. Everyone in the group is encouraged to vote on their favorite ideas, each person voting only once, and each vote is worth 10 points. Although everyone can view the ideas and their corresponding scores, only community members can vote. To determine the most popular ideas, Starbucks uses an algorithm based on an idea's number of points, number of customer comments, and how recently it posted.

The most popular ideas are considered, along with other customer ideas that may not be as popular based on voting scores, but are innovative and make practical sense. "We want customers in the community to vote up the best ideas, and then we'll give them a thread of conversation," says Bruzzo. "A mini-community starts to form around an idea, with community members talking about it and voting it up to get Starbucks attention. We then provide a moderator [for] the best ideas to let the community know we are listening and may consider those ideas."

The *My Starbucks Idea* community categorizes ideas as follows:

- **Popular Ideas.** Ranking determined by algorithm based on number of points, number of comments, and the freshness of the idea
- **Recent Ideas.** Most recently posted ideas
- **Top All-Time.** Top ideas, based on point value alone
- **Comments.** Ideas with the greatest number of recent comments

By viewing members' comments and the ideas' overall scores, customers can determine what others in the community think of their ideas.

Blogging About *Ideas in Action*

Starbucks can't possibly respond to every idea posted in *My Starbucks Idea*, but customers are kept abreast of which ideas Starbucks is considering through its *Ideas in Action* blog. Through *Ideas in Action*,

Exhibit 4.2 *Ideas in Action* Blog
Source: Reprinted with permission of Starbucks.

Starbucks keeps the community informed about which ideas have been recommended for implementation and their current status is. Starbucks gives each idea an icon indicating whether the idea is *Under Review, Reviewed, Coming Soon,* or *Launched.* Promising ideas are placed *Under Review* so that Starbucks can take a closer look at them. An idea's status eventually may be elevated to *Reviewed, Coming Soon,* or *Launched* (see Exhibit 4.2). Customers can comment on the *Ideas in Action* blog and share it with their friends in other social networks.

Real-Life Results

In the first two years of its life, *My Starbucks Idea* has contributed approximately 100,000 ideas for enhancing the Starbucks experience. Not all ideas are practical or possible to implement, but Starbucks uses its community to help filter and prioritize the best ideas. "We're now up to 70 ideas that have been implemented and that we've credited back to mystarbucksidea.com," comments Bruzzo. Seventy ideas out of 100,000 may not sound like a lot, but in just a couple of years, to succeed in rolling out even one idea to over 16,000 stores requires operational discipline, time, and energy.

My Starbucks Idea is now managed under the direction of Matthew Guiste, director of Global Social Media, and his team. Both Guiste and Bruzzo talk enthusiastically about some of the customer ideas that have made Starbucks a better experience.

- **Splash Sticks.** "The introduction of Splash Sticks was one of the first and most popular ideas," says Guiste.[6] [A Splash Stick is a plastic guard to help alleviate spills from the hole in the coffee cup's lid.] "They were in Japan at the time and we had no thought of bringing [them] to the U.S. until the community suggested it," adds Guiste. Splash Sticks can now be found in Starbucks stores nationwide.

- **Pour-over method.** "One of best ideas was around bold coffee," says Bruzzo. In the afternoons, Starbucks stores didn't always have a freshly brewed pot of bold or decaffeinated coffee on hand for the occasional customer request. Through *My Starbucks Idea*, a suggestion was made to use the pour-over method. This method involves putting finely ground coffee into a cone-shaped filter and pouring boiling water over the coffee. To implement this idea, Starbucks has provided pour-over kits to all U.S. and Canada stores.

  The idea around being able to get bold coffee in the afternoon was debated in the *My Starbucks Idea* community for over a year. "People are really passionate about their ideas, and it wasn't always a positive discussion," admits Bruzzo. "We revealed all of our constraints, and one of our customers recommended the pour-over method. It was truly an example of a company and its customers wrestling [with] an issue and ultimately getting to a positive resolution."

FINDING OUT WHERE CUSTOMERS ARE HANGING OUT

Through *My Starbucks Idea*, the company figured out how to reach its customers and create a very human connection online. Once *My Starbucks Idea* had plenty of traction, Bruzzo and his team began looking for other sites where their customers were forming online conversations and could perhaps help Starbucks join in. "We asked ourselves the question, 'Where else (online) are our customers hanging out?' That led us to Facebook and Twitter. We went there because that's where the customers are. We learned what mattered to our customers in these environments." Rather than jumping right into the conversations, Starbucks was deliberate in its approach, initially spending time just listening.

The task of replicating the in-store conversations online was put in the hands of Matthew Guiste and his small but capable team. Guiste's four-person social-media team is part of Bruzzo's 15-person Digital Strategy team. In Guiste's view, "The local coffee shop is the original social network. We needed to figure out how to replicate what it feels like in our stores, online—in other words, what is the digital analog of that in-store experience?" Starbucks has a unique and well-defined culture; therefore, in order to translate those conversations with the same "voice" in the digital channel of social media, the key was to involve a handful of people with considerable in-store experience.

With the full support of the Starbucks leadership team, Bruzzo, Guiste, and their teams have done a remarkable job of catapulting Starbucks into the position of being viewed by many as the most successful brand utilizing social media. A recent study entitled *Engagement: Ranking the Top 100 Brands* looked at the *BusinessWeek/Interbrand* "100 Best Global Brands 2008" and evaluated how those brands are engaging with consumers in social media. This Wetpaint/Altimeter Group study tracked how that engagement correlates with the companies' financial metrics. Of all the brands on the Engagement Index, Starbucks was ranked Number One (see Exhibit 4.3).[7]

Joining the Conversation on Starbucks.com

The Starbucks Web site is the launch pad for the *My Starbucks Idea* community, the *Ideas in Action* blogs, and the Starbucks V2V social network, as well as other company blogs covering everything from music, to menu items, to community outreach. The Web site also includes links to the Starbucks Facebook, Twitter, YouTube, and Flickr company-sponsored pages (see Exhibit 4.4).

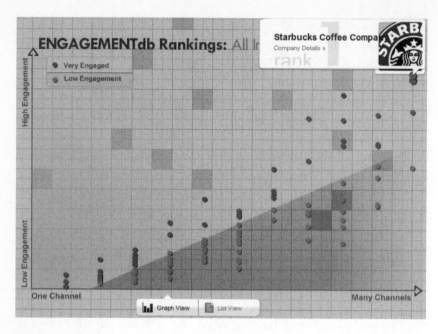

Exhibit 4.3 Wetpaint/Altimeter Group Brand Engagement Index
Source: Reprinted with permission of Starbucks and Altimeter Group.

Exhibit 4.4 Join the Conversation
Source: Reprinted with permission of Starbucks.

Facebook

With its 12 million-plus fans, Starbucks is both the Number-One retailer and the Number-One brand on Facebook.

Starbucks views Facebook and other social-media platforms as new ways to engage with customers. The Starbucks Facebook community originated organically. When Starbucks began looking at creating its own fan page in 2008, several fan pages built by others already existed. Starbucks quickly built its own fan page by investing in resources, engaging with its customers, and using paid digital advertising on Facebook.

Going onto the Starbucks fan page is like entering a virtual coffee shop. The Starbucks Facebook Wall is filled with hundreds of daily posts from customers, mostly a lovefest for the brand, along with the occasional requests and complaints. Starbucks Facebook posts are not only about offers, but also about brand stories, community outreach, customer experience, and even an occasional joke such as on April Fool's Day. "If you just build relationships on offers, it's a surface relationship," says Guiste. "We take a deeper approach." The global impact of the company's Facebook efforts has been compelling, with friends joining almost as fast as the original fans. This phenomenon is representative of both the equity of the Starbucks brand and the power of social media.

The Starbucks Facebook page also includes the following features:

- **Starbucks Around the World.** Click on one of the 20 country flags shown on the global map and launch into the Starbucks Facebook page for that particular country (see Exhibit 4.5).
- **Starbucks Card.** Find information about joining the Starbucks loyalty program and a test feature that allows Facebook users to manage their card balances and track rewards.
- **A Featured Product Offer.** Starbucks infuses content and sometimes a viral contest along with the offer. For Starbucks Via® Ready Brew, it featured an "Instant Story," asking the customer to fill in a few blanks in a precrafted story. Starbucks then "brewed" the story and sent it to the customer's fans, and

Exhibit 4.5 Starbucks Around the World
Source: Reprinted with permission of Starbucks.

in return the customer got a $1 coupon toward the purchase of Starbucks Via.

- **Other.** The page also contains photos, events, customer polls, and a lively discussion forum covering hundreds of topics.

Twitter

Brad Nelson of Starbucks is a popular guy. In fact he's so popular that since June 2008, he has built a following of nearly 1 million people conversing with him. Although many people don't know Nelson by name, they do recognize him as the main human face behind @starbucks on Twitter. Following Brad's conversations is fun and informative, and his personality shines through his Tweets, which are characterized by a distinct style and a sharp wit. Every day, Nelson busily tweets and answers questions about customer service and Starbucks promotional campaigns. According to Chris Bruzzo and Matthew Guiste, when Nelson takes a vacation, Starbucks has to explain that fact to the Twitter community, letting everyone know they "are introducing a 'guest DJ'" in the interim. "When Brad returns, it's like a celebration," says Guiste, who is Nelson's manager.

Starbucks grew Twitter organically. In fact, it was Nelson who first made the point that the company didn't have a Twitter account. "I told him, 'Go get it!'" says Guiste, and he did, with passion. As is true of other Starbucks social-media venues, Nelson brings authenticity to Twitter. In the virtual Twitter coffee shop, Starbucks wants to have that same kind of conversation that a barista has with in-store customers. What makes Nelson so authentic is that he not only understands how to converse in 140-character sound bytes and to build great customer relationships, but he is also a former barista.

Increasingly proud of Nelson's accomplishments, Guiste still recalls his favorite Nelson Tweet, which he describes as "magical" (see Exhibit 4.6):

> On this day in history: Hank Aaron hit #715 & the Clash released their first album. Suddenly I feel like I have a lot to live up to. #April 8

Guiste continues: "The reason I think it's magical is because it's just a typical example. You might say this isn't about Starbucks at all, but I'd argue this is everything about Starbucks. In 140 characters we managed to:

- Pass along an interesting tidbit that you [could] then share.
- Share in a celebration about baseball, music, and human achievement.
- Give people a motivational message.
- Reinforce Brad's personality—he's known as a fan of both baseball and music.

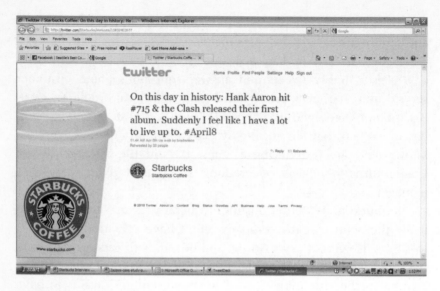

On this day in history: Hank Aaron hit #715 & the Clash released their first album. Suddenly I feel like I have a lot to live up to. #April8

Exhibit 4.6 Nelson's Twitter
Source: Reprinted with permission of Starbucks.

- Reinforce the company's position as a curator of good things.
- Replicate the sort of experience you have on your best Starbucks visit.

It's that sort of thing that we do day in and day out, [and] that is why nearly 1 million people follow us on Twitter."

In addition to @starbucks, the company maintains other Twitter accounts such as @mystarbucksidea, @starbucksjobs (Starbucks job postings), and @starbuckslive (used to follow a Twitter stream during live events such as Starbucks' annual meeting of shareholders).

When it comes to the use of social media, Starbucks thinks holistically. Customers engage with the Starbucks brand both online and in the stores, not just on social media. The company understands what is right for each specific social-media channel, but always views it from the overall brand experience. "Twitter and Facebook are incredibly rewarding in terms of whether you're hitting on what matters," says Bruzzo. Every time we put up a post on social media, we look at how many comments we got in return, as well as how many 'Like' votes we got, not just how many followers."

YouTube

With millions of views, Starbucks has one of the most popular brand channels on YouTube, which also lists Starbucks as being in the top 60 "Most Subscribed" channels of all time and in the top 100 "Most Viewed" channels of all time. And if that isn't enough, there are tens of thousands of Starbucks-related YouTube videos uploaded by others.

The Starbucks YouTube channel is both educational and entertaining. You can sit at home, sipping a cup of morning coffee and watching videos about the same subjects you'd find baristas conversing about in a Starbucks store. The channel is well organized, with Playlists for Coffee, Music, Giving Back, new Starbucks Via Ready Brew product, Starbucks TV commercials, and more. As is the case with Starbucks' approaches to its other social-media venues, its YouTube channel is first and foremost about building relationships, not just promotions (see Exhibit 4.7).

Exhibit 4.7 The Food Project—Youth Growing Together: A Starbucks Community Outreach Project
Source: Reprinted with permission of Starbucks.

Flickr

For the photography buff or just those people who enjoy looking through photo albums, Flickr contains over 300,000 images tagged with Starbucks. The Starbucks Flickr fan club formed organically before Starbucks engaged in its company-sponsored group, which now offers thousands of photos and a lively discussion thread.

STARBUCKS MOBILE

From the Starbucks perspective, mobile is a "green field" of opportunity. "We are just at the very beginning of what the potential is, when it comes to mobile," says Bruzzo. "The number of customers that are coming into our stores with mobile devices is continuing to skyrocket, and as Wi-Fi is becoming more accessible, that number is growing geometrically." Starbucks currently has two iPhone/iPod touch-enabled mobile applications: myStarbucks and Starbucks Card Mobile (see Exhibit 4.8). These applications focus on the company's strengths in customer loyalty, gift cards, payment, and social engagement.

myStarbucks

The myStarbucks application combines practicality with a little fun. Using GPS technology to identify your current location, Store Locator displays the closest Starbucks stores, as well as their amenities, store

Exhibit 4.8 iPhone Apps: myStarbucks and Starbucks Card Mobile
Source: Reprinted with permission of Starbucks.

hours, and directions. Also available for viewing are a complete listing and detailed description of Starbucks whole bean coffees, as well as nutritional information and ingredients for all of its menu items. If you aren't able to meet your friends at Starbucks, you can do the next best thing with the Drink Builder, which allows you to custom-build your favorite coffee drink and share it with all of your friends through Facebook, Twitter, SMS, or email. In addition, you can save your favorite custom-built drinks, coffee blends, menu items, and stores for recall.

Starbucks Card Mobile

The Starbucks Card Mobile application combines the My Starbucks Rewards loyalty program, Starbucks Cards (stored value cards), and payment. With Starbucks Card Mobile, iPhone, and iPod touch users can:

- Create virtual gift cards by electronically storing multiple Starbucks Cards on their phones.
- Check the remaining balances on any number of Starbucks Cards.
- Reload Starbucks Cards with additional value via credit card.
- Track the Stars earned toward free beverages through the My Starbucks Rewards program.
- Use the phone for electronic payment (in limited markets).

Starbucks Card Mobile is currently the largest mobile-payment initiative in the United States. While the application is still being tested, customers can use it to pay for their order at any of the 1,020 Target® Starbucks stores and select stores in Seattle and Silicon Valley. Customers can pay for their order simply by flashing the bar code on their phones against an in-store scanner and no longer need to worry about carrying their Starbucks Cards; they just have to carry their phones. Once a phone is scanned, the remaining balance on the card is shown (see Exhibit 4.9).

This application is loaded with the functionality that Starbucks customers use most often. Starbucks sees an unusually high use of

Exhibit 4.9 Starbucks Card Mobile: Card Balance and Bar Code for Payment
Source: Reprinted with permission of Starbucks.

cards, and some people even have several cards, so they constantly need to ask about the remaining balance on a particular card. Entering a card's identification number and security code into the application will store its balance in the phone. Customers can reload the electronic card directly from their iPhone or iPod touch.

Customers in the United States who register their Starbucks Cards either online or through their mobile devices are included in the My Starbucks Rewards program. When paying by phone, they will receive the same reward benefits as customers paying with a physical Starbucks Card. Using their phones, customers also can track their progress in the loyalty program since the application shows the number of Stars earned toward a free drink.

Both fast and easy, the application even includes a video clip that appears on the phone and gives step-by-step directions for how to use the phone to make a payment. Mobile payment is still in its very early stages, and Starbucks is on the cutting edge with this application.

"GeoLocation Sharing" for Social Engagement

Starbucks is now experimenting with "geolocation sharing" social games such as Foursquare and Brightkite, using them to build customer loyalty. The popular mobile-based social games work on the following premise: Users "check in" at particular locations, letting friends in their network know exactly where they are. Players who frequent a particular location can earn badges from that location. The person who checks in the most at a particular location is given a badge of honor. For example, in Foursquare, the person who checks in most often is given a badge designating him or her as "mayor" for that location. Although the badges have no monetary value associated with them, they do have "status" value in the game.

In Foursquare, Starbucks rewards frequent customers with the Barista badge. With its "Nationwide Mayor Special," Starbucks has added a time-based financial incentive to the game. Mayors of individual Starbucks stores can now unlock the Mayor Offer and receive a discount on a select drink. The deal offers customers a $1 discount on a Frappuccino® blended beverage for a limited time. Brightkite, a game similar to Foursquare, also is working with Starbucks to develop locally targeted and time-sensitive brand integrations across its mobile social network.

Starbucks promotions such as the Frappuccino Happy Hour are being highlighted across all of Starbucks digital channels, including Starbucks.com, *My Starbucks Idea*, Facebook, Twitter, YouTube, Foursquare, and Brightkite.

Although the mobile revolution is just beginning, Starbucks is taking this phenomenon very seriously. Bruzzo compares it with the ways in which Starbucks has embraced social media. "Social was two-and-a-half years ago a big green field—we've now opened up a new green field called mobile. We're excited to expand our presence in that field."

The Starbucks mobile strategy is clear. As Bruzzo explains: "What you see us doing in our apps is informed by where we have strengths and where mobile has a unique ability to deliver against those strengths. An unusual amount of transactions are done through Starbucks Cards. Mobile, as it relates to payment, preferences, and how customers order and buy, is a continuation of that strategy. We want to continue to stay in front of how customers are using stored value on the Starbucks Card. We are just at the very beginning of what the potential is for mobile."

DIGITAL LEADERSHIP

Its no accident that Starbucks is considered the leading consumer brand in its use of social media and mobility to engage with customers. Starbucks has invested in its competency in these areas. Chris Bruzzo and Matthew Guiste are two examples of talented Starbucks partners dedicated to driving its program forward.

Although the Starbucks digital strategy has led to several early successes, its team modestly believes it's only the beginning of the journey. The strategy's potential was demonstrated in July 2009, when Starbucks announced a "Free Pastry Day": All customers who came to a participating store before 10 AM would receive a free pastry along with their purchase of coffee. The company used social media as the primary channel for spreading the word, and the event proved to be highly successful.

"The community made this take off," says Bruzzo. "It significantly exceeded our expectations. The number of people standing in line with this offer in hand was unbelievable." Having played a major role in the early test launch of Starbucks Via Ready Brew, digital media also served as a major vehicle for the company's national launch in the fall of 2009.

With global expansion already a key part of the company's strategy, Bruzzo is enthusiastic about supporting it with Starbucks' digital efforts. As he points out, "Starbucks is a social experience everywhere in the world. The way we engage with customers is very different in different parts of world, but we're applying this approach globally." Committed to establishing a presence wherever its customers congregate—and determined to bring value and relevance to that relationship—Starbucks will continue to develop its competence in these areas.

Starbucks is a company with a foundation based on social responsibility and interaction. Schultz built the company with passion, intellectual curiosity, and a foundation of values found in the Starbucks Mission Statement, producing spectacular results. When the new worlds of social media and mobility burst into the market, Starbucks seized this major opportunity to use these new channels for communicating its strategy and culture worldwide. What an impressive beginning for the company's foray into the digital world.

NOTES

1. The authors are not employees of Starbucks nor have they received any consideration for materials contained in this chapter.
2. "Social Media Top Restaurant Players," *Nation's Restaurant News*, July 2009.
3. Howard Schultz and Dori Jones Yang, *Pour Your Heart Into It: How Starbucks Built a Company One Cup at a Time* (New York: Hyperion, 1999).
4. Starbucks Corporation, Fiscal 2009 Annual Report, fiscal year ended September 27, 2009.
5. Interview with Chris Bruzzo, conducted via phone, May 14, 2010. All subsequent quotes from Bruzzo are from this interview.
6. Interview with Matthew Guiste, conducted via phone, May 14, 2010. All subsequent quotes from Guiste are from this interview.
7. The world's most valuable brands. Who's most engaged? ENGAGEMENTdb, Ranking the Top 100 Global Brands, Wetpaint/Altimeter Group, available at http://www.engagementdb.com (accessed August 10, 2010).

5

Zappos: "Your Culture Is Your Brand"

H ow many retailers do you know that have done all of the following:

- Had a couple get engaged while touring its headquarters and later come back to hold the actual wedding ceremony?

- Hosted a contest to see who can eat eight Ding Dong snack cakes the fastest, then posted the resulting video on YouTube?

- For employees' birthdays, presented them with a customized "CelebriDuck" wearing tennis shoes and bearing a birthday cake?

- Given daily guided tours of its corporate offices to anyone who wanted to visit, invited the visitor to wear a crown and be photographed sitting in a VIP Royalty Chair, and then posted all photos at the corporate headquarters?

- To celebrate being acquired by Amazon, hosted a wedding-themed holiday party where employees dressed as brides and grooms and could get married (this time, for make-believe) by an Elvis impersonator.

■ Posted an April Fool's Day video of the CEO claiming he was suing Walt Disney for false advertising because he believed his retail company was the "happiest place on Earth"?

Only one retailer goes to this much trouble to share its culture with the world: Zappos. How does it pull off all this "fun and a little weirdness" while continuing to show remarkable growth? It's because of the Zappos culture, which is based on core values that include delivering the "WOW" factor through customer service, fostering a family spirit, being adventurous, embracing change, remaining open-minded, and creating a caring and trusting environment. This corporate culture translates into employees with a positive attitude and a natural passion for customers; and employees who treat custom-ers the same way they are treated within the company. Ultimately, the mission is for everyone to become a fan of Zappos. The company doesn't call itself a retailer; it characterizes itself as "a service com-pany that happens to sell shoes, clothing, handbags, eyewear, watches (and eventually a bunch of other stuff)." That is why this culture and its underlying attitude have enabled Zappos to become a leader in the use of social media (see Exhibit 5.1).

In fact, its culture and service are so successful that Zappos runs a culture-training center called Zappos Insights (www.zapposinsights. com) that anyone or any company can join to "learn how to create a strong culture where people love to work with service that WOWs your customers." Zappos Insights offers tours, meetings, a one-day training course, and a two-day culture boot camp. While Zappos

Exhibit 5.1 Zappos Facebook Post: Culture Webcast
Source: Reprinted with permission of Zappos.

Power of repeat customers and word of mouth...

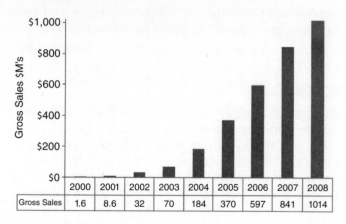

	2000	2001	2002	2003	2004	2005	2006	2007	2008
Gross Sales	1.6	8.6	32	70	184	370	597	841	1014

Exhibit 5.2 Zappos Year-to-Year Growth
Source: Reprinted with permission. From "Extending the Customer Experience" Slide Presentation of Zappos by Aaron Magness, April 26, 2010.

shares its culture with individuals from a variety of industries, it also uses its Insights program as an opportunity to learn from those who attend, for the program supports another of the company's core values: to pursue growth and learning.

Many elements are required for a business to attain brand equity. A company that uses a powerful culture and strategy to communicate effectively with consumers will be a powerful brand. Zappos definitely possesses these characteristics. This Web retailer, which has done an outstanding job of achieving these objectives, has become a leader in today's retail industry. With less than $2 million in sales in 2000, today, just a decade later, Zappos exceeds $1 billion in gross merchandise sales (see Exhibit 5.2). This enormous growth has been powered by outstanding customer experiences, as evidenced by the fact that 75% of the company's sales are from repeat customers, extremely loyal ones who love the experience and service that Zappos provides.

This reality runs counter to the overall retail trend of vast reductions in customer loyalty. Under the leadership of CEO Tony Hsieh, Zappos is committed to the belief that "Your Culture Is Your Brand."

His principles clearly guide the company's unique culture. Tony is passionate about promoting his company's values, staying focused, and learning from everyone. It would be impossible to communicate Zappos' culture without directly citing Tony Hsieh's own words. Following are excerpts from one of his many blogs, this one posted on January 3, 2009:

> Building a brand today is very different from building a brand 50 years ago. It used to be that a few people got together in a room, decided what the brand positioning was going to be, and then spent a lot of money buying advertising telling people what their brand was. And if you were able to spend enough money, then you were able to build your brand.

> It's a very different world today. With the Internet connecting everyone together, companies are becoming more and more transparent whether they like it or not. An unhappy customer or a disgruntled employee can blog about a bad experience with a company, and the story can spread like wildfire with tools like Twitter.

> The good news is that the reverse is true as well. A great experience with a company can be read by millions of people almost instantaneously.

> The fundamental problem is that you can't possibly anticipate every possible touch point that could influence the perceptions of your company's brand.

> At Zappos.com we decided a long time ago that we didn't want our brand to be just about shoes, or clothing, or even online retailing. We decided that we wanted to build our brand to be about the very best customer service and the very best customer experience. We believe that customer service shouldn't be just a department—it should be the entire company.

> So what's a company to do if you can't just buy your way into building a brand? What's the best way to build a brand for the long term?

> In a word: culture.

> At Zappos, our belief is that if you get the culture right, most of the other stuff—like great customer service, or

building a long-term brand, or passionate employees and customers—will happen naturally on its own.

We believe that your company's culture and your company's brand are really just two sides of the same coin. The brand may lag [behind] the culture at first, but eventually it will catch up.

Your culture is your brand.

http://blogs.zappos.com/blogs/ceo-and-coo-blog/2009/01/03/your-culture-is-your-brand

These are compelling words from a CEO, but what makes them even more impressive is that Zappos has delivered on its statements and its promise in every way possible, resulting in a high percentage of repeat customers, strong brand loyalty, and significant sales growth in the company's short history.

COMMITTED TO "WOW'ING" EVERY CUSTOMER

In 2009 Zappos was recognized by the National Retail Federation (NRF) in its Customer Choice Awards as one of the top retailers for customer service. The company also was selected by *Fortune* as one of the 2009 100 Best Companies to Work for. Zappos actively pursued this goal, and initially entered at Number 23, the highest ranking newcomer to the list for 2009. In 2010 Zappos moved up to the Number 15 position in this category. The NRF also recognized the company as 2010 Retail Innovator of the Year.

It is no surprise that Amazon, the largest online retailer, acquired Zappos in 2009 for approximately $1.2 billion, based on the value of Amazon stock at the time of close. Responding shortly after the acquisition, Amazon CEO Jeff Bezos stated, "Zappos has a customer obsession which is so easy for me to admire. It is a starting point for Zappos. It is the place where Zappos begins and ends. And that is a very key factor for me. I get all weak-kneed when I see a customer-obsessed company, and Zappos certainly is that."

The *Zappos 2009 Culture Book* clearly defines the "10 Core Values" of the company:

1. Deliver WOW through service.
2. Embrace and drive change.
3. Create fun and a little weirdness.
4. Be adventurous, creative, and open-minded.
5. Pursue growth and learning.
6. Build open and honest relationships with communication.
7. Build a positive and family spirit.
8. Do more with less.
9. Be passionate and determined.
10. Be humble.

These inspiring, yet practical, core values were not developed by a management team in isolation: Instead, Tony Hsieh invited all employees via a 2003 email to actively participate in determining the company's core values. He clearly made a conscious effort to understand what everyone thought would be important in order for Zappos to be a successful and fun company. This action gave a clear sign that Zappos wanted to be a unified team, communicating internally and developing an open dialogue with its customers and vendors. These simple, yet powerful statements exemplify the Zappos culture. It is also important, however, to understand how these principles translated into a successful retail business. The rapid sales growth for a specialty retail startup speaks for itself.

A VISION TO EMBRACE E-COMMERCE

In the early era of e-commerce, many constituent groups strongly believed that apparel, including footwear, would not have much revenue potential. Despite the fact that apparel catalogues represented a $2 billion business at that time, the prevailing view on the part of retailers, investors, and analysts was that building an online apparel business was an enormous challenge and would not likely produce significant revenue. Zappos, however, had the foresight to view the footwear business as a major online opportunity and was one of only a few companies to blaze this trail. Because of this early success,

Zappos also has expanded its merchandise categories to include apparel and accessories, housewares, and more.

Because of courageous merchants and consumer acceptance, much has changed in the ensuing years. On today's Web, apparel, shoes, and accessories represent almost $15 billion in annual sales, ranking behind only the retail and wholesale computer, electronics, and office-supply businesses. Customers have proven that they enjoy—and are comfortable with—the experience of shopping online for apparel and goods in related categories.

Because its many characteristics must be understood for a company to build and service customers successfully, the shoe industry has always presented a significant challenge for retailers. It is one of the most difficult retail businesses in which a company can satisfy customer needs. Consider the significant challenges of the various categories of women's, men's, and children's; then within them, the subcategories of dress, casual, athletic, and so forth. Now add the variations of size, color, and seasonality (e.g., boots for winter; sandals for summer). The number of stock-keeping units (SKUs) required to service a shoe store is the highest in the retail industry. Suffice it to say that this reality creates a significant logistical problem. Listen to most consumers' discussions about shoe-shopping experiences, and you will find that they are seldom positive. The sheer magnitude of unique SKUs makes it very difficult for a company to keep adequate in-stocks and provide good customer service.

Zappos became the Number-One online shoe seller by providing compelling assortments, supported by an engaging online shopping experience and outstanding customer service. Today it stocks over 3 million pairs of shoes, as well as a wide variety of handbags, accessories, and apparel from over 1,000 brands. Its strategy of providing stylish merchandise at value prices is consistent with that of other successful retail-industry brands. (See Exhibit 5.3 for a timeline showing Zappos' key milestones.)

The company is driven by its culture and open communication, along with superior merchandising, online store quality, logistics, and human-resource success. Anyone involved in online retail realizes that simultaneously developing high-quality performance in all these areas is an enormous achievement. When you consider the realities of

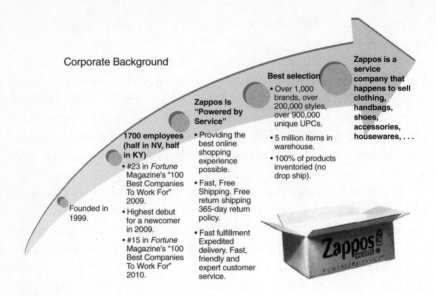

Corporate Background

1700 employees (half in NV, half in KY)
- #23 in *Fortune* Magazine's "100 Best Companies To Work For" 2009.
- Highest debut for a newcomer in 2009.
- #15 in *Fortune* Magazine's "100 Best Companies To Work For" 2010.

Founded in 1999.

Zappos Is "Powered by Service"
- Providing the best online shopping experience possible.
- Fast, Free Shipping. Free return shipping 365-day return policy.
- Fast fulfillment Expedited delivery. Fast, friendly and expert customer service.

Best selection
- Over 1,000 brands, over 200,000 styles, over 900,000 unique UPCs.
- 5 million items in warehouse.
- 100% of products inventoried (no drop ship).

Zappos is a service company that happens to sell clothing, handbags, shoes, accessories, housewares, . . .

Exhibit 5.3 Zappos at a Glance
Source: Reprinted with permission. From "Extending the Customer Experience" Slide Presentation of Zappos by Aaron Magness, April 26, 2010.

providing industry-leading customer service while managing a $1 billion-plus business— with an average transaction of $135 and four million items in the warehouse—Zappos' success is nearly mind-boggling.

WOW SERVICE ONLINE

Going to the Zappos site is an exciting experience that offers a broad merchandise assortment, with clear messages on key issues such as free shipping both ways and a 365-day return policy. A significant added dimension is the creative, service-oriented content that Zappos consistently includes at every customer touch point. Zappos adds blogs, videos, and updated information about what is going on in the company. In January 2010, the company was selected as one of the top-performing retailing businesses-to-consumer (B2C) sites for online customer service as part of the twelfth Annual Mystery Shopping Study conducted by the e-tailing Group, Inc. Retailers were ranked on speed, efficiency, effectiveness, accessibility, and customer service, and Zappos easily rose to one of the top positions in the study.

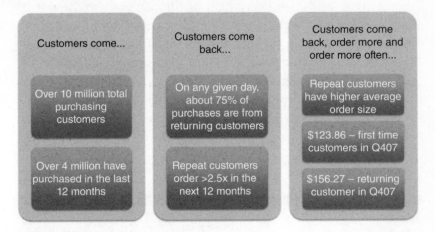

Exhibit 5.4 Zappos Customer Service Value Proposition
Source: Reprinted with permission. From "Extending the Customer Experience" Slide Presentation of Zappos by Aaron Magness, April 26, 2010.

Zappos believes in forming authentic personal and emotional connections with the customer (see Exhibit 5.4). The company's strategy has always been that face-to-face or telephone communication is the best way to form these attachments. The company currently engages in 6,000 phone calls per day with its customers, and its goal is to WOW every customer who calls. As the company has grown, however, it can't possibly talk to every customer by phone, so it also incorporated "live chat" on its Web site, currently participating in 400 live chats per day.

Take a look at the Zappos Web site, www.zappos.com, and you will experience an easy-to-navigate, function-rich Web 2.0 interaction with written and video-based customer reviews, testimonials, and quality feedback; live-chat help; and the ability to share an item with friends by email or on over 250 social-media sites. When customers view product information, "Zap.me" links enable them to share detailed product pages with their friends by allowing them to copy and paste a tiny URL about the product into blogs, Twitter, email, or a variety of other social sites. Also available is source code that can be copied and pasted into any blog, creating an "I Like: this item at Zappos!" blog badge for every item on the Zappos site. Zappos has already added Facebook's Open Graph functionality, providing customers with the ability to click the Facebook "Like" button on any Zappos product page and see which of their friends—complete with their Facebook photos—like that same product. Products can be enlarged and viewed from seven different angles, offering a more lifelike experience (see Exhibit 5.5). Zappos's site has been built on the following goals:

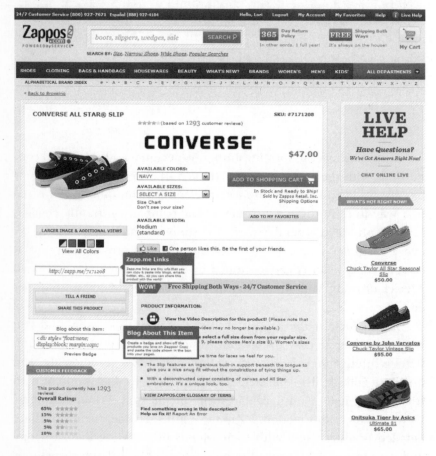

Exhibit 5.5 Zappos Web Site: Product Description Page
Source: Reprinted with permission of Zappos.

- **To give customers a voice on the site.** Customer reviews and a feedback mechanism provide a better user experience, useful information, and lower return rates. They also build empathy, a sense of community, and repeat visits; for Zappos, the strategy builds search-engine-optimization (SEO) value.
- **To enable product sharing.** The site provides free link-backs and community engagement while creating referrals that lead to customer acquisition.

There are also other Zappos Web sites that can be accessed: My.zappos.com, for example, allows a customer to add Zappos merchandise to a personal closet, share items with friends, and then see what those friends think of items in the customer's "activity stream."

For more specialized categories such as surfing, snowboarding, running, hiking, and even high fashion, Zappos offers such Web sites as rideshop.zappos.com, running.zappos.com, outdoor.zappos.com, and couture.zappos.com. Included in these sites are blogs, articles, and educational videos. To learn how to "have fun in an elevator," "wear your boyfriend's clothes," or "make frozen hot chocolate," customers can go to www.zappos.com/how-to, which includes videos featuring products sold at Zappos that allow consumers to experience how products can be used or clothing can be worn. Some of these even allow the customer to purchase the product by clicking at the top of the video.

AN EARLY LEADER IN "ZOCIAL MEDIA"

With the introduction of social media, Zappos recognized that because the times were changing, it was imperative to extend the customer experience beyond its site. The company views social media as a way to create more touch points with its customers, which, in turn, enable more frequent and meaningful engagement with them, leading to brand longevity. By extending the customer experience through social networks such as Twitter, Facebook, and other sites, Zappos is extending its opportunities for daily customer interactions from its 6,000 daily calls and 400 daily Web chats to more than 1 million encounters. This number translates to more than 400 million annual opportunities. According to Aaron Magness, Director of Business Development

Exhibit 5.6 Zappos CEO Blog
Source: Reprinted with permission of Zappos.

and Brand Marketing, "Employees are encouraged to 'be real,' use their best judgment, and WOW the customer at every touch point."[1] As a result, Zappos is one of the most successful retailers in terms of its effective use of social media.

Blogs.zappos.com frequently provides entertaining blogs by CEO Tony Hsieh, other Zappos associates, customers, and vendors on everything from Zappos' corporate culture, to community outreach projects, to product reviews. For Easter 2010, the site featured a culture song about its 10 core values, sung by "The Core Values Bunny." Zappos blogs are both insightful and entertaining, and accordingly they turn customers into fans. These blogs reflect the total operation: an open, transparent business with few walls and only open doors (see Exhibit 5.6).

Everybody Tweets Zappos!

In the world of social media, Zappos is best known for using Twitter. With over $1 billion in gross-merchandise sales, the company is currently well below the top 100 U.S. retailers in overall revenue ranking. With regard to its Twitter followers, however, now close to 2 million, Zappos vies with Whole Foods for the Number-One position among all global retailers. The company created Twitter.zappos.com to track all of its employees on the social-media site, and approximately 500 employees—nearly one third of Zappos's overall staff—currently use Twitter. The company uses Twitter to connect with customers and vendors, as well as to communicate with its colleagues. The most popular Zappos Twitter-user is Tony Hsieh, using the handle @zappos, with over 1.7 million followers.

According to Aaron Magness, Zappos began using Twitter in 2007 when the tool was introduced at the South by Southwest (SXSW) Conference. The company originally used Twitter because it provided one-to-many, text-messaging capabilities between employees. But Zappos quickly realized that a secondary benefit was the ability of people outside Zappos to listen in. "People could break down this 'faceless' corporation and listen to what Zappos was saying internally," said Magness. "Zappos is a friendly, family environment at work and believes in open, transparent communication, so Twitter was just a good way to communicate," he added. Soon, it wasn't just other people listening to Zappos employees on Twitter; people began retweeting Zappos tweets, customers and vendors began interacting with Zappos employees on Twitter, and the Zappos culture quickly spread through the Twitterverse. As Magness pointed out, the Twitter ID @Zappos_service was launched last year "to show that we're here to help ... to solve a problem. If someone says they're going to a wedding, someone from Zappos may send them a link for interesting wedding shoes. But we don't try to insert ourselves in customer conversations where we don't belong. And we are authentic, [providing] answers from real people, not a 'Tweet bot.'"

Why such a focus on Twitter? It perfectly fits the culture. Zappos has a limited budget for marketing, and word-of-mouth is still its best marketing strategy. Twitter is easy, inexpensive, and quick. "Even if we type 140 characters, it probably takes eight seconds of time," said Magness. "People often ask what our return on Twitter is. We don't measure it. Social media is used to share our culture, not sell our product. So we don't need to know the value of every tweet that our employees send out."

vanityfairest: Thank you, **@zappos**, for delivering happiness the same day as my awful tax return! Molly preferred your box, too! :)
http://bit.ly/bbsJWh
about 1 hour ago from Tweetie

dhbook: @SumitBhanote such a gd Q that we had 2 dbl check our answer w/ **@Zappos**. It's actually Tony's stunt double. Did we pass the test? ~Angela
about 1 hour ago from Echofon

iamnotpretendin: @joshuaplus Starbucks and **zappos** have good Twitter presences for sure
about 1 hour ago from TwitterGadget

scottbelsky: Made my day to hear that Tony @zappos will be adding copies of #MIH to the **Zappos** "library." Among good company!
about 1 hour ago from CoTweet

kegsofduff: Hey @zappos thanks for the crazyfast overnight shipping free of charge. 14 hours! My new shoes are sweet.
http://post.ly/YuOr
about 1 hour ago from Posterous

imagination: I cant wait to read the book "Delivering Happiness" by Tony Hseih (CEO @ **Zappos**)! imagiNATION
about 1 hour ago from web

DNICE_DA_FRESH1: **Zappos**.com got free shippin RT @Mr_Meer5: I gotta get me some Creative Recs asap
http://myloc.me/5N700
about 2 hours ago from UberTwitter

Exhibit 5.7 Tweets Referencing Zappos
Source: Reprinted with permission of Zappos.

Doing a hashtag search on #Zappos in Twitter currently yields hundreds of daily tweets consisting of customer questions and service-oriented responses, links to Zappos products that customers want to show their friends, customer testimonials to Zappos' outstanding service, links to blogs, and countless discussions about Zappos' unique culture (see Exhibit 5.7).

Tony Hsieh and his entire company honor the objective of immediately answering any customer inquiry, and this commitment to service permeates rougly 500 employees who represent the Zappos brand on Twitter. At Zappos, social media is all about culture and "delivering on the promise to customers." Zappos is wholly committed to communicating with all customers and turning them into fans. The company listens and interacts on Twitter, with the objective, whether it begins with a positive or a negative experience, of engaging customers and drawing them into the culture of Zappos' world. Interaction always begins with servicing the customer and making her purchase a positive experience. The entire approach on Twitter is to connect with all constituents, helping them become members of a high-quality, high-integrity, and fun family, while providing excellent service.

Facebook

Beyond Twitter, this same upbeat communication threads its way through other social-media sites. On Facebook, for example, more than 50,000 followers can interact with Zappos associates on the Wall, read blogs and glowing customer reviews about the company, watch videos, share photos, and laugh with the "Zappets!" puppets—all with the same brand reinforcement. Fans literally can spend hours entertaining themselves on the Zappos Facebook page (see Exhibit 5.8).

YouTube, Flickr, and Other Social-Media Sites

Log onto Flickr, and you'll see thousands of photos posted by Zappos fans that create a visual image of the brand. Zappos has its own YouTube channel, where thousands of videos are posted, including skits, parties, contests, instructional videos, and other types of videos, providing positive entertainment that reinforces the company's culture. Zappos YouTube channel features humorous videos such as "What the Zappos Easter Bunny Does After Easter" (see Exhibit 5.9).

"ZOCIAL MEDIA" IS PERVASIVE

As a company, Zappos has extensive blogs, a YouTube channel, and a Facebook page. While extensively used by approximately 500 of its employees, Twitter is more individualized—with the exception of a few corporate accounts. Zappos extends its brand on many other social-media sites, not by maintaining corporate accounts, but by allowing employees to go where they are comfortable. Furthermore, the company continues to build the brand on many other sites,

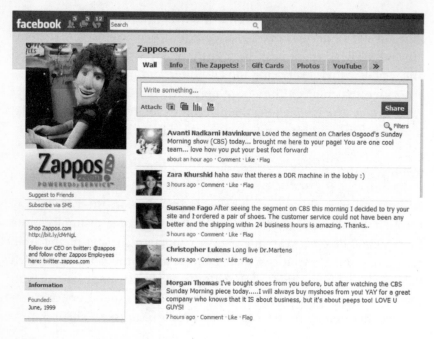

Exhibit 5.8 Zappos Facebook Page
Source: Reprinted with permission of Zappos.

Exhibit 5.9 Zappos Easter Bunny
Source: Reprinted with permission of Zappos.

including Flickr, friendfeed, LinkedIn, MySpace, Plurk, Pownce, tokbox, Ning, socialthing!, StumbleUpon, and Brightkite.

Zappos' use of social media clearly supports its culture and brand. The company makes effective use of a "communications architecture," with social media serving as the part of the overall architecture that focuses on personal and emotional connections with the customer at every touch point. "We don't have a social-media strategy or a goal specific to social media," said Magness. "In person or by phone is the best way to WOW the customer, but we can't always verbally speak to every customer, and therefore we look for other ways. Twitter is just a tool. Facebook is another tool. Internally we don't use the phrase 'social media.' We have a friendly, family environment at work, so it is just a good way to communicate."

Social media is all about bringing the brand and the store to wherever the customer spends time, rather than expecting the customer to find the store—or the Web site. While it may not have a formal social-media strategy, Zappos certainly has been successful at incorporating social media into its communications architecture. The company makes it easy for customers to engage with Zappos employees on most of the popular social-media sites, read one of their blogs, watch one of their videos, and—almost inevitably—all that communication leads to the customer's clicking on the Zappos Web site.

MOBILITY: THE NEXT CHANNEL

Zappos purposely has chosen not to introduce a mobile-based application until the company is confident that the chosen application will meet its stringent criteria for an engaging customer experience. As Magness pointed out, the original site was built to sell shoes. Now that Zappos is expanding in so many additional categories, the first priority has been to re-architect back-end systems to support the growing business. Zappos hasn't wanted to introduce a mobile application simply for technology's sake and risk a bad experience; its first priority is to ensure that customers will find it easy to shop with mobile technology. Accordingly, the company is scheduled to launch its mobile application in late 2010. Based on Zappos' track record with the communication channels currently available, the addition of a mobile channel undoubtedly will offer a significant growth opportunity for the company—especially considering Zappos' combination of strong brand identity and customer service with the more-than-285-million mobile subscribers in the United States.

When Aaron Magness described social media and mobility as part of Zappos' communications architecture, he talked passionately about branding: "Every interaction you have ... every communication you put out is 'branding.' The days of ad media are over," he said. "Your consumer is telling you what your brand is, and you need to embrace that. That is why we focus so much more on culture. If you get the culture right, you get the branding right!"

DELIVERING HAPPINESS: A PATH TO PROFITS, PASSION, AND PURPOSE

Tony Hsieh recently published the book *Delivering Happiness: A Path to Profits, Passion, and Purpose;*[2] in writing it, he was motivated by his desire to help entrepreneurs, and arguably the rest of the world, discover and instill happiness in others, all while pursuing their dreams. In *Delivering Happiness* (www.deliveringhappinessbook.com), he speaks humbly of his early beginnings as a childhood entrepreneur; his first successful startup, LinkExchange; and the many difficulties he encountered in building Zappos. Hsieh catalogs all the challenges that an entrepreneur must weather to pursue his dream; and in doing so, he focuses on what it takes to build a happy, fun culture that permeates an organization.

Having done extensive research on the "science of happiness," Hsieh truly believes that he can help make the world a better place through happiness; he has done much thinking about how to bring happiness to himself, to his employees, and to Zappos' customers. In this fascinating and humorous account, he discusses how people can increase their own happiness—and success—by increasing the happiness of those around them. Hsieh describes "how Zappos customers tell us they think of the experience of opening up a Zappos shipment as 'Happiness in a Box,'" and he explains how he turns his beliefs into actions that really *do* deliver happiness, while still continuing to passionately build a company with a strong purpose that delivers profits.

According to Hsieh, in 2009, Zappos simplified its vision and purpose in one statement: "Zappos is about delivering happiness to the world." If any leader—and his company—can ever come close to achieving such a lofty vision, we'd place our bets on this one!

NOTES

1. Interview with Aaron Magness, conducted via phone, April 5, 2010. All subsequent quotes from Magness are from this interview.
2. Tony Hsieh, *Delivering Happiness: A Path to Profits, Passion, and Purpose* (New York: Business Plus, 2010).

6

Wet Seal: iRunway Steals the Teen Fashion Scene

Soooo cutee! (:—AWESOME —Cool!—OMG SWEAR!!!—Loooveeee it! ♥—I am so wearing this outfit—ukno they r hot!—Cute(:—Adorable ☺—mye favorite place n da mall to shop—Woot, I am so there!—C my haul on YouTube—omygosh cute! ♥—LOVE IT!!!!(:

When you read Wet Seal's Facebook Wall or the flow of "#wet seal" tweets on Twitter, you may think you're reading your teen's text messages. What you're actually seeing is a steady stream of teens' comments about the latest fashions at Wet Seal, their favorite place to shop.

Many retailers are still refining how to effectively use social media by posting promotions and listening to feedback from customers. But at Wet Seal, because of the company's strategic, purposeful use of social media and mobile technology, something unique is happening: Teens enter their own virtual fashion world where they create and rate one another's outfits and chat with friends about the latest styles.

They also compete with one another to be voted a top "designer" on Wet Seal's site.

Using social media and mobility, teens can shop Wet Seal's latest fashions together, selecting and purchasing outfits that they or their peers have designed. Teens give plenty of feedback when Wet Seal posts the latest trends and styles on social-media sites like Facebook, but the beauty of this retailer's strategy is that most comments originate from teens socializing with one another about shopping at Wet Seal.

Wet Seal is a junior-apparel brand whose target market is 13- to 19-year-old-girls who seek trend-focused and value-priced clothing and accessories. Items can be purchased at one of roughly 425 stores throughout the United States and Puerto Rico or on the retailer's Web site (www.wetseal.com). Wet Seal also owns the brand Arden B (www.ardenb.com), an 80-store chain catering to 25- to 35-year-old contemporary women.

Wet Seal is known as a fast-fashion retailer for the fickle, style-conscious teen girl. The concept of fast fashion means offering a continuous flow of new styles that turn frequently and that drive the customer back into the store to see what's different. Fresh items build shopper frequency, and frequency builds loyalty. Buying decisions are made swiftly and must be accurate, or the retailer is left with excess inventory and markdowns. Trends in Wet Seal's market change quickly; seasons are many and short; and, unlike many other apparel retailers where items are purchased months before the season begins, in Wet Seal's fast-fashion world, the time from purchase to when the item hits the store floor is a matter of weeks. Fast fashion is a challenging business that is made even more difficult for a company catering to young adults whose tastes are influenced by peers and can change in a matter of days. These customers expect trendy, stylish clothing at affordable prices, or they'll quickly lose interest and go elsewhere.

FAST FASHION TAKES CENTER STAGE

Ed Thomas, Wet Seal's current CEO, initially served as the company's COO from 1992 to 2000. When he left in 2000, the company was performing well; fast-fashion competitors emerged in the late 1990s, however, and had gained significant momentum by the early 2000s. These competitors were building business models based on offering knock-offs of expensive fashion items that required no product development, had extremely short lead times, and offered low prices. Companies like Wet Seal and others were still operating with the slower cycle times and the higher prices traditionally associated with junior fashion brands. When Thomas was asked to return to Wet Seal in October 2007, he was faced with a difficult situation: Competitors in the fast-fashion world were growing rapidly, had more and larger stores, and could bring merchandise to the market faster than Wet Seal. Simultaneously, the United States was entering the worst recession in modern times.

To bring Wet Seal up to speed quickly, Thomas focused on three strategies:

1. **Sourcing and buying techniques.** To bring trendy merchandise to market faster, Thomas changed the company's buying structure from product development with lengthy lead times to domestic-market buying with short lead times. "We now source some of our merchandise as quickly as three weeks out,"[1] Thomas said. As a result, Wet Seal could make current, trendy buys and manage the quantities appropriately. Thomas also was able to broaden the assortment with the new buying model.

2. **Understanding customers.** Thomas also recognized that the customer age range was increasing, and his market was becoming more ethnically diverse: "We have a much wider demographic today than in the 1990s. We used to cater to 13- to 16-year-olds. Today, it skews a little older, going into the 20s, and is more ethnic, with more emphasis on African American and Latino customers."

3. **Enhancing the company's technology.** Thomas realized that the company needed to invest strategically in technology that would enhance performance. This strategy included a new merchandising system, a new point-of-sale system, business intelligence and sophisticated analytics, e-commerce upgrades, and innovations in social media and mobility.

A Customer-Focused Culture

In addition to implementing these fundamental changes, Thomas also focused on Wet Seal's market-driven culture: "Understanding what drives your customer and ensuring that your brand is appealing to that customer is what it's all about," says Thomas. "There's nothing more valuable than your customer base and your employee base to stay on top of trends." The company began bringing younger market-savvy merchants into the organization so they could better connect with the customer. According to Thomas, "Our culture is also entre-preneurial, with discipline and a lot of accountability."

Once he had his strategy and culture in place and integrated into the organization, Thomas looked for points of differentiation. He met with his CIO, Jon Kubo, who also leads e-commerce and Direct Marketing. Kubo was already experimenting with applying social media to Wet Seal's business. Thomas understood the teen market: "Each generation that comes up is more dependent on the Web for fashion advice than the last generation. Print media is nearly obsolete. The Web puts us on a level playing field with everyone else. It used to be in the junior market that a trend might start in Southern California and hit the East Coast in a year. Now the trend is instant across the country. The Web is critical in telling the customer what's new and what's exciting. What we also know about teens today is that they are incredibly good at multitasking. It's very different than it used to be. A teen can be on the Web, on Facebook, texting on her phone, doing her homework, watching TV, and whatever else at the same time." Understanding the value that social media and mobility could play in his strategy, Thomas embraced Kubo's early focus in these areas.

WET SEAL'S FASHION COMMUNITY

Social media and the use of mobile technology are second nature to Wet Seal's customers. Ninety-three percent of teens ages 12 to 17 go online, as do 95% of young adults ages 18 to 29. Seventy-three percent of American teens and 72% of 18- to 29-year-olds use social-networking sites. Since 75% of teens and 93% of 18- to 29-year-olds

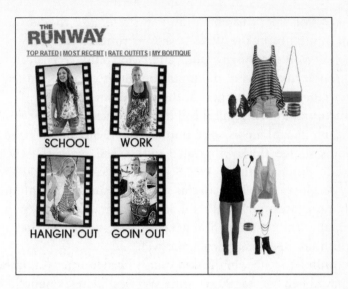

Exhibit 6.1 Outfitter Fashion Community
Source: Reprinted with permission of Wet Seal.

now have cell phones, cell phone ownership is nearly ubiquitous among teens and young adults.[2]

In 2007, based on Wet Seal's strategy, Thomas and Kubo were already building a unique differentiator with Outfitter, the company's online social community. By accessing Outfitter, which customers can tap into from Wet Seal's Web site, teens can become fashion designers (see Exhibit 6.1). Joining Outfitter is free, and when a teen uses the Outfitter application, she becomes part of Wet Seal's Fashion Community. By selecting clothing items, accessories, and shoes from Wet Seal's Web site and pulling selections into her virtual closet, a teen can create and name outfits for important occasions such as parties, dances, dates, school, or a day at the beach. Outfits can then be saved to a virtual runway that allows other teens from around the world to vote for one another's outfits and rank them based on popularity. It's the fast-fashion virtual equivalent of *American Idol*.

Because outfits with the most positive votes are ranked at the top of each category, teens can see which outfits are most popular among their peers. In addition to gaining the status that comes with being recognized among peers and being seen on the Web site as a "top designer," Wet Seal customers can view, rate, and click to purchase favorite outfits from the Web. Based on runway categories such as "School," "Work," "Hangin' Out," and "Goin' Out," teens can rapidly sort through hundreds of thousands of outfits created by their peers to determine which ones best fit their tastes.

Unlike traditional retail e-commerce, which is built around purchasing individual items, not outfits, Wet Seal makes it easy for customers to see trendy top-rated outfits and, with the click of a button, to purchase them. Wet Seal wins because, should the customer decide to purchase outfits in the Fashion Community, she usually purchases more outfits than if she simply had viewed items individually. The customer also wins because she knows she's buying an outfit that meets her peers' approval.

According to Kubo, in the two years since Outfitter was launched, teens have been constantly scouring Wet Seal's latest online fashions, designing outfits, and posting them.[3] To date, more than 400,000 outfits have been posted to the virtual runway, with between 20,000 and 30,000 available at any time. With an average of 20,000 new outfits being added every month, those numbers are growing daily. Once items in user-designed outfits are obsolete and no longer available for purchase in stores or online at www.wetseal.com, the company automatically removes them.

Based on customer-generated rankings, top designers are listed in Wet Seal's Fashion Community and can be viewed online. It's even become customary for a consumer designer to go to the digital airwaves of Facebook and Twitter with links to her outfits, asking others to cast votes to increase her outfits' ratings. The goal is to be ranked as one of the site's top designers. These outfits, along with the designer's username, outfit name, ranking, and number of views, are displayed prominently on the Wet Seal Fashion Community site for millions of other teens to see (see Exhibit 6.2).

iRunway

Wet Seal quickly followed the introduction of Outfitter with an iPhone application called iRunway, which allows customers to quickly sort, filter, and view outfits created in Outfitter, as well as to view rankings

Exhibit 6.2 Customer-Created Outfit
Source: Reprinted with permission of Wet Seal.

and related comments (see Exhibit 6.3). While the iPhone application is captivating, its major purpose is to drive cross-channel shopping and more purchases in the stores. When customers visit a Wet Seal store, they can use iRunway to scan a style number from an item's price tag and instantly view the wide variety of customer-generated outfits containing that item. Scan the barcode for a pair of skinny jeans, and the top-ranked, customer-generated outfits containing those jeans

Exhibit 6.3 Wet Seal iRunway Application
Source: Reprinted with permission of Wet Seal.

pop up, along with their rankings. One striped tank-and-shorts combination, complete with shoes and accessories, was viewed 33,315 times and given 23,441 positive ratings. More than 30,000 customers have already downloaded iRunway since its launch. The application is very sticky (meaning that customers stay on the site for a long period of time and visit frequently) and is already generating 500,000 outfit views per week.

Although Wet Seal is aware that iPhone access among teenagers is limited, it wanted to test the concept under the assumption that smart phones will continue to gain significant market share in the next few years. To further test the idea that teens will respond to content generated by their peers when shopping for clothing, Wet Seal piloted in-store kiosks in December 2008. The kiosks operate under the same premise as the iRunway application. Wet Seal's merchandise and inventory systems are integrated with the kiosk to ensure that customers are shown only those outfits that are immediately available for purchase in a given store.

While the kiosk tests provided a positive impact on sales, Wet Seal is refining its strategy because it believes that new mobile commerce devices such as smart phones and the Apple iPad will soon make kiosks obsolete. As for the value of this concept, Kubo tells a story about being in a store and using the kiosk to assist a customer. When she scanned the price ticket for a fashion top, a photo of all the outfits containing the item appeared on the screen. "She ended up purchasing related apparel, shoes, and accessories," he says. A $20 top sale became a much larger transaction because the customer could envision what to wear with the top.

FASHION—IT'S ALL SOCIAL

Wet Seal clearly recognizes that its most effective means of creating customer loyalty is to continue to build its Fashion Community where customers may share fashion tips and design outfits in a friendly, fun, and competitive environment. The company also uses more traditional social networks, such as Facebook, MySpace, Twitter, and YouTube. These tools offer Wet Seal a way to build brand awareness, gather customer feedback on new trends, and drive additional sales. These more mainstream social networks also provide a way for the company to gain Web traffic: In March 2010, Facebook surpassed Google as the top source for upstream traffic to www.wetseal.com.

Facebook

Wet Seal is rapidly building its Facebook presence. It began in Summer 2009 and by Summer 2010 it was closing in on 650,000 Facebook fans. Through its Facebook page, Wet Seal fans receive updates and share their opinions about promotions and new merchandise. They also can gain access to Facebook-exclusive coupons, view behind-the-scenes photos and videos, and interact with other fans of Wet Seal. The Facebook site also features its Virtual Runway application. This allows customers to post new outfits, view others' outfits, and share comments about their favorites with Facebook friends, creating a viral marketing effect for Wet Seal across hundreds of thousands of prospective customers.

Wet Seal's newest social-networking tool is an application called "Shop with Friends," created by San Diego-based Sesh, Inc. Shop with

Exhibit 6.4 Shop with Friends Facebook Application
Source: Reprinted with permission of Wet Seal.

Friends, available on both Wet Seal's Facebook page and its Web site, allows customers to shop with friends and family online in real time, seeing the same Web page even if they are separated by many miles (see Exhibit 6.4). Users can circle merchandise, make notes and suggestions, and even post to Facebook friends. During a Shop-with-Friends session, a customer can, for instance, click on a pair of skinny jeans, show them to a friend, circle them, and add a comment such as, "Would these go with my new red tank?" The friend can respond, and together they can browse through all of Wet Seal's merchandise to suggest alternatives.

Wet Seal also has plans to use the Shop-with-Friends tool as a customer service and personal-shopping application. Instead of chatting with a friend, a user would be able to initiate a Shop-with-Friends session with a company stylist to receive help. "Wet Seal will soon have Mobile Shop with Friends," said Kubo. "You'll be in the store, your friend will be on the Web site, and you'll shop together. Or you may be in the store, and your mom can be on the Web site. Tendering will come next. Teens generally don't have credit cards, so the idea of being in the store with a phone and being able to shop with your mom from home has a lot of appeal to our customers."

Twitter

Despite Twitter's not being as popular with teens as it is with adults, dozens of comments about Wet Seal can still be seen daily. As shown in Exhibits 6.5 and 6.6, teens also use Twitter to solicit others to vote for their outfits generated in Wet Seal's Outfitter application. In turn, Wet Seal experiences increased exposure and traffic every time someone clicks on the link to cast a vote.

Exhibit 6.5 Wet Seal Fan Tweet
Source: Reprinted with permission of Wet Seal.

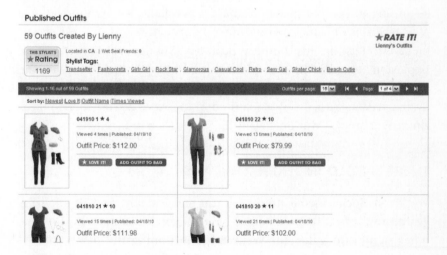

Exhibit 6.6 Link from Outfitter Attached to Exhibit 6.5 Fan Tweet
Source: Reprinted with permission of Wet Seal.

Other Social Networks

YouTube and MySpace also attract plenty of attention from teens. While Wet Seal maintains a YouTube channel with videos showing company photo shoots, fashion contests, and hot fashion picks, fans also frequently post videos displaying their "Wet Seal Haul" to show off recently purchased items and discounts. Wet Seal also maintains a presence on MySpace, where it posts news about trends and promotions.

MOBILE: SHOP ON THE GO

In addition to its iRunway application, Wet Seal has developed an m-commerce site launched in October 2009, when it partnered with Digby, a company specializing in developing mobile solutions for retailers. Mobile shoppers can purchase online and also have access to real-time inventory updates and location-based store look-ups. "Mobile is the next step in the e-commerce process, and it offers us a very powerful platform to communicate with our customer, regardless of which channel she is using to shop," says Thomas.

Despite its relatively small size compared with some of the larger retail brands discussed, Wet Seal has developed effective, innovative, and customer-friendly social-media and mobility tools. Wet Seal is beginning to receive plenty of market accolades for its innovations. *New York Times* business writer Steve Lohr featured Wet Seal's social-media strategy in his January 3, 2010, Sunday column, "A Data Explosion Remakes Retailing." In April 2010, Wet Seal received the Mobility Customer Engagement award from *RIS* (Retail Information Systems) *News* and also was featured in the April 2010 *Apparel* magazine cover story, "Wet Seal Nails its Social/Mobile Strategy."

THERE'S GOLD IN THOSE THREADS

Wet Seal's social-media strategy is fun and friendly, and its appeal is geared toward its teen customer base. Beyond customer loyalty, the other significant value for Wet Seal is in mining the data collected through these tools. The customer-generated outfits help Wet Seal identify exactly what trends and which combinations of merchandise are selling. "We can get a read on where our customer is headed faster than ever before," said Thomas. "It gives us unbiased, immediate feedback on what the customer is doing with the merchandise. She's voting on it. So we get a lot of information about trend." Buying decisions can be adjusted accordingly.

Through its Fashion Community, Wet Seal also has gathered customer-specific information on tens of thousands of teens, including names, email addresses, mobile phone numbers, and style preference, giving it the ability to target these customers based on their individual preferences. Similar to Web analytics from its traditional e-commerce site, Shop with Friends also allows Wet Seal to record each session, including which products customers were browsing, what product feedback friends shared during the session, and whether they made a purchase.

Even more powerful are the generated data showing the cross-channel impact of Wet Seal's Fashion Community. The iRunway application captures the mobile phone ID of the person who scans products using the in-store bar code. The company uses those data to look at customers' Facebook-post characteristics. "After we know the scans are there, then we will decide how to do promotions that are very personalized to what they [the customers] are doing," commented Kubo. While the program is still very new, Wet Seal can already track the scanned bar codes to determine cross-channel impact. "On good days we get 1,000 scans currently in the stores . . . we want to get to 100,000."

Despite two years already under its belt, Wet Seal still considers itself in the early stages of the social-media and mobile programs that integrate data collection and data mining. With social-media analytical tools being developed rapidly to analyze customer sentiment, find the most powerful customer influence networks, and personalize content, Wet Seal is creating a dynamic database of its customers.

Advice, Authenticity, and Affiliation

Thomas and Kubo are creating a steady flow of ideas for the next generation of social-media and mobility applications. Everything is done with a cohesive brand extension and customer-loyalty strategy. Wet

Seal's innovative approach is about understanding, listening to, and engaging with its customers, and then turning those customers into true brand advocates who carry the message forward for the company.

First and foremost, Wet Seal understands what interests its teen customer base. It engages with customers on new, trendy merchandise to determine what customers like and dislike. Through its Fashion Community, Wet Seal gives customers a worldwide virtual stage to display their creativity as fashion designers and instantly be ranked against their peers. Wet Seal then steps out of the way and lets customers engage with one another and sell the merchandise through peer reviews and outfits their friends and other fashion "experts" have designed.

Wet Seal is very clear about its social-media and mobility strategy. As Kubo describes it, retailers like Wet Seal need to address three questions:

1. How do we get customers into the store?
2. Once the customers are in the store, how do we engage them via a better shopping experience (e.g., Outfitter) or a personalized deal?
3. How do we enlist their social network to get additional viral sharing of the brand?

Wet Seal's Web site no longer starts with the traditional categories such as "tops," "bottoms," "dresses," and "accessories," which allow the customer to shop only by item. Instead, it features "Browse by Outfits" and "Shop with Friends" as more prominent home-page categories.

Traditional e-commerce design is not ideal for incremental related sales, since the customer is not presented with all that could go with an item to create an outfit. "Think about it," says Kubo. "All the systems are built around items. Electronic commerce is all about items today, and it should be about ensembles. We want to transform our customers from looking for products to getting a long tail from the overall trend. Social media gives us the long tail. User-generated content is the way to do it to get the long tail. We enable the customers to tell our brand story. The customers can tell each other what the trend is about. We just provide the shopping experience and give them the tools and let our customer brand advocates talk about the merchandise, what trends work, and what makes sense."

Wet Seal's approach to Facebook also differs from that of most other brands. The number of Wet Seal–originated posts is relatively small compared with those by customers. "When you're on Facebook, you want to be socially engaged," said Kubo. "You need to put that above anything else. It needs to be entertaining. People have to have fun. That's what Wet Seal does with Shop with Friends. Everything we do on Facebook is in a social context. We used to post our own outfits on Facebook. Now we post outfits from customers; we rarely post our own outfits. We determine the item that we are really trying to promote, go find the highest rated outfit that contains that item, and then we post that customer-designed outfit. Instead of saying, 'This is a cool item,' in order to better engage the customer, we say, 'What item would you wear with this outfit?'" Wet Seal has found that user-generated content elicits between 50 and 100 times more responses than company-generated posts. Exhibits 6.7 and 6.8 show

Wet Seal **Official Page**'s Photos - Wall Photos
Photo 324 of 329 | Back to Album | Wet Seal **Official Page**'s Photos | Wet Seal **Official Page**'s Profile

Check out our Hot Item right now- the Poppy Girl Dolman Tee! Here's a super fun outfit that one of our fans made in the boutique. Would you wear it?
http://www.wetseal.com/outfitter/outfit.jsp?outfitId=410851

Exhibit 6.7 Wet Seal Facebook Wall Post
Source: Reprinted with permission of Wet Seal.

Exhibit 6.8 Wet Seal Facebook Wall Fan Responses
Source: Reprinted with permission of Wet Seal.

a Wet Seal post designed to gain feedback about a user-generated outfit.

There's a lot of talk about using social-media channels to listen to what the customer wants. That's important, but Wet Seal has taken this idea a step further. Kubo explains it as "The Three A's of Social Media: Advice, Authenticity, and Affiliation." Elaborating on this concept, he adds, "It's about empowering your brand advocates to speak passionately about all your merchandise and your brand so the rest of your customers have all the information they need to make important decisions about the brand. Instead of seeking an influencer who may affect buying decisions in her circle of friends, make all of your brand advocates influencers. It's more about giving these brand advocates great tools so influencers become viral."

Wet Seal has a clear vision of how it will continue to build its base of brand advocates. "In social media, there are two kinds of people we talk about: experts and influencers. Most companies are focused on the influencers," says Kubo. "Wet Seal concentrates more on experts than influencers. We want a lot of experts who generate great content. We're not necessarily targeting influencers who have a lot of friends. The next step is to determine which of these experts will help you as a consumer to better make your decision. In other words, we believe in identifying the experts, then [we] pair them with consumers who have like tastes. The experts may not currently be part of those consumers' network of friends. They are not necessarily friends on Facebook, but they drive huge decisions. We'd rather pair up an expert that has your taste and that you're affiliated with instead of just friends."

SOCIAL + MOBILE = A GAME CHANGER

As for Wet Seal's mobile strategy, the tendering or convenience of buying is not the biggest benefit, according to Kubo. The bigger benefit is coming from its iRunway mobile application, which allows a customer to scan an item in the store to see what outfits other teens are wearing with that item. "We want the customer in the store, and we want to make the experience better. With iRunway, we are trying to make the best cross-channel strategy by engaging the customer in the store by taking the best of mobile," Kubo adds.

The company's social and mobile strategies are tightly integrated. "These are two huge technologies, but the real power comes at the intersection," says Kubo. "Mobile plus social is absolutely a game changer for retail. Wet Seal's iRunway application makes good use of this theory." Thomas clearly agrees: "I think the smart phone and the social-media part tie hand in hand," he says, "certainly from a marketing standpoint and soon from a payment standpoint."

Thomas is already thinking about how to give teens the ability to pay from their smart phones at some point in the future: "With our iRunway application, they scan items in the stores, they see the outfits, they have a store locator, but adding the ability to pay like an electronic gift card will be the big win. A disproportionate amount of sales are done in cash because teens have no credit. I look at my own daughter. If I could electronically send money to her iPhone, this would be an easy way to do it."

Measuring Results

At approximately $550 million in sales, Wet Seal is a relatively small retailer, with a lean culture, a limited marketing budget, and fewer resources at its disposal relative to larger companies. But Thomas has a clear vision of customer engagement; he believes in testing innovative ideas and proving return on investment (ROI) along the way, with a focus, making them essentially self-funding. Kubo brings the entrepreneurial creativity that is required in such an environment.

Wet Seal's social-media strategy is creating a lot of buzz, but the real value lies in the customer loyalty and analytical data it's generating, as well as in the increased sales and profitability to its bottom line.

"The true measure of these tools' usefulness is whether sales increase. And they have," says Thomas. "Our conversion rates [from browsing to buying] are over 40% higher for customers who have viewed a user-generated outfit, and the average dollar sales are over 20% higher. I look at ROI this way: It's a marketing expense. We're not expecting miraculous results [on] Day One, but we think it's critical that we invest in it now and not play a game of catch-up later."

Eighty-five percent of all items in the chain are associated with outfits from user-generated content, and Wet Seal can already tell that the Outfitter application generates 20% of its e-commerce revenue. "Conversions are far less from people that didn't use it [Outfitter]," says Kubo. "Average dollar per sale and average order per sale are also far better. The cross-channel value is the biggest opportunity for Wet Seal. The idea is to bring great things from the Internet into the store to increase sales. It's about bringing the best user-generated content into the store to allow the customer to see entire outfits she can buy along with that item she's thinking about purchasing."

Tone At The Top

Many otherwise great retailers are still uneducated about the powerful impact of social media and mobility. Thomas credits his being more up-to-date than some retailers to his dealings in the teen market, but he admits, "There is still a lot we don't know." He reviews customer feedback daily, and, despite having other means of monitoring social media, he personally looks at Wet Seal's Facebook fan page weekly. In the long run, for a social-media program as comprehensive as Wet Seal's to be effective, it must have organizational buy-in, not only from marketing, but also from merchandising and operations. "To engage the overall staff, what's critical is [the] tone at the top," says Thomas. "We are educating our executives on this technology. It starts with the tone at the top, but if I understand it better than they do, it's a problem."

Thomas admits that as CEO, his biggest challenge has been to motivate the rest of the company to become engaged in social media, especially buyers and others who may not be technology-savvy. Consequently, Wet Seal holds regular internal social-media training classes for its staff. "Every time we do something differently on social media, we do a launch with our employees," Kubo explains. Thomas adds that in order to spread the tone from the top down into the merchant ranks, he personally did a live demo of Shop with Friends, using one of his staff members as a co-presenter to demonstrate how social-media tools can be utilized and to show the type of information that can be monitored.

FARMVILLE FOR FASHION

Consumers spend time on Facebook primarily to socialize, not to shop, and Wet Seal has proved it understands that fundamental premise. Consumers also spend a significant percentage of their time on Facebook playing games; gaming is, in fact, the largest socially acceptable activity that occurs there. FarmVille, the most popular game on Facebook and other social networks, has more than 80 million players and 29 million active daily users. Other social-media games like Cafe World, Mafia Wars, Fishville, Petville, and Happy Aquarium all capture

Exhibit 6.9 Home Page for Wet Seal's New Fashion Game "Chic Boutique."
Source: Reprinted with permission of Wet Seal.

the attention of millions of players every day. Rarely do consumers post about retailers' products to their friends. What is seen on friends' Facebook pages is constant game comments posted by consumers playing other popular games. "The game guys have broken the consumer code," Kubo comments.

Not surprisingly, Wet Seal's latest introduction is a social-media game called "Chic Boutique" that Thomas describes as "our own version of FarmVille. It fully integrates into Outfitter and our mobile technology." The premise of the game is that the teen gets to play retailer, opening a Wet Seal store, then getting to design outfits in the store. Having selected and placed these outfits in the store, she then has her friends rate them. As she posts outfits on her friends' walls, that action gives Wet Seal viral impact. And, as the outfits earn more positive ratings, her store sales increase (see Exhibit 6.9).

As the teen's sales increase, she moves up a level in a strategy similar to that used by FarmVille and other Facebook games. Then, as she advances from level to level, she can buy marketing dollars, move the store to a better location, buy additional fixtures, add more floors to the store, and do other things that actual retailers do to increase sales. She can even work to build multiple stores, selecting new locations on maps to ultimately build a Wet Seal empire.

Wet Seal also plans to tie the game to the real world. Instead of charging the players to level up as most games do, Wet Seal instead will offer players discounts and promotions in the real world. Using these promotions in a real Wet Seal store will give players more points to level up in the game. If the teen is actually in a real Wet Seal store, she can scan an item from her outfits within her game's virtual store and accumulate extra points in the game. The key here is tying the gaming experience, which is very popular among teens, to real-world shopping. Kubo observes that this is one more way to give tools to the retailer's brand advocates to celebrate and spread the word about Wet Seal.

Regarding the competition's tapping into these tools, Thomas says, "The reality is that I'm sitting here with 4,000-square-foot stores, and my biggest competitor has 20,000- to 100,000-square-foot stores. I look at all of this as a point of differentiation. The more we do here, the more customer loyalty we get. We also have to get the right product or nothing matters, but this also gives us enormous customer feedback, which allows us to improve our merchandise mix. Outfitter may become obsolete. The game we are developing may become obsolete. My strategy is to keep 10 steps ahead of everyone else."

NOTES

1. Interview with Ed Thomas, conducted via phone, April 29, 2010. All subsequent quotes from Thomas are from this interview.
2. Pew Internet Study: Teens and Mobile Phones, April 20, 2010.
3. Interview with Jon Kubo, conducted at SAS Global Forum Conference, April 12, 2010. All subsequent quotes from Kubo are from this interview.

7

Macy's: Shooting for the Stars!

When it comes to retail brands, Macy's has always been in a unique position. With its larger-than-life image, it represents incredible excitement—the 2,169,000-square-foot Herald Square flagship store, the Macy's Thanksgiving Day Parade, Macy's Fourth of July Fireworks, flower shows, movies, songs, celebrities, and so much more. With its storied past, many famous entertainers and movie stars who have been affiliated with the company, and its quest to give customers a magical shopping experience, Macy's bright red star logo is a timeless symbol of the all-American brand. Nearly everyone has a Macy's recollection, and yet it was not a national department store chain until recently.

TWO GREAT BRANDS

Macy's, Inc., comprises Macy's and Bloomingdale's, two of the most well-known department store brands with worldwide exposure. Millions of visitors from other countries travel to major U.S. cities—New York, San Francisco, Chicago, Los Angeles, Miami, and others—and experience the joy of shopping at Macy's and Bloomingdale's. These two iconic brands are supported by 161,000 motivated employees. Although our major focus in this chapter will be on Macy's, as it has 810 stores and is undergoing enormous and exciting changes, let's first take a quick look at the iconic Bloomingdale's.

Bloomingdale's

Bloomingdale's is America's only upscale, full-line department store chain with an international fashion reputation. The company's 40 stores offer upscale contemporary brands, supported by outstanding amenities and service. Bloomingdale's anchor stores are located in the highest quality fashion malls across the country. The power of the Bloomingdale's brand was exemplified when a store opened in Dubai, the first international location for Macy's, Inc. This 146,000-square-foot store and a separate 54,000-square-foot home store now anchor one of the world's largest shopping centers. With an impressive store presence and a rapidly growing Web presence at Bloomingdales.com, this is a unique upscale cross-channel retailer.

Four Bloomingdale's outlet stores, a new concept for the company, launched in 2010. These stores offer a wide range of apparel, accessories, and jewelry in spaces of approximately 25,000 square feet. Additional Bloomingdale's outlet stores are expected to open in the coming years, and this strategy represents strong potential for growth.

Macy's

Macy's converted about 400 former May Company stores to the Macy's nameplate in 2006. Combined with about 400 existing Macy's stores, this brand became a powerful national presence. While this was a clear strategic decision, the name change created an emotionally charged debate in local markets. Chairman, President, and CEO Terry Lundgren made this decision at a critical time marked by the emergence of cross-channel retailing. Although the decision to operate all of the stores under the Macy's name required a great deal of reorganization and communication, all signs point to the strategy working. For the first time, Macy's was named as one of

Interbrand Design Forum's 2010 Most Valuable U.S. Retail Brands[1] based on its three-year focus on becoming a "master brand." Even more important, serving customers under one name allows the company to capitalize on the new world of digital engagement with consumers. With 2009 sales of $23.5 billion, 850 retail stores, and a growing cross-channel business, Macy's, Inc., has been making many innovative changes over the past few years and is poised for significant sales growth.[2]

MACY'S STRATEGY REFRESHED

Macy's updated its business strategy in early 2010, reviewing the market dynamics and positioning the brand to achieve its revenue and profit growth plans. The company "refreshed" its four strategic priorities (i.e., assortment, value, shopping environment, and marketing) with new tactics, including a strategy to engage with customers in the rapidly evolving digital world. An important part of these changes focused on creating a company culture that embraces innovation and testing, an inclusive work environment, and the development of its people.

Macy's four strategic priorities are:

1. Differentiating merchandise assortments and tailoring them to local tastes
2. Delivering obvious value
3. Improving the overall shopping environment
4. Enhancing customer engagement, loyalty, and traffic through more brand-focused and effective marketing

Branding and Value

The dynamics between the department store industry and its branded suppliers have changed dramatically over the past several years, and Macy's is benefiting from these changes. Of the major national department store chains, Macy's has the broadest range of well-known and prestigious brands in apparel, accessories, cosmetics, and home furnishings. Exclusive, private, and limited-distribution brands, most developed by or with Macy's, represented more than 42% of the company's total sales in 2009, and this penetration continues to increase.

Today's consumer demands brand authenticity, fashion, and value, and Macy's meets these needs, supported by its suppliers and product development organization. Macy's plans, designs, and sources these brands at affordable prices, giving customers a reason to shop more frequently. The company now has an unprecedented opportunity to communicate this message through national marketing, as well as direct customer engagement through social media and mobility.

Private Brands

Because of the confidence that customers have in Macy's, the company has developed 15 successful private brands of merchandise, including Alfani, American Rag, Charter Club, Hotel Collection, I.N.C., and Style Co., and each has a strong following. In 2009, private brands and labels exceeded 19% of Macy's sales. With this percentage of the total business, maintaining fashion-right merchandise, in-stock positions, and high quality, private brands will continue to be an important element of Macy's business.

Exclusive Brands

A major element of Macy's store-brand strategy is to provide customers with well-known, fashion-right merchandise from market brands sold exclusively at Macy's. This strategy has been highly successful with brands such as Martha Stewart Collection, Tommy Hilfiger, Donald Trump, and others. In 2009, Macy's launched "Rachel Rachel Roy only at Macy's" and several other new exclusive brands. In the spring of 2010, Ellen Tracy–branded sportswear was launched, and Sunglass Hut eyewear began its rollout in the fall of 2010. Macy's will become the exclusive department store retailer of Kenneth Cole Reaction men's sportswear, Sean John men's sportswear, and a new junior line called "Material Girl" being developed in conjunction with Madonna. Exclusive brands and national fashion brands that are exclusive to Macy's, they thus form an important strategy for Macy's to provide its customers with well-recognized fashion at affordable prices.

Macy's focuses on speed-to-market and has selected certain merchandise categories as "Fast Track," which means reducing cycle time to 10 to 15 weeks. This strategy, supported by the product development team, enables the company to maintain fresh, fast-changing inventory, thereby inviting the customer to shop Macy's more frequently.

My Macy's

Despite its status as a national department store, Macy's remains highly sensitive to the unique needs of its customers in local markets. Department store customers have always been loyal to their local store because they believe it is "their" store. Macy's is now responding to these needs with its key strategy—My Macy's—which is all about making the company's merchandise specific to customers' needs in every store and local market. In particular, it involves tailoring merchandise by focusing on such major factors as style preference, climate, customer diversity, and size. The company also is gearing its marketing and promotions so that the customer feels that her local store is "My Macy's."

The company cites an excellent example of the success of this strategy: The Menlo Park, New Jersey, Macy's trade area has experienced a demographic shift, with Asian Americans now representing 35% of the customer base, up from 16%. The district team identified this demographic shift and responded with necessary merchandise changes. With refined data, the company continues to focus on local customer needs and will be able to further serve those customers through directed digital media.

Peter Sachse, Macy's Chief Marketing Officer and Chairman of macys.com, provided insights into the implementation of My Macy's. He discussed the challenging process of integrating all of the operating divisions under the Macy's banner. "In 2009, we took the bold step of consolidating them down to one very large operating division. While there were compelling reasons to do this, we also wanted to keep the localization to better serve our customers—therefore My Macy's was born."[3]

Sachse discussed both the structural and process changes that were required in the company. The major advantage is that the company redeployed some of the savings from consolidation and invested in a field organization sourced by much of the merchandising talent that existed in the former operating divisions. Sachse commented, "As an example, we are utilizing our West Coast buyers and planners as members of the new team in the field. This is a major competitive advantage because we already had the talent in the company."

Deborah Weinswig, Managing Director and Senior Retail Analyst at Citigroup, said in the 2010 first-quarter Macy's financial update that "management believes the company is only in the early innings with respect to My Macy's localization initiative. We were pleased to learn that Macy's best performing stores are its smaller volume doors, as it serves as evidence of the My Macy's initiative taking hold and delivering top line benefits."[4]

Macy's Online

Macys.com is growing strongly in e-commerce and serves as the customer-interaction hub for all channels.

Online

Macy's online business performed strongly in 2009, with an increase of over 20% in a very difficult economic environment. In the Spring 2010 analysts' meeting, Terry Lundgren said, "A bright spot in our business is the Internet. We remain very excited by the possibilities for our direct-to-customer strategy and it is becoming increasingly integrated with our stores." An excellent example of this synergy is Macy's Search and Send Web tool, which allows associates to complete a sale when a product is not available in a local store. Lundgren added, "In the past several years, Macy's has invested heavily in its e-commerce channel and its direct-to-consumer fulfillment capability." Macy's has invested hundreds of millions of dollars to upgrade site functionality, e-commerce, order management, warehouse management, and fulfillment.

According to the *Internet Retailer 2010 Edition Top 500 Guide®*, Macy's ranked Number 20 in the top 100 e-retailers in 2009, a rise of three positions from 2008.[5] With apparel representing over 24% of retail-industry Web sales in 2009—and housewares/home furnishings another 10% of all retail Web sales—Macy's, with its strong penetration in these categories, clearly is poised to experience strong sales growth. With a sales increase of over 35% for the first half of 2010 over the same period in 2009, the company is capitalizing on its large e-commerce opportunity.

The Hub of the Brand: Macys.com

Macy's views its Web site as the central connection point between its brand and its customers. Sachse is responsible not only for the company's brand, but also for its Web site and e-commerce. In addition to the Web site's contribution of over a billion dollars in annual revenue (Macys.com and Bloomingdales.com combined), Sachse describes how it must facilitate customer interaction across all channels: "We believe the Web site is the hub of the brand," said Sachse. "It's not just an e-commerce vehicle. The Web site has to be the giant facilitator for all of these channel strategies—from mobile, to social media, to store." Consider that the company can "bring the store" to the customer in so many ways, regardless of which channel she chooses to shop. The more Macy's knows about the customer, the better it can anticipate her needs, inform her, and provide her with superior customer service. This is the power of cross-channel, utilizing all elements of customer contact. We will further review these opportunities as we discuss Macy's social media and mobility strategies.

ENGAGING THE CUSTOMER

Macy's is an exciting place to work. Customer focus comes to life in My Macy's, where local merchandising teams listen to and respond to customer needs. At Macys.com, the company solicits and closely monitors customer ratings and comments, again taking action as appropriate. These engagements represent a commitment to providing a rewarding experience for customers regardless of where they choose to shop Macy's. This service to customers will grow as the company expands its Web platform as its hub for all information.

Sachse describes Macy's focus, innovation, and customer engagement as the heart of the culture of the company. In describing the period in 2010 when Macy's refreshed its strategy, placing the customer at the center of all decisions, Sachse said, "When we talked about the tipping point being the customer, we asked the question, 'do we really act that way?' Terry Lundgren immediately deemed himself the Chief Customer Officer and appointed me as Customer Champion. We have always made P&L [profit and loss] decisions but we didn't necessarily look at it from the customers' perspective." Sachse further discussed a plan for focusing on, listening to, and engaging with the customer. "We focused on and encouraged innovation among the employees. We start all meetings by asking 'What will our customer get out of this discussion?'" Sachse says. "If there's no answer, the meeting is over."

Happy customers often make for happy employees, as evidenced by the 2008 and 2009 Macy's "Believe" campaigns, during which the company matched every letter to Santa that was sent to Macy's by customers with a $1 donation to the Make-a-Wish Foundation. Sachse discussed the positive—but unintended—outcome of the campaign. "The company received thousands of emails from its own employees about how proud they were of Macy's campaign that gives back to the communities. We all know when employees feel good, that ultimately leads to better customer service—a positive attitude is contagious." Combine this with Macy's priority of attracting, training, and growing what it believes to be "the most talented people in the industry," and you have a workforce that is committed to strong customer service.

SOCIAL MEDIA IS FASHIONABLE

Macy's had begun using social media several years ago, but in 2009, with significant enhancements to Macys.com, its launch of Facebook and Twitter pages, and its iPhone commerce application, the company became very engaged in this dynamic new platform. That said, Sachse believes that the potential of this new channel is in its early stages for Macy's. Its longer-term social-media strategy is still unfolding, but it will tie closely with the company's broader strategy for My Macy's.

"We believe social media is an incredibly powerful medium and we want to get engaged with the consumer. You can either ignore that or get into the conversation," says Sachse. My Macy's brings all kinds of possibilities for personalizing the shopping experience to individual customers, and that is clearly where Macy's sees its biggest opportunity with both social media and mobility.

To date, the company has leveraged social media for the launch of most of its fashion and marketing campaigns. Its spring and summer 2010 "Fashion Director" outfit-building contest has received an "enormous amount of engagement," according to Sachse. Macy's Material Girl Madonna-designed fashion line is being launched through blogger and social outreach. And the company filmed a series of entertaining and humorous Webisodes of its fashion designers Clinton Kelly, Martha Stewart, Rachel Roy, and Donald Trump performing "Fashion Interventions" across America (see Exhibit 7.1). The Webisodes drove traffic to YouTube and also can be viewed on Macy's TV, which is featured on Macy's Web site.

Social media also played a hand in the success of the previously mentioned "Believe" campaign, during which customers were asked to write letters answering the question, "Why do I believe?" As a

Exhibit 7.1 Donald Trump Fashion Intervention at a Grade School "Bake Sale"
Source: Reprinted with permission of Macy's, Inc.

result, people wrote inspirational and heartfelt letters detailing why they believe in Santa Claus or perhaps why they believe in a spiritual way. A gallery prominently displayed each letter, some with pictures and videos, on Macys.com along with its votes and ranking, and the company awarded a trip for four to the Macy's Thanksgiving Day parade to the letter writer with the highest number of votes. People took to social networks such as Facebook, Twitter, and MySpace to help solicit their friends' votes.

As for building its fan base on Facebook and Twitter, Sachse states that the company wants to do so organically. Macy's views these sites as brand builders. Therefore the company doesn't offer a promotional incentive for becoming a fan. "We believe our fans are therefore zealots," says Sachse. "If someone starts to rant on one of these social networks, the community defends us!" Macy's employs both an internal team as well as media agencies to monitor these social sites.

Macys.com—It's Social!

Previously we discussed the fact that Macy's views its Web site as not just an e-commerce vehicle but also, as Sachse describes it, "the giant facilitator of all strategies." This relates to using all relevant data to inform and serve the customer regardless of where she chooses to make her Macy's purchase: Web, store, or mobile. As the data and technology improve, the possibilities grow proportionally. The Web as the "hub" provides customers with information never before available to them, and the better informed store employees have the tools to provide outstanding customer service.

Customer Reviews

Every product is given a one- to five-red-star (Macy's logo) rating based on customer votes, and customers are encouraged to write reviews (see Exhibit 7.2). Ratings and reviews, both positive and negative, are prominently displayed, and shoppers also can send their reviews to their friends through a variety of social networks such as Facebook, MySpace, Twitter, and Digg. Some products sold on Macys.com have hundreds of reviews.

Exhibit 7.2 Rant. Rave. Win.
Source: Reprinted with permission of Macy's, Inc.

At the National Retail Federation's Shop.org annual summit, Lundgren shared his perspective on customer-generated reviews, a topic that causes some retailers to hesitate. "We were worried about what customers would say on product reviews. We realized that if you start getting bad reviews on a product, get rid of that product," Lundgren said. "If you start getting bad reviews on a particular product …guess what? The product is bad! It's not the customer. To me, all product reviews are good. When they're bad, you have to get it off the site, get rid of the product. We do that."[6] Macy's even goes so far as to display the category "CUSTOMERS' TOP RATED ★★★★★" (5 red stars), which shows customers only the top-rated items in each product line (see Exhibit 7.3).

Fashion Director

Macy's recently introduced "Fashion Director," an interactive outfit maker, to its women's fashion categories. Fashion Director is prominently displayed along with a series of videos of the latest fashion

Exhibit 7.3 Customers' Top Rated
Source: Reprinted with permission of Macy's, Inc.

trends and the previously mentioned humorous Webisodes of Fashion Interventions by Macy's celebrity designers.

Fashion Director helps the customer create a complete ensemble of clothing, shoes, handbag, accessories, and even the perfect perfume. Customers create outfits by clicking and dragging items into a virtual fitting room and then can save them in Macy's virtual collection, share them with friends across multiple social-media sites, and enter them into Macy's monthly contest. Customers can shop the collection of outfits for purchase and vote for their favorite outfits. The outfit that receives the most customer votes wins the monthly

Exhibit 7.4 Macy's Fashion Director
Source: Reprinted with permission of Macy's, Inc.

contest, and the Web site displays each outfit and its popularity (see Exhibit 7.4).

Macy's has many other interactive touch points on its Web site. For holidays like Father's Day, with an assortment of gift ideas, customers can vote for their favorite gifts, and each is shown with its number of votes. The most popular gifts are displayed in rank order. Customers also can take an online survey that collects information on the gift recipient and receive customized gift recommendations, along with the popularity of that gift among other customers. Customers also can share the survey with friends through a wide variety of social networks (see Exhibit 7.5).

Interactive touches like Fashion Designer, surveys (such as for Father's Day and Mother's Day), and fashion videos, which can be shared with friends on social-media sites, drive more traffic to macys .com, as well as to external Macy's social-media sites such as its

Exhibit 7.5 Hard to Shop for Pop?
Source: Reprinted with permission of Macy's, Inc.

Facebook page, YouTube channel, and Twitter stream. While it focuses on higher-end fashion lines, bloomingdales.com offers a socially interactive experience similar to that on macys.com.

Facebook

Macy's launched its Facebook site in 2009, and by the beginning of 2010 it had approximately 250,000 fans; since then its fan base has grown to almost 500,000. In addition to promoting its Facebook page on its Web site, in its early days Macy's also promoted it through display advertising campaigns around the Web. The strategy appeared successful as Macy's fan base grew substantially month over month during that time period (Exhibit 7.6).

Macy's Facebook Wall is filled with fan mail and customer-service-related topics. Macy's posts are typically a mixture of fashion trend information, community service program notifications, and queries to customers about their choices in fashion. Most posts receive hundreds of positive affirmations from the "Like" button and dozens of customer comments (see Exhibit 7.7).

Exhibit 7.6 Become Our Fan
Source: Reprinted with permission of Macy's, Inc.

Other tabs on the Facebook page include:

- Trend Report, which includes videos showing the latest fashions and a customer comment page.

- Seasonal promotion. Exhibit 7.8 shows Fashion Director, which links directly to the outfit maker and the associated Summer 2010 contest. This tab also allows the customer to purchase the outfit by providing a direct link back to macys.com. In other seasons, the promotional tab has been used for events such as Prom 2010.

- Give Back, a detailed list of Macy's community outreach programs, including Feeding America, Make-a-Wish Foundation, Go Red for Women, and Rwanda Path to Peace.

- Photos, videos, events, customer polls, discussion threads, and company reviews.

Bloomingdale's has its own Facebook page and is actively building its fan base. With its wide array of designers, its Wall is filled with posts about designer events, fashion trends, and exclusive offers. It also contains a wide variety of fashion photos, videos, links to its

Exhibit 7.7 Macy's Facebook Wall
Source: Reprinted with permission of Macy's, Inc.

design partners' Facebook pages, and events where customers can swap beauty and fashion tips and mingle with some of fashion's most elite designers (see Exhibit 7.9).

Twitter

As of 2009, Macy's maintained two Twitter addresses: @macysinc, its main voice, and @macysjobs, which tweets about job postings at all Macy's sites. The voice behind @macysinc, the company's official Twitter handle, is authentic and conscientious (see Exhibit 7.10). Macy's engages directly with individual customers, resolves and follows up on customer service issues, and keeps customers abreast of hot fashion trends, Macy's many promotions, celebrity events, and

Exhibit 7.8 Facebook Macy's Fashion Director
Source: Reprinted with permission of Macy's, Inc.

Macy's cause marketing and community service events. Macy's does not use the channel to pitch sale products.

Macy's is using Twitter successfully for promotions and community outreach programs such as the holiday "Believe" campaign mentioned earlier. Macy's also used Twitter to do a sleigh tour with Santa Claus, and Santa tweeted his whereabouts. Macy's best known Twitter-specific campaign was its "Sweetest Tweets" campaign for Valentine's Day 2010 (see Exhibit 7.11). Macy's gave away one quarter-carat diamond daily from February 1 to February 13, and a three-stone diamond anniversary ring as the grand prize on February 14, to the person who sent the "sweetest tweet" that included the hashtag #sweetesttweet. Macy's promoted the contest in direct mail pieces, e-commerce, Twitter, Facebook, and in-store channels. "Sweetest Tweets" drove up the number of Macy's Twitter followers because the winner had to follow @macysinc in order to receive

Exhibit 7.9 Bloomingdale's Facebook Page
Source: Reprinted with permission of Macy's, Inc.

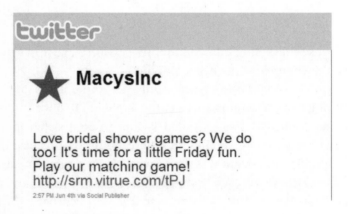

Exhibit 7.10 Macy's Twitter Feed
Source: Reprinted with permission of Macy's, Inc.

Exhibit 7.11 Sweetest Tweets
Source: Reprinted with permission of Macy's, Inc.

notification of winning by direct message and had to respond, via Twitter, within 24 hours.

Bloomingdale's can be followed on Twitter at @bloomingdales. Like Macy's, Bloomingdale's voice is authentic and engaging. Bloomingdale's follows a similar Twitter strategy to Macy's.

YouTube

A search for Macy's on YouTube returns more than 25,000 videos. With a brand as iconic as Macy's, one can spend hundreds of hours touring videos of fashion, celebrities affiliated with the brand, Macy's famous Herald Square flagship store, Macy's 150-year commemoration, current and former television commercials, and, of course, the Macy's Thanksgiving Day Parade from years gone by. Macy's and Bloomingdale's both have their own YouTube channels where each posts videos of fashion trends, company events, commercials, and Webisodes.

Flickr

Flickr contains more than 100,000 photos tagged to Macy's. More than a dozen user-generated groups have spawned, all having to do with Macy's. Macy's has formed its own Flickr Group (Macysinc), but to date it has not had much activity.

Blogging

Macy's Web site doesn't include blogs generated by its own staff. However, a quick search of blogs mentioning Macy's returned about

3.8 million results, exhibiting the brand's stature. Macy's uses blogger outreach for getting the word out about new product launches and campaigns. Instances where Macy's used bloggers to help spread the digital word include the "Believe" campaign, Madonna's Material Girl fashion line, as well as the Fashion Intervention Webisodes.

MOBILE MACY'S

Macy's is approaching the mobile channel with a vengeance. In the fall of 2009, it launched a robust iPhone e-commerce-enabled application and currently is testing various ad media programs and customer-loyalty applications tailored to mobile. Macy's sees mobile as a major growth channel and one that helps complete the 360-degree view of the customer. Lundgren commented in a September 2009 address to Shop.org's annual conference that "our mobile commerce sales are expected to grow [exponentially] in the next three years."[7] Mobile is emerging rapidly, and Macy's is investing heavily to ensure that mobile becomes part of its overall business model.

Mobile Alerts

Macy's provides various ways to opt in to receive its mobile alerts: Short message service (SMS) calls-to-action appear on traditional media—with both a keyword and short code. Consumers also can opt in for mobile alerts from Macy's by texting MACYS to short code 62297 or by signing up for mobile alerts on Macy's Web site. Macys. com has a mobile component encouraging registration to receive Macy's text alerts and discounts. The company has been successful using traditional media-supported mobile campaigns, seeing high double-digit opt-ins for its mobile initiatives, especially when combined with special offers such as discounts.

Macy's has launched several successful mobile initiatives with co-op marketing. One example is a promotion Macy's ran with Anne Klein featuring an ad with a mobile call-to-action in the March 2009 issue of *Elle* magazine. People who texted were entered to win a Caribbean vacation; this provided an added incentive to sign up for mobile alerts.[8] In 2009, Macy's mobile database doubled year-over-year and continues to grow. The retailer has experienced a very low opt-out rate.

Bloomingdale's also is dipping its toes into the mobile space through various interactive mobile contests that engage the consumer through SMS text and build Bloomingdale's mobile marketing database for future use. Bloomingdale's used a mobile contest, "Lights, Camera, Fashion," for its fall fashion campaign. As part of the theme, a variety of short films shot and produced in New York were shown in all Bloomingdale's stores and on bloomingdales.com. Shoppers were given the ability to vote for their favorite film via SMS or through Bloomingdales.com. bloomingdale's also used mobile marketing in its Lexington Avenue store windows to engage the customer. The retailer's windows were transformed into three studio vignettes, with Bloomingdale's, Apartment Therapy, and Elle Decor each designing one window. A call-to-action was included in the window display that encouraged consumers to vote for their favorite vignette via text message or online.

Macy's iShop

The description of Macy's e-commerce iPhone/iPod touch application says it all: "Your favorite store now fits in your pocket!" Macy's iShop combines a full e-commerce application with a GPS-enabled store locator, calendar of in-store events, and listing of promotions for both e-commerce discounts and location-specific, in-store savings passes. Customers shopping a physical Macy's store who forget their savings passes can access them from their iPhone. They simply show the on-screen, bar-coded coupon at checkout to have the discount applied.

Customers can shop the entire assortment of Macy's products easily from their iPhone. A three-way rolling wheel, designed like a slot machine, allows the customer to easily select the category, brand, and/or price point by which to shop. Customers also can shop the "Top Rated" section of consumer five-star-rated items or sale items, both of which filter items in each category meeting those criteria. In addition to being able to order online through the mobile device, the customer can scroll down the page to see whether an item is available for sale in a nearby store.

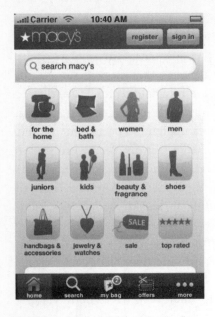 

Exhibit 7.12 Macy's iShop Application
Source: Reprinted with permission of Macy's, Inc.

If a fashion item such as a dress is available in different colors, tapping the color swatch changes the color of the item. Tapping again provides customer reviews available for that item. Many other retailers' mobile apps are simply generic versions of the company's existing Web site, modified for a phone. Macy's iShop is a mobile application, built from the ground up, taking advantage of the iPhone user interface. Fun and easy to use, iShop is one of the most comprehensive mobile commerce shopping applications available (see Exhibit 7.12).

Mobilized Print Ads

Macy's leads the way in mobilized print ads that allow customers "tap-to-buy" e-commerce functionality. Macy's has been working with Zinio, a company that provides digital versions of popular magazines to devices like the iPad, to embed digital versions of Macy's print ads into the magazines. Macy's two-page advertisement can be found in 20 magazine titles offered within the Zinio iPad application, including

Exhibit 7.13 iPad Journey Ad
Source: Reprinted with permission of Macy's, Inc.

Country Living, Elle Décor, Harper's Bazaar, Marie Claire, O (Oprah Magazine), *Redbook, Seventeen,* and others.

A recent ad for Macy's spring/summer collection features an interactive mobile element that allows consumers to tap the ad. Headlined "journey," the ad asks consumers to leave the cold winter months behind and take a journey into the colorful world of spring and summer, through vibrant colors and designs.[9] Consumers are asked to tap the ad to see more (see Exhibit 7.13). Those who do so are taken to Macy's Spring/Summer Journey catalog, which can then be browsed through the iPad. When the consumer wishes to purchase an item in the digital catalog, she can simply tap to automatically add it to the shopping cart on Macys.com.

While this strategy is in its infancy—few people have iPads and even fewer subscribe to these digital magazines—this marriage between print ads and digital mobile devices has enormous potential. The ability to simply tap on an ad provides Macy's with a whole new level of interaction with its customers that could never happen with print media. Macy's can track engagement by knowing which readers actually will opt in to view the catalog. Furthermore, Macy's takes it a step further by seeing which consumers take the next step and tap to purchase through Macys.com. The advertisement marries the two worlds of print media and mobile, first by bringing Macy's catalog to life and then by bringing its merchandise directly to consumers with an option to purchase right then and there. Should this phenomenon catch on, it would alleviate one of Macy's most expensive marketing costs: printing an extensive number of catalogs.

My Macy's Goes Mobile

Another exciting pilot program that Macy's began in Summer 2010 is an application that will push personalized offers to customers' mobile phones or pad devices. Macy's is working with ShopKick, a startup company, to build the mobile loyalty program.[10] The GPS-enabled application keeps track of what consumers buy and then promotes items the customer would likely buy in the future. For some time, retailers have envisioned the potential of personalized mobile loyalty marketing that can be tailored to the individual customer when she walks into the store. Macy's is now doing it!

Macy's logic is that most consumers have their mobile phones with them when they walk into a store. As an incentive for the consumer to receive in-store marketing messages on her phone, Macy's will offer loyalty points to customers who opt in, just for walking into the store. When a customer enters the store, the application will help Macy's understand who the customer is and what her preferences and past purchase history are, and then deliver personalized, relevant offers to her mobile device. The app will reward consumers in a variety of ways. Shopkick is keeping quiet about how it works, but describes itself as bridging "the mobile and retail worlds"[11] and portrays the launch as "a mobile application that turns offline stores into interactive worlds, dramatically improving your shopping experience." Macy's started the pilot rewards program in Summer 2010, in Miami, Los Angeles, New York, and San Francisco.

My Macy's is about localizing the shopping experience to the customer. Nothing could be more tailored than a loyalty program that follows a customer around the store and rewards her according to her personal shopping habits. While it's too early to predict, this program could be a winner; one thing is for sure—Macy's is investing in technologies that help provide a 360-degree view of each of its customers.

Sachse is excited about the potential of the partnership with Shopkick, which he describes as true location-based loyalty and marketing—something that fits perfectly into the My Macy's strategy.

JUST THE BEGINNING . . .

Macy's has invested hundreds of millions of dollars in its digital strategy, in its Web site, and in the analysis of the rich customer data that it produces. "We monitor how many customers are influenced by the Web site," says Sachse. "We are reviewing what activity those same customers had in the store within the past 10 days, how much does search drives in-store behavior, and how much social media drives in-store behavior." Sachse talks about the transition the company has made in its marketing mix from less print to more digital media. Not everyone has been quick to jump on board, but the company is sticking to its strategy. "An old-school merchant still may want a big ad in the local city newspaper and instead we invest in a keyword from Google. Slowly but surely we convince them."

In terms of return on investment from its digital strategy, Sachse says Macy's is encouraged. "We formed a very strategic partnership with Google three years ago. We proved that search has an absolute positive impact on traffic in stores. With Google, we will feed them our store data every day. Google will be able to show the inventory in the store as well as the price of the dress." The impact of social media and mobile is just starting to be measured.

That said, Sachse, like other retail executives we've spoken to, is careful to say that Macy's is just beginning to understand, embrace, and execute its strategy in these new channels. "When you bring My Macy's into the social and mobile world, there are all sorts of applications," he says. "Mobile is going to be the epitome of local and the poster child of social media."

Sachse talks about the fact that Macy's is going to need to figure out how to offer relevant, personalized messages to the customer at point-of-sale. Every customer is different. Whether it's through direct mail, email, Macys.com, an offering over social media, or a point-of-purchase offering on a mobile device, it is all the manifestation of My Macy's.

Macy's has undergone one of the most dramatic transformations of any major retailer in history. It has been a well-planned, yet methodical movement, and accordingly, at times, not totally visible to the observer. Think about consolidation, reorganization, movement to Macy's name nationally, My Macy's, improved customer service, a compelling merchandise brand strategy, reclaiming fashion authority, improved value to customers, and more. In a previous retail environment, these alone would have been remarkable achievements—and they still are. But now, marry these strategic improvements with the new digital world, and the opportunity is even more powerful. Many times in the past, retailers have made important changes within their stores, but were not able to effectively communicate them to consumers.

Today's multiple channels of customer engagement are ubiquitous. In maximizing this engagement, using the Web as the hub for customer information is a significant move for Macy's. Engaging with customers wherever they are is a huge opportunity—in stores, online, through social-media networks, and through the various proliferating uses of mobility. The company is moving full speed ahead in installing 50,000 new point-of-sale registers that offer customers the ability to order products online if they can't be found in stores and further delving into social-media, mobile, and other digital strategies to better reach younger shoppers. Terry Lundgren has provided the vision and leadership to place Macy's in one of the most enviable positions in retail. Coming off first-quarter 2010, when retailers were still dealing with the aftermath of the recession, Macy's posted excellent sales and profits. Lundgren summed it up best in a recent interview about the impact of some of the company's investments: "We didn't waste a good economic crisis in 2009. We made every change we could think about."[12]

NOTES

1. "The Most Valuable U.S. Retail Brands 2010," Interbrand Design Forum, available at www.interbrand.com/images/studies/-1_MVRB_Ltr_updated .pdf (accessed June 15, 2010).

2. Macy's, Inc. 2009 Annual Report/Fact Book, available at www.macysinc .com/Investors/AnnualReport/ (accessed June 15, 2010).
3. Interview with Peter Sachse, conducted via phone, May 13, 2010. All subsequent quotes from Sachse are from this interview.
4. "M/Quick Thoughts After Macy's 1Q10 Earnings Conference Call," Citi Investment Research, Retailing/Broadlines, Food & Drug, and Home Improvement, Deborah Weinswig, May 12, 2010.
5. "The Top 500 Guide 2010," *Internet Retailer*, May 27, 2010, available at www.internetretailer.com/2010/05/27/top-500-guide?p=3, (accessed June 15, 2010).
6. "Tracy Mullin's Burning Questions for Terry Lundgren," NRF's Digital Division Shop.org Blog, Ellen Davis, September. 22, 2009, available at http://blog.shop.org/2009/09/22/tracy-mullins-burning-questions-for-terry-lundgren/, (accessed June 15, 2010).
7. Giselle Tsirulnik, "Macy's CEO Unveils Mobile Retail Plan during Shop. org Keynote," *Mobile Commerce Daily*, September 23, 2009, available at www.mobilecommercedaily.com/macys-ceo-unveils-mobile-retail-plan-during-shoporg-keynote/, (accessed June 15, 2010).
8. Dan Butcher, "Macy's, Domino's and Unilever's Dove Case Studies Shared at Mobile Marketing Day," *Mobile Commerce Daily*, March 5, 2010, available at www.mobilecommercedaily.com/mobile-marketing-day-case-studies-macy%E2%80%99s-domino%E2%80%99s-unilever%E2%80%99s-dove/, (accessed June 15, 2010).
9. Giselle Tsirulnik, "Macy's Mobilized Print Ad Lets Consumers Tap-to-Buy Merchandise," *Mobile Commerce Daily*, May 27, 2010, available at www .mobilemarketer.com/cms/news/commerce/6395.html, (accessed June 15, 2010).
10. Ibid.
11. ShopKick home page, www.shopkick.com/ (accessed June 15, 2010).
12. Mercedes Cardona, "Macy's Marks Up 2010 Sales and Earnings Forecasts," *AOL Daily Finance*, April 27, 2010, available at www.dailyfinance.com/story/company-news/macys-marks-up-2010-sales-and-earnings-forecasts/19455856/, (accessed June 15, 2010).

8

1-800-Flowers. com: "Build a Relationship First—Do Business Second"

Jim McCann's "Build a relationship first, do business second"[1] articulates the premise underlying everything that he has done in his professional life, from being a social worker helping troubled youth in New York City to being the founder and CEO of 1-800-Flowers.com today. Jim's brother Chris McCann, the company's president and COO, cites Jim's words as he describes the mission of 1-800-Flowers in the 2010 season finale of the CBS reality TV series *Undercover Boss*. Working undercover, Chris meets a human testament to the company's mission in the form of a long-time employee and store manager named Dee. "Dee is a perfect living example of what my brother always says: 'Build a relationship first—do business second.'" Watching Dee in action, Chris could see how much rapport and trust she brought to the genuine, caring relationships she had built with the customers who frequented her store. "One thing I've always admired about Jim, says Chris, is his ability to understand people and connect with them very quickly."

Describing the company's corporate culture, Chris McCann says, "1-800-Flowers.com is all about relationships. Our mission is to help people create smiles every day. We do that with wonderful products —flowers and great food gifts. Every time someone sends one of our gifts, it means someone is smiling on the other end. We do this in ways that make it easier for customers to shop and build bigger, deeper relationships with our company."[2]

Over 33 years, Jim, Chris, and their team have built the company from one retail flower shop to the largest online floral and gift retailer with over $700 million in annual sales and an unaided 90% brand awareness. 1-800-Flowers.com is a company with a strong culture and a strategy that effectively leverages these strengths through social media and mobility. The early success that the company enjoys in these new channels of communication is based on the innovative drive of its leaders and the social-occasion premise of its core business.

GOING UNDERCOVER IS REVEALING

The entrepreneurial culture of 1-800-Flowers.com became evident to millions of television viewers as Chris McCann appeared on *Undercover Boss*, with Jim McCann playing a supporting role in this event. This CBS television series features a senior executive at a major corporation working incognito as a new recruit to find out what's really going on inside his company. The disguised executive learns how the company operates and how its employees and customers perceive it; during this process, he also discovers some of the unsung heroes within the organization.

While undercover, as a "new" 1-800-Flowers.com employee, Chris learned a great deal about the quality of his employees and management's need to better connect with them. In each of their individual roles, it was apparent how much care and commitment the employees demonstrated; but perhaps not as clear to them how much management appreciated their efforts. Chris looked at how to better equip his employees with the necessary tools to be more productive and make their jobs more enjoyable. He realized the need for his brand managers to immerse themselves in their employees' work on a regular basis, not only to better understand their roles, but also to build the culture. He also recognized the importance of showing employees that the company was thankful for each of their individual contributions and ensuring that they understood how each of their roles added value to the overall success of 1-800-Flowers.com.

Chris's *Undercover Boss* experience relates directly to his and his brother's focus on company culture and its people, with the goal of delivering passionate customer service. The *Undercover Boss* show also provided viewers with a real look at the focus, commitment, and interactions of the McCann brothers with their team at 1-800-Flowers. com. Going undercover revealed that relationships come first, from employees to customers, and from company to employees. This leads to better business.

PLANTING THE SEEDS OF SUCCESS

To understand 1-800-Flowers.com, it is important to briefly review the company's history, its entrepreneurial moves, and its culture and strategy as the strengths of the business. The company represents a great example of how vision, intelligence, persistence, and relationships have come together to build a very successful business.

In 1976, Jim started the company, then under the name of Flora Plenty, with one flower shop on the Upper East Side of Manhattan. By 1984, the business had grown to 12 stores, and Jim, still a full-time social worker, persuaded Chris, then a student, to join the business full-time. Chris states, "We grew the business to 12 stores, but most of them were unprofitable, so we brought it down to three stores." This move was an insightful decision by the two brothers. In analyzing the business, Chris saw a significant change in the way customers were shopping for flowers: Specifically, they were becoming more comfortable calling in orders over the phone, rather than having to visit the store. Concurrent with closing 9 of the 12 stores, the McCanns opened a basic call center in the basement of one store and focused on the new retail channel that telephone ordering presented.

Also in 1984, the McCann brothers were presented with a new opportunity. They reviewed a phone-order floral business, named

800-Flowers, based in Dallas. There were several iterations, but ultimately the McCanns gained control of that company. They joke about it today because, in fact, they ended up acquiring not only the company phone lists and the name "800-Flowers," but also $7 million in debt. Chris remembers Jim's comment: "We have to get out of Dallas—how fast can we build 30 telemarketing stations?" The large infrastructure in Dallas was shut down and a call center, built out of plywood, was assembled in the back of one of their New York stores. At this point, Jim's days as a social worker ended and he became the company's full-time CEO. Thus, the new 1-800-Flowers had been launched; the company went public in 1999 and has been growing ever since.

A simple chronology of 1-800-Flowers.com follows:

- First wave: Retail stores
- Second wave: Telephone commerce, building a brand around 800 numbers
- Third wave: The Internet and e-commerce (.com added to company name)

In the early 1990s, as early online services were becoming popular through technology companies like Prodigy and CompuServe, Jim and Chris both recognized that the company "better get involved in this new communications channel." So 1-800-Flowers.com opened a digital store on CompuServe, selling flowers, candy, and gift baskets. The idea and foresight were on target, but the money to fund it was not there, and the technology had not yet evolved enough to provide a customer-friendly shopping experience. The McCanns believed that this online-service model would be an enormous opportunity for the future of the company, but they also realized that getting the flower business to a compelling position was their first priority. Additionally, while they wanted to become an early entry into the online business, they recognized that several years would elapse before technology matured into what is now known as the World Wide Web.

As technology evolved, 1-800-Flowers.com became the first company to sell its product on AOL. During that time, numerous skeptics questioned why the company was spending time on what seemed like a risky strategy. "Back then, we were early adopters of technology, and we learned that there was more customer purchase frequency online than with telephone shoppers," says Chris. "We saw customer behavior changing because of technology. We launched 1-800-Flowers.com on Netscape in 1995, and then when the World Wide Web became popular, we added the .com to our company name and became 1-800-Flowers.com, Inc."

As a result of this early vision, the company has demonstrated great success in what has now become known as e-commerce on the World Wide Web. The company learned many lessons from its early entry into this new channel of customer shopping and interaction. Equally important, the business developed by 1-800-Flowers.com through its cross-channel strategy has set a base for significant additional growth opportunity through social media and mobility.

BEYOND FLOWERS

Today 1-800-Flowers.com, Inc., is the world's largest florist and gift shop. The market leader in the $18 billion floral segment, the company also continues to expand its market presence in the $16 billion gourmet and gift-basket market. Additionally, the company's BloomNet wire service helps independent florists grow their businesses profitably.

With 35 million customers in its database, this nearly $700 million-plus business is well positioned for growth. In 2009, the 1-800-Flowers.com e-commerce business had more than six million customers transacting with the company to express themselves and connect with important people in their lives. Equally important, 52% of the consumer transactions came from existing customers. These important metrics demonstrate the company's focus on customer service.

Through its expansion into new categories and brands, 1-800-Flowers.com is rapidly improving its loyalty and multibrand cross-marketing strategies. The company focuses on improving customer satisfaction along the way, an important part of the customer relationship. It also is emerging as an early market leader in the new consumer communication channels of social media and mobility. Through its focus on organization and teamwork, 1-800-Flowers.com has a unique culture, along with a solid cross-channel business strategy, positioning itself to provide significant benefits to its customers.

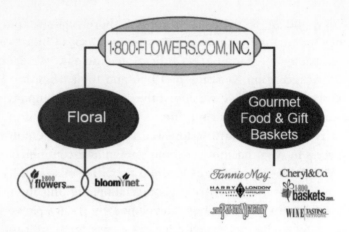

Exhibit 8.1 1-800-Flowers.com Categories of Business
Source: Reprinted with permission of 1-800-Flowers.com.

1-800-Flowers.com Business Platform

The company has two major categories: Floral and Gourmet Food & Gift Baskets (see Exhibit 8.1). The Floral category consists of 1-800-Flowers.com Consumer Floral and the BloomNet wire service. The Gourmet Food & Gift Basket category comprises growing brands such as Fannie May and Harry London chocolates, The Popcorn Factory, Cheryl&Co. cookies and brownies, 1-800-Baskets.com, Geerlings and Wade, and The WineTasting Network.

Customer Channels

1-800-Flowers.com is a comprehensive cross-channel retail company with presence and growth opportunities in all important retail channels: stores, Web, catalogs, call center, B2B (BloomNet), and now social media and mobility (see Exhibit 8.2). Few retail specialty companies have as many areas for potential growth as 1-800-Flowers.com.

LEVERAGING SOCIAL COMMERCE THROUGH TECHNOLOGY

1-800-Flowers.com is a social business. It's all about relationships and providing gifts and services for celebratory occasions. There-

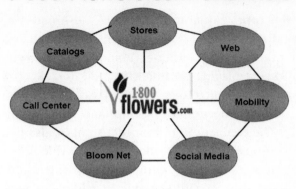

Exhibit 8.2 1-800-Flowers.com Channels of Business
Source: Reprinted with permission of 1-800-Flowers.com.

fore, with Jim and Chris McCann's track record of focusing on innovative technology and customer engagement, it's not surprising that the company is enjoying early success in social media and mobility.

In 2007 1-800-Flowers.com was already beginning to learn about Web 2.0 and its potential impact on the business. The McCanns look at today's rapid surge in social media and mobility as being similar to the early days of the dot-com revolution that transformed 1-800-Flowers.com into a top e-commerce business: "In 1992–1997 (the early Internet era), we knew that technology would significantly change our company but we didn't know how at the time. The same is happening now with social media and mobility. We know it will have a profound impact on our business. We're just not sure how," says Chris McCann.

McCann describes the recent changes in consumer behavior that are largely attributable to social technology: "First, there's a power shift from the retailer to the consumer. Second, it's all about friends sharing with friends. Consumers don't make a decision without checking with their network. And there's plenty of conversation taking place about our brand. We need to ensure we are involved in those conversations."

SOCIAL MEDIA BLOSSOMS

1-800-Flowers.com's social-media strategy is broad and deep. In addition to its flagship 1800flowers.com Web site, each of the company's other seven consumer brands has its own Web site, with social media playing an important role for all of them: 1800 baskets.com, cherylandco.com, fanniemay.com, harrylondon.com, geerwade.com, thepopcornfactory.com, and winetasting.com (see Exhibit 8.3). The company's social-media strategy also is woven into its business-to-business units: BloomNet® (mybloomnet.net), the company's international floral wire service provider, and Designpac (designpac.com), the company's product development and production subsidiary for specialty gifts.

The company's social-media strategy is based on five goals:

1. Build individual brand awareness.

2. Drive customer engagement.

3. Position 1-800-Flowers.com as a gifting and celebratory destination.

4. Drive traffic to the company's Web sites.

5. Ultimately drive sales.

 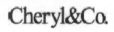

Exhibit 8.3 1-800-Flowers.com Consumer Web sites
Source: Reprinted with permission of 1-800-Flowers.com.

Exhibit 8.4 1-800-Flowers.com Web Site
Source: Reprinted with permission of 1-800-Flowers.com.

Social Media on 1-800-Flowers.com

In addition to its award-winning commerce functionality, the 1-800-Flowers.com Web site provides live chat with customer service representatives, customer product reviews, and the ability to comment on and share an item with friends through email, by instant messaging, or across one of the popular 40-plus social networks such as Facebook, Twitter, Google Buzz, and MySpace (see Exhibit 8.4).

The site also contains a Floral Lifestyle blog written by one of the company's top floral designers.

External Social Networks

The 1-800-Flowers.com team's aggressive move to utilize external social networks such as Facebook, Twitter, and YouTube actually occurred several years ago. "We looked at what customers wanted to get out of these,"[3] says Kevin Ranford, who leads the company's social media and mobile efforts. "Like most retailers, we first pushed out promotional offers. Customers quickly let us know that what they really wanted was an open dialogue with our brand. Now, we allow our fans and followers to shape our communication plan."

Exhibit 8.5 1-800-Flowers.com Facebook Wall
Source: Reprinted with permission of 1-800-Flowers.com.

Facebook

The 1-800-Flowers.com Facebook page is unique and innovative; its Wall is filled with comments about company posts and customer service questions (see Exhibit 8.5). The company quickly engages with its customers about relevant issues. The page also provides links to company-sponsored contests, photos, videos, customer reviews, polls, quizzes, and other events.

Facebook Shopping and Virtual Gifting

The most innovative part of 1-800-Flowers.com's Facebook page is its Shop tab, which offers customers a chance to enjoy the full benefits of e-commerce without ever having to leave Facebook (see Exhibit 8.6). It also gives customers the ability to send the actual products featured on the commerce site as a virtual gift to friends on Facebook. 1-800-Flowers.com pioneered the idea of "social com-

Exhibit 8.6 1-800-Flowers.com Facebook Shopping Site
Source: Reprinted with permission of 1-800-Flowers.com.

merce" and has been acknowledged for launching the first e-commerce store on a Facebook fan page. The company partnered with Alvenda, Inc., a business specializing in developing tools for brands that enable customers to shop directly on social-media sites. Customers can now shop the full 1-800-Flowers.com catalog directly from its Facebook page.

The company discovered that while customers found it convenient to shop on Facebook, they enjoyed spending time on their own Newsfeeds rather than venturing onto a brand's fan page. Therefore, bringing these two elements together would be beneficial to customer convenience. In first-quarter 2010, the company launched Storecast, which brings the 1-800-Flowers.com gift shop right into fans' Facebook Newsfeeds so they don't have to leave their own Facebook pages to make a purchase.

Storecast allows 1-800-Flowers.com fans to compile wish lists from its Facebook store and push notification to their friends. It also allows the company to recommend a product from its own Fan page and enter it in its fans' Facebook Newsfeed, along with a comment or question such as, "Do you like this bouquet of pink roses?" In addition to giving feedback on the item, fans can purchase it directly from their own Newsfeed. While it's early, the company is seeing an increase in both fans and traffic. The new functionality makes 1-800-Flowers.com more viral as fans spread the word to all of their friends.

Facebook "Like" Button

Facebook recently introduced the capability to insert its "Like" button directly onto companies' Web sites, and 1-800-Flowers.com has embedded that functionality. The mechanism allows a user to connect with Facebook directly from another Web site. If a customer on the 1-800-Flowers.com Web site likes a particular product, she can simply click the "Like" button next to the product, thereby accessing the option of sharing that item, along with a personalized comment, with her entire network on Facebook. Within Facebook, anyone who sees the post can click on that item and be transported right onto the 1-800-Flowers.com site to see a list of all their friends, along with their pictures, who like that item, as well as other products.

The 1-800-Flowers.com Web site can now be personalized to show which friends like which products. Friends' birthdays and other important dates from Facebook also will appear automatically on the 1-800-Flowers.com site, thus tailoring the shopping experience to each user's own personal network. In tying products to friends' personal tastes, this new functionality has the potential for transforming the way searches work.

Twitter

1-800-Flowers.com uses the corporate Twitter account @1800flowers to engage with customers about service issues, as well as other relevant information about upcoming events, holidays, and company promotions. Probably most well known in the Twittersphere are the company's frequent contests, which also generate a lot of activity on the company's Facebook page. Each Wednesday is the celebrity birthday contest in which people tweet answers to clues given about a particular celebrity. Floral Ambush occurs every Friday, and three winners are chosen at random, receiving free floral bouquets, as well as other prizes.

YouTube

1-800-Flowers.com has an active YouTube channel, where it promotes its commercials, contests, and other company events such as a recent episode featuring Chris McCann on the CBS reality hit show *Undercover Boss*.

Social Contests

1-800-Flowers.com engages customers in various contests promoted through social media. One very successful contest has been the company's "Spot A Mom" campaign for Mother's Day, which was highly promoted through Facebook and Twitter, as well as the company's Web site and television commercials (see Exhibit 8.7). The company first ran the campaign in 2009; because it was such a success, it has now become an annual event. The Spot A Mom "Lessons Mom Taught Me"

Exhibit 8.7 1-800-Flowers.com Spot A Mom Contest
Source: Reprinted with permission of 1-800-Flowers.com.

contest encourages consumers to log on to a special Web site, where they can share imaginative and passionate lessons they've learned for the chance to honor mom and win her a dream vacation. Visitors are encouraged to enter stories about their mothers, grandmothers, sisters, best friends, or any of the special moms in their lives for the chance to win daily prizes, with one grand prize winner receiving a getaway vacation for four to Hawaii and a year's supply of flowers.

After last year's contest, CEO Jim McCann published a keepsake book, *Celebrating Mom*, which features customers' heartwarming stories and real-life accounts based on lessons learned from mom. Offered on 1-800-Flowers.com company Web sites as an additional gift for mothers, the book is expected to be the first in a series created from contestants' testimonials about their moms and other important people and celebratory occasions in their lives.

Mommy and Lifestyle Bloggers—Key to Strategy

Blogging and value-added content are key parts of the 1-800-Flowers. com social strategy. In addition to writing its own blogs, the company is engaging with hundreds of lifestyle bloggers and so-called mommy bloggers in an effort to bring them closer to the brand. "We invite them to peek behind the curtain and see our company from the inside," says Yanique Woodall, Vice President of Enterprise Public Relations.[4] The company invites these bloggers to company events, makes them aware of new initiatives, and gives them products to test. "For example," adds Woodall, "during the launch of 1-800-Baskets. com, we invited bloggers to visit our headquarters. They learned how to design and assemble a holiday gift basket."

"They walked away with a skill, but they also walked away better understanding all that is involved in designing and producing high-quality holiday gift baskets. Then, the bloggers were able to journal their experience to their blog readers and Twitter followers. We are encouraging these bloggers to share their experience with their readers, and we are also engaging other consumers, creating organic chatter about the launch of a new brand. We understand that consumers are looking for real users and are seeking their feedback. We work directly with mommy bloggers and lifestyle bloggers because if the experience is great, they'll write about it and if it's not, that's okay too, because we'll learn from it."

Celebrations.com: Plan a Party

1-800-Flowers.com also has established celebrations.com, its own social network for party planning (see Exhibit 8.8). Customers can join celebrations.com at no cost: The site includes a community where participants can share party ideas, recipes, photos, and videos. On the Web site, experts in the party-planning industry provide advice about decorations, gifts, favors, and crafts projects for children. The site also offers a question-and-answer forum, how-to videos, and rich content for every type of party imaginable. It describes itself this way:

> The best place to plan your party with simple party-
> planning tools, including invitations you can create and
> design yourself, budgeting tools, and drink calculators.
> Celebrations.com is a comprehensive resource for all of
> life's most important celebrations including Bridal Showers,
> Baby Showers, Kids' Birthday Parties, Dinner Parties,
> Tailgating, Halloween, Thanksgiving, Christmas, the entire
> Holiday Season, and more.

Exhibit 8.8 Celebrations.com Web site
Source: Reprinted with permission of 1-800-Flowers.com.

Celebrations.com also includes its Life of the Party blog, which offers a constant stream of tips, gift ideas, crafts, and recipes for celebrating and creating parties around the calendar's current events— Valentine's Day, Mothers Day, Cinco de Mayo, birthdays, and so forth. It also contains Platinum Celebrations, an insider's blog on celebrity parties.

References to 1-800-Flowers.com brands on the celebrations.com site are subtle, although they appear frequently, along with relevant content. In a section called "Mother's Day Ideas," one will find a variety of ideas, including a Mother's Day Coupon Book, Cupcakes, Gift Ideas Under $50, and Fun and Easy Bouquet Ideas for Mom. For these special items, one finds references to the 1-800-Flowers.com and the 1-800-Baskets.com Web sites.

"Celebrations is a core part of our social-media strategy," says Jim McCann. "The idea is to get customers exposed to our brands and products. Through celebrations.com, our customers are giving us permission to be involved in their celebrations. While it could be a good business for us, it's also a learning bed for content and social media. What we learn about user-generated content and social media on our celebrations.com site, we apply to our commerce businesses." Celebrations.com is all about content, the idea being for the content to build engagement with customers of the 1-800-Flowers.com family of brands.

MOBILE: APP OF THE YEAR

As in social media, 1-800-Flowers.com has been an early pioneer in mobile commerce. As far back as 2005, the company started experimenting with Mobile Wireless Application Protocol sites, and it began developing downloadable applications in 2008. The company now has such applications for the iPhone, Blackberry, and Android. Its mobile shopping site recently won *RIS* (Retail Information Systems) magazine's 2010 Mobile App of the Year (see Exhibit 8.9).

When customers launch the mobile application, they are presented with an easy-to-use menu that allows them to order gift items directly from their phone. It includes categories such as Birthday, Get Well, Anniversary, Congratulations, I'm Sorry, Sympathy, Business

Exhibit 8.9 1-800-Flowers.com iPhone Application
Source: Reprinted with permission of 1-800-Flowers.com.

Gifts, Gourmet Food Gifts, Exclusive Offers, Same-Day Delivery, and Gifts under $50. The customer can email an item to a friend for review or put it right in her shopping cart and purchase it through a digital wallet.

The Celebrations Ultimate Party Guide App is currently available for both the iPhone and iPod touch. It includes party tips, food-and-drink recipes, crafts, and decoration ideas for all occasions.

1-800-Flowers.com also is engaged in short message service (SMS) messaging campaigns and in growing its SMS Mobile Club; it is doing so using best practices around double customer "opt-ins."

The company recognizes tremendous potential in mobile commerce and has already seen hundreds of thousands of downloads for its mobile applications. "Mobile commerce is now growing 1000%, and numbers are starting to become meaningful," says Chris McCann.

INNOVATION IS A CORE STRATEGY

At 1-800-Flowers.com, social-media and mobile initiatives are cross-functional in accordance with the company's belief that cross-department coordination is critical to success. Customer service is tied in; marketing and public relations are tied in, as are product development and merchandising. As with most companies, cultural acceptance of these new channels within 1-800-Flowers.com has not come without its challenges. The McCanns have made organizational changes and are investing in internal training to enable employees in all departments to understand the value of these initiatives. 1-800-Flowers.com also is actively training its network of approximately 800 home-based customer service agents to become active in the company's social-media efforts.

Investing in such innovations as social media and mobility is one of three core corporate strategies that 1-800-Flowers.com highlights in its 2009 Annual Report. Plenty of skeptics question the focus on ventures such as mobile commerce, but the McCanns are confident in their strategy. "One year ago, people were telling us that we were wasting our time on mobile commerce," says Chris McCann, "but they're the same people who were telling us in 1994 that we were wasting our time on the Internet. We're just in the early stages of something very big and still have a lot to learn."

1-800-Flowers.com is determined to keep a high-energy culture of innovation. Vincent Raguseo, the company's Vice President of Web Marketing & Merchandising, comments, "Chris McCann always pushes us to innovate. We know that we will make plenty of mistakes, but we'd never get to where we are if we weren't willing to take some risks and learn from our mistakes. That's what innovation is all about."[5] Seth Lasser, the company's Vice President of Marketing, says that what makes innovation so exciting is that "we're trying to create a new kind of relationships. This is much more than just selling people stuff. Transactions are just one piece of what we do. Helping people celebrate is a way for our brand to stand for something much better."[6]

In Chris McCann's words, "This is 1995 all over again. We know it's going to change our business. We don't yet know how, but we do know that we will be better off if we are involved in shaping the path. Ultimately, we know that embracing new technologies will help us in our mission to help deliver smiles every day."

NOTES

1. Interview with Jim McCann, conducted at 1-800-Flowers.com headquarters, April 30, 2010. All subsequent quotes from Jim McCann are from this interview.
2. Interview with Chris McCann, conducted at 1-800-Flowers.com headquarters, April 30, 2010. All subsequent quotes from Chris McCann are from this interview.
3. Interview with Kevin Ranford, conducted at 1-800-Flowers.com headquarters, April 30, 2010. All subsequent quotes from Ranford are from this interview.
4. Interview with Yanique Woodall, conducted via phone, May 10, 2010. All subsequent quotes from Woodall are from this interview.
5. Interview with Vincent Raguseo, conducted at 1-800-Flowers.com headquarters, April 30, 2010.
6. Interview with Seth Lasser, conducted at 1-800-Flowers.com headquarters, April 30, 2010.

9

JCPenney: Digital Transformation

When people think of JCPenney, words like reliable, dependable, fashion-forward, high quality, and moderately priced spring to mind. The brand has been a pillar of American retailing for more than a century. JCPenney is a tradition.

Now take a minute and visualize a JCPenney board of directors' meeting. Probably the last thing you'd envision is for this meeting to be held at Facebook's offices in the heart of Silicon Valley, but that's exactly what JCPenney Chairman and CEO Myron (Mike) Ullman did. Due to a rapidly changing digital world, Ullman held the company's February 2010 board meeting at Facebook's Palo Alto, California, headquarters. His mission: to give the JCPenney board a crash course on the impact of digital media. Ullman understands the importance of technology in his business. Even through the recession, he has been investing heavily in digital initiatives to make sure that JCPenney gets a head start. He has, for example, committed several hundred million dollars to support its "Digital Center of Excellence."[1] Ullman believes that people today think and behave digitally, and the survivors in the industry are going to lead in this space. He's making sure JCPenney is one of those leaders.

BUILDING A BRAND BY "WINNING TOGETHER"

JCPenney's vision is to be "America's shopping destination for discovering great styles at compelling prices."[2] In 2009, the company recorded $17.6 billion in sales and operated more than 1,100 retail stores in addition to its e-commerce site, jcp.com. While the company previously had introduced a long-range plan for growth, it put that plan on hold in 2008 and 2009, the latter part of the most difficult economic times in modern history. A bridge plan was activated as the proper course for that period. It proved to be the right decision for the company as it ended its fiscal year 2009 with $3 billion in cash on its balance sheet, which is providing the necessary capital to execute its 2010–2014 long-range growth plan. In preparation for the long-term plan, key investments in technology and infrastructure were made. The long-term plan includes four strategies that support the company's vision:

1. Our customers—Become America's favorite destination for apparel, home, and fashion.
2. Merchandise—Consistently delight our customers.
3. Associates—Invest in our people, our greatest strength.
4. Performance and shareholders—Establish JCPenney as a growth leader in the industry.

JCPenney's strategy and culture, reflected in its long-term plan, are built on a strong platform of "WINNING TOGETHER," which supports all decisions and actions necessary for it to become a top-of-mind brand that remains foremost in the mind of today's consumer.

WINNING TOGETHER™ Principles:

associates . . . We value, develop, and reward the contributions and talents of all associates.

integrity . . . We act only with the highest ethical standards.

performance . . . We provide coaching and feedback to perform at the highest level.

recognition . . . We celebrate the achievements of others.

teamwork . . . We win together through leadership, collaboration, open and honest communication, and respect.

quality . . . We strive for excellence in our work, products, and services.

innovation . . . We encourage creative thinking and intelligent risk-taking.

community . . . We care about and are involved in our communities.

we do this for our . . .

customers . . . We build lasting relationships by offering superior service and value.

shareholders . . . We aspire to superior financial performance.[3]

Brand As a Value-Generator

There has been profound change in the way department stores position their brand in recent years. Department store consolidation, underway for decades, has positioned a small number of major retailers operating nationally. As a result, prominent retailers now have the opportunity to strengthen brand-product development, purchasing strength, marketing efficiency, and cross-channel leverage. Branded suppliers are selling to fewer chains and see the need to develop brand exclusives with major retailers. Additionally, licensing companies now offer well-known brand names for retailer-exclusive relationships.

JCPenney seized this opportunity and built a merchandising strategy around private brands, exclusive brands, and destination national brands. JCPenney's private brands represent nearly half of its annual revenue, resulting from strong customer loyalty over many decades. These private brands, referred to by JCPenney as "power brands," maintain a strong market position; examples include Arizona, Ambrielle, St. Johns Bay, Stafford, Worthington, and Linden Street.

Through the addition of exclusive brands, JCPenney's brand positioning has improved substantially. Outstanding examples of this strategy include:

- **American Living®.** This brand was developed exclusively by Polo Ralph Lauren's Global Brand Concepts for family apparel and home at JCPenney.

- **Cindy Crawford®.** The Cindy Crawford Style™ brand of home furnishings launched in 2009. Because of the brand's success, "One Kiss™" by Cindy Crawford, a fine jewelry line, was introduced in early 2010.

- **Liz Claiborne®.** In 2010, JCPenney became the exclusive department store destination in the United States for Liz Claiborne and Claiborne-branded merchandise.

Through collaboration with top designers, JCPenney is becoming a fashion leader. Mango, a world-renowned leader in design and fast fashion, has signed with JCPenney as its exclusive MNG by Mango® U.S. department store retailer. Designer collections such as I Heart Ronson® by Charlotte Ronson, Olsenboye™ by Ashley and Mary-Kate Olsen, and Allen B® by Allen Schwartz bring the kind of fresh, branded names required to maintain JCPenney's style authority. Although these strategies are primarily about branding, they allow JCPenney to assume better control of its businesses, ensuring shorter merchandise cycle times. The strategies also provide freshness of product, high quality, and dominant in-stock position, resulting in a more enjoyable customer experience.

Sephora—Quality Cosmetics—New Demographic

Cosmetics and its related services are key to driving loyalty with women and important elements in the "theatre" of a department store. JCPenney introduced Sephora beauty shops in select stores in 2006, setting up "SiJCP" shops carrying the top brands in makeup, skincare, fragrances, and accessory products. The plan is to have these shops in 230 JCPenney stores by the end of 2010 and continue to roll out SiJCP with an ultimate target of 600 stores. This well-known, high-quality brand is supported by a staff of beauty consultants who have been trained in the "Science of Sephora" educational program. As you walk through these impressive in-store shops, you feel a new sense of energy and excitement at JCPenney. Sephora attracts a younger and more affluent customer. The outstanding SiJCP strategy strengthens JCPenney as a style leader. The Manhattan flagship JCPenney store has a 2,000-square-foot Sephora boutique, offering its finest products.

Manhattan Flagship Unveiled

From Herald Square, to Midtown, to SoHo, New York City has always been home to the famous flagship retailer stores. To demonstrate its fashion leadership, JCPenney opened its flagship store in 2009 at 33rd Street and 6th Avenue, right in the heart of America's fashion capital. This sleek and exciting 153,000-square-foot store provides a window to the fashion world; it also gives JCPenney a stage for the millions of commuters from the New York metropolitan area, and travelers from around the world who come to this great city for entertainment and shopping. The flagship store–shopping experience provides fashionable merchandise, superior service, and new technologies that represent the digital direction of JCPenney. With New York being the media center of the country, the Manhattan store has had a positive halo effect on the entire JCPenney brand.

CustomerFIRST!

The ever-changing competitive landscape challenges department stores to effectively provide excellent customer service. JCPenney exceeds customers' expectations by focusing on this important relationship. JCPenney has exceeded customer expectations. JCPenney's "CustomerFIRST" initiatives, executed through the efforts of its associates, have created highly satisfied customers. The company's 2009 Annual Report states: "Our Associates treat each customer's visit as an interaction—not a transaction. This creates shopping experiences that are more likely to generate return visits and cultivate loyal relationships with our customers." In 2009, for the second consecutive year, JCPenney ranked Number One in customer service among department stores ranked in the American Express/National Retail Federation Foundation Customers' Choice Survey.

JCP Gets "RACIE": Award-Winning Marketing

JCPenney emerged as a marketing leader in 2009 by being the recipient of 12 Racie Awards. The Racie Awards, distributed by the Retail Advertising and Marketing Association, honor the year's best print advertisements, broadcast commercials, digital efforts, and other communication materials in the retail industry. In receiving this award, Mike Boylson, Executive Vice President and Chief Marketing Officer, said, "Our recognition at this year's Racie Awards—taking home more awards than any other retailer—it's a testament to the continued innovation and exceptional work of our marketing and agency teams."[4] The number of awards is impressive, notably the two gold medals awarded for marketing in new and growing strategic initiatives. JCPenney received gold in the "outdoor" category for its flagship store grand-opening campaign in Manhattan and gold in "Web site experience" for its "Return to the Doghouse" campaign.

FROM BIG BOOK TO DIGITAL LEADERSHIP

In late 2009 JCPenney made a transformational decision to discontinue its semiannual "big book" catalog. With its high cost of production, the productivity of the once-popular paper catalog had faded in terms of its ability to drive profitable revenue. The company now engages customers through integrated marketing, incorporating stores, catalogs, online applications, and emerging digital platforms, including social media and mobility. JCPenney now has the ability to focus on growing its jcp.com business. Mike Ullman summarizes this strategic move: "To ensure we are keeping pace with consumers' changing media habits and continued migration to online versus catalog shopping, we have increased our investments in new technologies, as well as successfully integrated the merchandising and marketing teams serving stores, jcp.com, and catalog into one enterprise-wide team that is able to consistently and seamlessly serve our customers, no matter how they prefer to shop with us."[5]

JCPenney's Direct-to-Consumer Marketing Evolution

Jcp.com was run as a separate operation for many years, with separate buyers and different merchandise assortments. As a result, the company was unable to leverage the synergy and benefits of cross-channel retailing. Those days are over. As Boylson said, "We are becoming much more enterprise-focused, breaking down silos, connecting the pieces internally. Marketing and e-commerce have evolved to put the customer in control. More and more, the customer is deciding what's relevant, and marketers can no longer simply push their message down."[6] Boylson further discusses the shifts in overall media mix. The company had relied on weekly newspaper inserts and other traditional print media, which are now becoming less effective and more expensive. "We are planning on spending the same amount of marketing money," said Boylson, "but will be much more targeted in how we do so, redeploying money into digital."

According to Boylson, JCPenney is executing a strategy that marries fashion leadership with digital communication: "We have a tremendous amount of innovation going on in the entire digital space. We are dramatically changing our entire infrastructure. Tom Nealon, our CIO, is leading this process so that we can be faster and more nimble. Our entire customer database is being merged—direct and stores—so it can accommodate our social-media and mobile strategies." Its new strategy includes re-launching jcp.com, investing in mobile shopping, and adding in-store interactive touch-screen FindMore™ kiosks that allow shoppers to order merchandise items, colors, and sizes not available in-store. JCPenney has now positioned itself to have the customer lead—and that is the ideal place to be in this new digital world.

CULTURE OF TRANSPARENCY

JCPenney has undergone significant change over the past decade. The merchandising focus, which had been within the store organization, had served the company well for a long time. However, store-merchandise buying was no longer competitive in a highly centralized and evolving retail market. Boylson comments, "In February of 2001, we centralized the organization on a Sunday morning—everyone's role changed that day. Stores no longer bought merchandise; buyers now not only had to buy goods, but also do the planning. This was an enormous change, and many people couldn't adapt and left the company. This was the time that we started bringing in top talent from the outside." This change initiated a dramatic cultural shift from a decentralized model to a centralized one.

In discussing the next phase of massive change at JCPenney, while noting organizational changes and a growth culture, Boylson said, "Mike Ullman deserves credit for the incredible culture that we now have. Our whole effort to become a leader in this space started with this new culture." Mike Theilmann, Group Executive Vice President of JCPenney human resources, started branding many of the associates' initiatives. He started the WINNING TOGETHER principles that reflect how JCPenney values its people, and these principles became the company's cultural foundation. "Every Day Matters" is now the organizing thought, and the call-to-action for JCPenney associates and their customers. The company's goal is to be a great place to work and a preferred place to have a career. Building leadership development is a top priority, and associate surveys score high on engagement. The company embraces diversity and treats its associates with respect and kindness. During the 2009 recession, for example, the company froze merit increases, but didn't have layoffs—an exceptional decision. It's this kind of culture that builds a winning team for the long term.

At the core of JCPenney's brand strategy is its internal communication, which begins with treating its associates as its first customers. Every month Mike Ullman has a one-hour live fireside chat with them. Always beginning with an overview of what's going on in the company and a discussion of strategies, Ullman encourages associates to submit questions directly to him. "Everyone hears straight from Mike Ullman what's going on," said Boylson. "We have a culture of transparency."

SOCIAL AMBASSADORS

JCPenney's social-media strategy focuses on both internal communication with its associates and external communication with its customers. To enable associates nationwide to interact more effectively, JCPenney's social-media efforts began internally.

Winning Together: jLife and jChat

JCPenney publishes a monthly internal magazine called *jLife*. *jLife* not only is available in paper copy, but also is emailed to all associates' email addresses via URLinked. This allows all associates to stay connected to the business and to one another. Through the use of 2D barcodes placed throughout the paper copy of *jLife*, associates can "Snap it" with their smart phone and immediately link to relevant information such as benefits updates, training, or the latest happenings at the home office.

jChat is an online forum that allows associates to share their views on topics such as JCPenney's corporate culture, human resource concerns such as internal culture and diversity, corporate social responsibility initiatives like recycling and energy usage, and operational topics such as logistics. Connected to the company's Intranet, jChat can be accessed from any of the 40,000 in-store, point-of-sale terminals (see Exhibit 9.1).

Customers Reaching Customers Through Digital Word of Mouth

JCPenney is focused on the goal of "customers creating other customers," a tactic that Mike Boylson refers to as "digital word of mouth." Customer referrals have always been the best testimonials a company

Exhibit 9.1 *jLife* Digital Magazine and jChat Online Forum
Source: Reprinted with permission of JCPenney.

can receive, and the social-media strategy provides that capability—digitally. Ratings and reviews are a key feature of JCPenney's Web site. Facebook's "Like" button and associated customer comments are other examples of customers' spreading reactions by digital word of mouth. Customers want to hear about the value and benefits of a brand—or the products that make up that brand—from other customers. Marketing and e-commerce are both evolving in a way that puts the customer in control, deciding what is relevant, how to engage with the brand, and how to view the assortment of products. Marketers can no longer push messages down to customers, as consumers are in control. "Customers trust their friends much more than they trust a marketer," Boylson continues. "So we are asking—how do we best put the customer in control of our brand? How do we become relevant so that customers want to share our brand with their friends?"

In many large corporations, a marketer's nemesis is often the information technology (IT) organization, but in JCPenney's push to expand its digital word of mouth, Boylson has found his closest partner to be Group Executive Vice President Tom Nealon, who is also responsible for the company's digital innovations. "In a lot of companies, IT and marketing are like oil and water, but not here," said Boylson. "Today, I spend more time with our CIO than anyone else in the company. We work hand-in-glove on all of these initiatives."

Social Interaction Begins with Jcp.com

As an early leader in e-commerce, JCPenney built a large portion of its Web site in house, without the benefit of sophisticated design and software packages that have since become available. The site is now being redesigned to offer more social media and support for mobile devices. "We have a tremendous amount of innovation going on in the entire digital space," said Boylson. "Tom Nealon is re-platforming the entire digital infrastructure so that we can be faster and more nimble. This is a digital infrastructure that will support every customer touch point—regardless of where they are, including JCPenney stores."

Despite the overhaul of its Web platform, JCPenney's current site provides a number of Web 2.0 interactive and social functions. It features customer product reviews and allows the customer to share any item with friends through Facebook, MySpace, Stylehive, Kaboodle, or email. The link to JCPenney's Facebook site is prominently displayed on the company Web site.

The Look Book

JCPenney's "Look Book" provides an online experience that lets customers design, share, and save outfits from the Contemporary Style selection of women's and junior apparel and accessories. Customers can try their hand at designing an outfit and posting it to the Look Book to see how popular it becomes among other online customers. They also can view outfits designed by other customers, cast a positive "Love this" vote on any outfit, "Remix" outfits by swapping out items with a personal selection, share an outfit with Facebook friends, and finally purchase the outfit. JCPenney's socially interactive site won Silver in the "Social Commerce" category and Bronze in the "Web Site Experience" category of the 2010 Racie Awards (see Exhibit 9.2).

Online Runway Experience

The "Little Red Book" runway experience on jcp.com is an interactive application that highlights the latest styles and trends from the fashion runway. Fashion models come to life as they walk down the runway in select outfits available for purchase. Trends such as "Island Escape," "Re-Vintage," and "Keep It Simple" are highlighted through a series of outfits and online videos. Island Escape, for example, depicts a series of complete outfits in sea-blue and green color tones. An accompanying video discusses the modern fashion trend and how best to wear sea-inspired tones and patterns, along with tips for jewelry and other accessories. The customer can share outfits with friends via social media and then purchase various items as a complete outfit.

Teens Vote

JCPenney also uses interactive voting on its Web site for select junior apparel runway outfits. Customers can compare a series of outfits, vote for their favorite, and see how other teens voted. When viewing

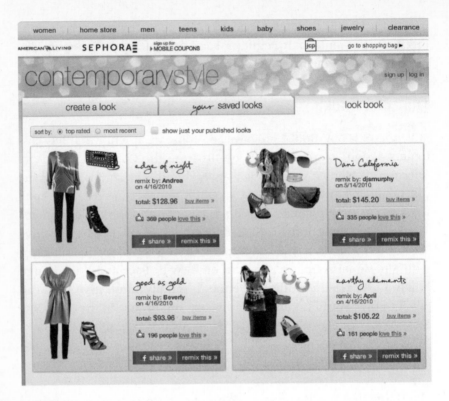

Exhibit 9.2 JCPenney Look Book Outfit Builder
Source: Reprinted with permission of JCPenney.

teen apparel, a "Let's Be Friends" tagline provides a link to the JCPTeen Facebook page (see Exhibit 9.3).

Facebook

With more than 930,000 fans of its main JCPenney page and more than 173,000 fans of its JCPTeen page, JCPenney has more than 1 million Facebook fans. The company also maintains a separate fan page for JCPenney Optical and JCPenney Portrait Studios.

JCPenney Facebook Page

JCPenney's Facebook Wall contains a good mix of company and fan posts. Company posts address such topics as fashion, community outreach, and promotions, and JCPenney receives a large number of

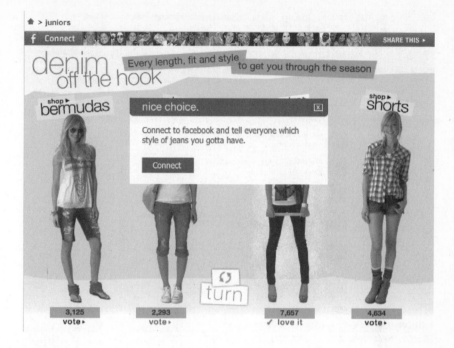

Exhibit 9.3 Jcp.com Interactive Teen Page
Source: Reprinted with permission of JCPenney.

responses to its posts (see Exhibit 9.4). Fan posts include plenty of fan mail, as well as the typical mixture of customer service questions and suggestions. JCPenney quickly views and responds to these inquiries. The Facebook page also provides links to the "Little Red Book" fashion runway, weekly specials, sweepstakes contests, its weekly circular, and its mobile advertisement alerts. Additionally, the page includes sections for reading and sharing reviews of the company's offerings and postings of customer polls about fashion preferences. Videos, photos, events, and a career page listing current job openings add to the page's attributes.

Exclusive Facebook offers are provided for JCPenney's Facebook fans. By entering a promotion code, they can receive discounts for limited-time sales sometimes lasting only a few hours. Judging from the fan posts about one such recent exclusive women's lingerie sale, these events generate a lot of traffic and a lot of Facebook comments—210 fans commented within the first couple of hours.

JCPenney The Sex and the City gals are back! Celebrate with Sarah Jessica Parker's new Carrie Bradshaw-inspired fragrance, SJP NYC, available at Sephora inside JCPenney stores. Which character's return to the big screen are you most excited about?

Sephora inside JCPenney Store Locator
bit.ly
SJP NYC is available at Sephora inside JCPenney Stores. Check to see if your JCPenney has a Sephora inside.

5 hours ago · Comment · Like · Share

50 people like this.

Martha Mena-Ramirez Samantha ; ?))
5 hours ago · Flag

Michelle Godfrey Well only one school friend responded...
5 hours ago · Flag

Kimberley Ayres Mr Big! ♥
4 hours ago · Flag

Christina Michelle Willmon-Mettlen SJP of course....and i wore the perfume to the premiere last night! I love it!!!
4 hours ago · Flag

Amy Dawn Ringering I like Miranda's hubby... I think he's adorable! :)~
4 hours ago · Flag

Kimberly Swan Downham aiden
4 hours ago · Flag

Exhibit 9.4 JCPenney Facebook Page
Source: Reprinted with permission of JCPenney.

JCPTeen Facebook Page

JCPTeen is hip! It's a fast-growing Facebook page with strong engagement from teens and preteens. The company includes posts about the latest teen fashions, including its popular Olsenboye line of clothing. Teens are active participants on the Wall and highly responsive to company posts eliciting fashion preferences, both through the Facebook "Like" voting button and specific comments. Other page tabs include "Weekly Crush," which highlights a favorite teen item that the company is promoting—quick-dry beach towels, for example; "Olsenboye," which contains videos, virtual gifts, and downloadable wallpaper, all with its current Southern California beach-life theme; and "Mash," an interactive game that will predict a teen's future (see Exhibit 9.5). By interacting with teens in a series of questions about their current "crush," favorite types of cars, dream places to live, and career aspirations, the game processes answers to the questions and creates a fun prediction about the teen's future that can then be shared with Facebook friends.

Exhibit 9.5 JCPTeen Facebook Page
Source: Reprinted with permission of JCPenney.

JCPTeen also links to several Facebook gaming applications designed specifically for teens:

- **JCPTeen "Stuck on You."** Teens select a friend's Facebook profile picture and then enhance that portrait with a beard, mustache, glasses, a new hairdo, and more. The new masterpiece photo can be put on exhibition in the Stuck on You photo gallery or on a teen's Facebook wall.

- **"Board Builder."** This application allows teens to design a custom surfboard that can be added to the profile page or sent to friends through Facebook.

Other Facebook Fan Pages

JCPenney Optical has its own fan page containing coupons and photos of the latest fashion eyewear, as well as an online Optical Fitting Room. Visitors to the site can upload a photo and select styles of eyeglass frames from the list, and the virtual fitting room superimposes the frames onto the photo. Visitors can try on various eyeglasses and even share their new look with friends on Facebook or by email.

In addition to promotions and a portrait-studio location feature, the JCPenney Portrait Studios Facebook Fan page contains an active Wall where fans enjoy posting portrait photos of their children.

YouTube

JCPenney maintains a YouTube channel where it uploads videos about style and the latest fashions available at the company, as well as promotional and community outreach videos. In addition, a search on JCPenney yields several thousand other videos about the company uploaded by other parties (see Exhibit 9.6).

Exhibit 9.6 JCPenney YouTube Channel
Source: Reprinted with permission of JCPenney.

Twitter

JCPenney is in the early stages of leveraging its own Twitter accounts. Both @JCPenney and @JCPenneyOptical are establishing followings and thus far have tweeted primarily about promotional events. The company's more widespread use of Twitter is for following celebrities like Charlotte Ronson and Cindy Crawford, who design exclusive lines for JCPenney. As part of its Cindy Crawford line of home products, the company invites consumers to follow Cindy Crawford's tweets (@cindycrawford) and posts them on its Web site. With more than 530,000 followers, Cindy Crawford's tweets about JCPenney get plenty of exposure. Likewise, Charlotte Ronson (@cjronson), who designs the exclusive I Heart Ronson line for JCPenney, also tweets about the fashion line to her 25,000 followers. Twitter offers JCPenney an excellent opportunity for customer engagement through product introductions, fashion direction, and customer service.

Blogger Influence

Although JCPenney does not have its own public blogs, the company works actively to get its message out among influential bloggers. The efforts are made not at an overall company-brand level, but rather by working with bloggers more targeted to specific customer segments, such as young moms and teens. The company also works actively with bloggers to spread the word about celebrity brands such as Charlotte Ronson's I Heart Ronson or Olsenboye. In 2010, it developed a holistic contact strategy directed to young moms primarily through blogs like ivillage, cafemom, and others that reach this engaged customer in a highly targeted way.

JCPENNEY LOVES MOBILE

In 2009 JCPenney implemented a 2D bar-code coupon program that allows customers to download and carry promotional incentives on their mobile phones. The incentives include coupons, events, polls, giveaways, downloads, and information alerts. The coupons can then be redeemed at the register. This program was the first of its kind among U.S. retailers. New imaging scanners capable of reading these 2D bar-code coupons have been deployed at point-of-sale registers in 16 Houston metro-area JCPenney test stores. JCPenney believes that mobile discounts, rather than clipping or printing coupons, will provide customers with an incentive to go to JCPenney. The company is also in the process of integrating 2D bar codes into its JCP Rewards loyalty program to make it easier for members to redeem earned rewards monthly.

The company offers its weekly promotional circular via any mobile phone. It also offers iPhone, iPad, and Android applications called JCPenney Weekly Deals (see Exhibit 9.7). Both the Apple and Android versions show weekly deals at JCPenney. And both applications offer a preview of weekly in-store sales and promotional offers; a favorites list to take to the store; the ability to share items with friends on Facebook, Twitter, or email; and a store locator to find nearby JCPenney stores. JCPenney is also one of Apple's Charter Partners on the new iPad application-based marketing program.

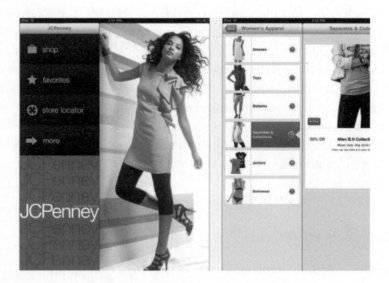

Exhibit 9.7 JCPenney iPad Weekly Deals App
Source: Reprinted with permission of JCPenney.

JCPenney is one of the first retailers with an interactive iPad application version of its weekly print circular. The app also provides one-tap access to the week's color newspaper insert, the latest sales, a "Little Red Book" with apparel deals, and more. Users can save favorites, locate the nearest JCPenney stores, watch the latest videos, and configure mobile alerts right within the app for mobile phone access to additional deals and discounts.

JCPenney was recognized with a Mobile Retailer of the Year Award, sponsored by *Mobile Commerce Daily*, for covering the whole range, from feature phones to smart phones, with its iPhone application. During the 2009 holiday season, JCPenney launched a holiday-themed mobile Web site. The Wireless Application Protocol site let customers browse the company's gift assortments and send gift "hints" to friends and family. A customer also could find a store and register for an early-riser, wake-up call to attend the Day-After-Thanksgiving Black Friday and the Day-After-Christmas sales. In addition, customers could choose a wake-up call from one of JCPenney's partners, including Cindy Crawford (style expert for JCPenney's Cindy Crawford Style brand), Kimora Lee Simmons (designer for JCPenney's Fabulosity brand), or Rascal Flatts band members Gary LeVox, Jay DeMarcus, and Joe Don Rooney, whose recent Rascal Flatts American Living Unstoppable Tour, presented by JCPenney, promoted the company's American Living brand.

JCPenney is bullish on mobile, and Mike Boylson talks energetically about the company's aggressive expansion plans for later this year: "We like social [media] but we love mobile," he said. "Mobile Internet usage is growing eight times faster than the adoption of traditional Internet usage, and this shift in mobile will fundamentally change the way customers and brands interact. The intersection of mobile and social will be very powerful." Boylson hints at the possibilities, especially among JCPenney's highly targeted teen market: "Imagine a teen taking a picture of an outfit she likes on her mobile device, sending it to her dad, and asking permission to purchase it. The father then sends money to her phone to complete the sale." JCPenney is now working on a strategy that will align itself with strategic partners within the mobile shopping space, giving it "first mover" advantage among its competition. The company is launching a new mobile site in the fall of 2010.

A DIGITAL FUTURE FOR A TRADITIONAL PLAYER

In discussing JCPenney's future, Boylson is focused and excited about the role that social media and mobile will play. With its new fashion styles and brands, JCPenney has a major opportunity to reach a broader market of young customers through these digital channels. "All these tactics add up to something much bigger," said Boylson. "I believe this really puts a halo on our brand!" What is Mike Ullman's role in all of this? "Our most innovative person is our CEO, Mike Ullman," Boylson replies. "Therefore, innovation permeates the culture. This has to be leader-led—Mike has an extreme sense of urgency, and he drives the organization hard on innovation." Boylson's statement is reflected in Ullman's actions: Expose the board of directors to the company's digital strategy by holding a board meeting at Facebook's headquarters. The real opportunity is reflected by Ullman's statement:

"The way that people think and behave today is digital."[7]

That's what's driving the digital transformation of JCPenney.

NOTES

1. "JC Penney CEO and CIO Put IT at Heart of New Strategy," *Information Week*, Bob Evans, April 22, 2009, available at www.informationweek.com/blog/main/archives/2009/04/jc_penney_ceo_a.html;jsessionid=NKDVVHFTMOCD1QE1GHPSKHWATMY32JVN, (accessed June 16, 2010).
2. J.C.Penney Company, Inc. Summary Annual Report 2009, available at http://media.corporate-ir.net/media_files/irol/70/70528/2009IAR/2009IAR/images/JC_Penney-AR2009.pdf, (accessed June 15, 2010).
3. J.C.Penney Company, Inc. Summary Annual Report 2009.
4. "JCPenney Wins Big at Racie Awards," JCPenney Press Release, March 8, 2010, available at www.jcpenney.net/about/jcpmedia/corporatenews/articles/JCPenney_Wins_Big_at_Racie_Awards,118.aspx, (accessed June 15, 2010).
5. J.C.Penney Company, Inc. Summary Annual Report 2009.

6. Interview with Mike Boylson, conducted via phone, May 7, 2010. All subsequent quotes from Boylson are from this interview.
7. "Penney's 'Smart Fixture' Rolls Out as Next Technological Step," *Dallas Morning News*, April 22, 2009, available at www.dallasnews.com/sharedcontent/dws/bus/stories/042209dnbuspenney.3961610.html, (accessed June 15, 2010).

10

Pizza Hut: Creating the Perfect Pizza—Digitally

There is nothing like a great pizza, particularly one that you've personally created. Or your favorite pasta dish or really good chicken wings—all at affordable prices. And imagine creating, ordering, and then having that favorite meal delivered to you without your ever having to say a word! You actually can do just that—from Facebook—while you're catching up with old friends or playing FarmVille. You can even share your suggestions for new menu items with your pizza community.

How do you get this intimate, engaging relationship with the largest pizza company in the world? Just go to www.pizzahut.com, Facebook, or your iPhone, and watch it happen! Step into the digital kitchen and create your own custom pizza, from crust, to size, to toppings. Want half pepperoni, half green peppers, and mushrooms on the whole thing? No problem: Just click or tilt your phone and watch your toppings move. Want to add some wings? Click on your favorite type, pour your favorite sauce, shake your phone, and coat your wings

189

to perfection. And a quick click serves up your favorite restaurant-quality pastas. Looking for a great deal? Check out the coupons on your virtual fridge. You have just prepared a delicious meal, compliments of Pizza Hut and its unique innovations in the socially connected digital world.

TOPPING THE PIZZA MARKET

With more than 13,000 outlets in 92 countries and territories, Pizza Hut, Inc., a unit of Yum! Brands, operates the world's largest pizza chain. The Pizza Hut chain serves a variety of pizza styles, including the flagship Pan Pizza, as well as Thin 'N Crispy®, Stuffed Crust, and Hand-Tossed Style. Additional menu items include Tuscani Pastas and WingStreet® wings, as well as a variety of side dishes and desserts. Pizza Hut was named as one of Interbrand's "2010 Global 100 Best Brands" and profiled in *BusinessWeek*. While its global achievements are very impressive, it is equally important to note that a business of this size and complexity also can focus on its franchisees and customers in a more intimate way than most small companies. Pizza Hut was named a Top 10 franchise in 2009 by *Entrepreneur* magazine, demonstrating that this large multinational company has a strong reputation and excels at communicating with its franchisees.

Pizza Hut focuses on attaining similar relationships with its customers. Through the new communication channels of social media and mobility, Pizza Hut has demonstrated early and successful engagement with consumers. Of the "2010 Global 100 Best Brands," Pizza Hut was ranked in the top half for social-media engagement. The study, conducted by Wetpaint, Inc., and Altimeter Group, evaluated how well these top 100 companies are engaging their consumers by using social media and—even more important—how that engagement correlates with their most important financial metrics. Only five leisure (casual food) companies made the list, and Pizza Hut, the only pizza company so named, landed in the top three.[1]

Pizza Hut was founded in 1958 in Wichita, Kansas. As the entire casual food market has grown and changed over the past 50-plus years, the company has grown both nationally and internationally, as well as through various creative formats. Customer-focused and innovative, Pizza Hut has adapted well to changes in the marketplace. This achievement is consistent with the progressive strategy of its parent company, Yum! Brands, an industry leader with a true entrepreneurial spirit.

BUILDING THE YUM! DYNASTY

With its 2009 revenue of nearly $11 billion, Yum! Brands is the world's largest restaurant company; it includes more than 37,000 retail units in over 110 countries and territories. The company's brands, KFC, Pizza Hut, Taco Bell, Long John Silver's, and A&W Restaurants, are the global leaders of the chicken, pizza, Mexican-style food, and quick-service seafood categories. Yum! is also the Number-One retail developer of units outside the United States, opening more than 1,000 for the ninth straight year (1,467 were opened in 2009).

Yum! Brands Chairman and CEO David Novak is a powerful communicator and an effective leader. In the Yum! Brands "2009 Annual Customer Mania Report," he commented, "I know you would agree the only way you can be recognized as 'The Defining Company that Feeds the World' is to get the results again and again, which is what we've coined as 'Building the Yum! Dynasty.'"

Yum! Dynasty Growth Model

Our goal: Be the Best in the World at Building Great Brands and Running Great Restaurants!

Our passion: Customer Mania ...put a YUM on customers' faces around the world.

Our formula for success: People Capability First...satisfied customers and profitability follow.

How we lead [with intentionality]: Step-Change Thinkers, Know-How Builders, Action Drivers, People Growers

The Company is focused on building leading brands in China in every significant category and driving aggressive, international expansion and building strong brands everywhere.

A Famous Recognition Culture: Everyone Counts

Using reward and recognition to drive results is key to David Novak's management style and he has built Yum!'s entire global culture around it. This culture is evident throughout the company in the various types of "fun recognition" awards that are given and events that are held. All leaders around the world, at every level of the organization, have their own recognition awards. Novak's Yum! Award is an oversized set of walking teeth given to employees who "Walk the Talk" of leadership.

Pizza Hut shares this same passion for its people, and its culture serves as a catalyst for innovation in the digital worlds of social media and mobility. "A major benefit to being a Yum! brand, is that we share one of the strongest company cultures in an organization," said Brian Niccol, Pizza Hut CMO. "The Yum! culture encourages a spirit of innovation throughout our business, which allows us to fearlessly pursue new digital and emerging media opportunities."

VALUE PLUS FAVORITES = A WINNING STRATEGY

Pizza Hut has a significant platform for leveraging its global brand in a number of areas: value pricing, menu expansion, customer service, marketing, and its use of the new consumer channels of social media and mobility. In 2009, with the global economic recession, the dinner-occasion segment showed the greatest decline as more consumers than usual chose to eat at home. Pizza Hut quickly examined the situation and dealt with both the strategic issues and the tactics necessary for effective execution.

Armando Garza, Senior Marketing Director for New Occasions, describes the strategy devised by the company to address this problem:

> Our strategy is around "Value" and "Favorites." In terms of delighting the consumer, you have to provide them their favorites. What are the right menu offerings? How do you maintain the competitive edge, and how do you use social media and all marketing disciplines to accomplish this? The biggest part of the strategy is around understanding the consumer. What our strategy hinges on

is providing the right value to consumers, as well as providing their favorites. Those are the two pillars we're leveraging in the marketplace today. What's going on in the economy pinpoints the importance of value. Also, we're trying to get back to the genesis of Pizza Hut, what they grew up with and loved.[2]

Because they responded directly to consumer demand, the actions taken by Pizza Hut have been well received.

Value Pricing

The quality of Pizza Hut pizza has always been well known. The 2009 challenges faced by the company included the economy's discerning, value-driven customers and heavy competition in the quick-service industry. In response, Pizza Hut introduced the "$10 Any Pizza/Any Toppings" pizza offering. This high-profile strategy, well marketed and supported by social media, has been extremely successful.

Menus

The strategic plan is to expand the Pizza Hut brand from "pizza" to a broader menu of "pizza, pasta, and wings." Accordingly, the company has taken actions that demonstrate the importance of this strategy and envisions additional opportunities in the future. As Garza states, "While we've had pasta in our menu options for a number of years, in the last couple of years we introduced Tuscani Pastas right to the customer's door, with great success. Carry-out units have the ability to deliver restaurant-quality pastas right to the customer at home. That's the same with the wing business. We now have a better quality wing that we can deliver to the customer's home."

Service

The company also is focused on improving speed of service and executing a "Heart of the Hut" program designed to improve overall hospitality.

Marketing

Along with its already-effective television strategy, Pizza Hut has recognized the critical importance of online marketing, tripling its investment in this channel. At the same time, the company succeeds in effectively engaging consumers through social media and leveraging this tactic into its marketing strategy.

Digital Consumer Interface

Having recognized the explosive growth of the digital consumer, Pizza Hut has assumed a leadership role in understanding this consumer, as well as utilizing the technological applications best suited to reaching and satisfying both current and potential customers. The company continues to do innovative work in the areas of social media and mobility.

ENABLING GLOBAL KNOWLEDGE SHARING

Any multinational company knows the challenges of spreading the corporate culture globally while serving the customer locally. Yum! Brands seized the opportunity to better connect its global employees through a virtual internal business collaboration network, named iCHING (see Exhibit 10.1). For employees, iCHING is a new, innovative way of working—across multiple time zones and geographies—in order to share best practices and foster breakthrough thinking and innovation in every area of the company's business.

As it relates to Yum! Brands' culture, the name iCHING is significant. As associates break through brand, geography, and functional silos to build global know-how, it is critical for each individual to build "CHING" along the way, meaning that making connections and building relationships is a key part of the Yum! culture. The "H" in iCHING is a visual representation of the power of collaboration, when two people come together to connect and build "know-how."

iCHING rolled out to "above restaurant" (corporate) employees in June 2009 and is in the process of being rolled out on a larger scale. Employees from Louisville to Dubai to China across Yum!, Taco Bell,

Exhibit 10.1 iCHING Business Collaboration Network
Source: Reprinted with permission of Pizza Hut.

KFC, Pizza Hut, Long John Silver's, and A&W Restaurants are using iCHING to share knowledge, join groups related to business-driving initiatives, and share best practices with their colleagues around the globe. On iCHING, discussions uncover success tips from one market or brand that can be applied to another. Employees can pose a question at the end of a business day and find dozens of responses from around the world waiting for them when they return to work the next morning.

iCHING was introduced to company employees through a creative internal marketing campaign. The "H," the key symbol in the iCHING logo, appears as part of this campaign in all relevant company communications. To ensure understanding and value, "brand activation squads" were formed at all of the company's branches. Five-foot-tall renderings of the "H" in the iCHING logo were strategically positioned throughout the company's major branches. When giant "Hs" began showing up in hallways, they generated much curiosity and excitement. This degree of leadership commitment within Yum! Brands— from the CEO throughout the entire organization—shows that this company's culture permeates all of its portfolio brands across the world.

AN INNOVATOR IN SOCIAL MEDIA

Describing the effectiveness of its social-media strategy, Chris Fuller, Senior Manager of Public Relations and Emerging Media, says, "At Pizza Hut, any time a customer has been socially discussing our brand, we've tried to become part of that discussion. In the world of online social media, we've been there since day one."[3] Pizza Hut's use of social media and mobility in its strategy and campaigns is woven throughout each of its digital media channels, while taking into account each specific channel's unique features and individual audiences. It is a formula designed to maximize engagement and excitement.

A Socially Engaging Website: "Your Place for Online Ordering"

When people visit a pizza company's Web site, chances are they want to place an order. With 6,200 domestic restaurants, Pizza Hut is expected to hit $2 billion in online sales in 2010. The website www.pizzahut.com is all about allowing customers to easily order their favorite Pizza Hut products at an affordable price. As Armando Garza says, "With technology, sometimes people don't want to talk to someone on the phone. They'd rather just do it themselves. We make it easy [for them] to just place the order themselves." For those individuals traditionally more comfortable ordering take-out by phone, the Web site makes ordering online so easy and fun that they may well be tempted to try the experience.

The Web site is simple. Its visual appeal makes online ordering faster, more intuitive, and less prone to error. It brings the menu to life, visually educating the consumer about variety and value. It coaches customers throughout the ordering process, even showing them how to save favorite items for easy reordering. When ordering a pizza, a customer encounters plenty of visuals to guide him through the process, including the ability to build a custom-made pizza, from selecting the crust, to watching the process of successively adding various toppings. One competitive differentiator is the availability of restaurant-quality wings and a variety of pasta dishes for home delivery. "Fan Us" on Facebook, "Follow Us" on Twitter, and "Watch Us" on YouTube are prominently displayed on the Web site's home page, as is the Pizza Hut "Killer App" iPhone application.

Pizza on Your Face

Pizza Hut has created a successful social-media presence, with more than 1.4 million fans on Facebook as of August 2010, and it continues to add fans rapidly. The company was actually an innovator in utilizing Facebook, having launched its fan site in early 2008. In October of that year, the company added more features, including an application that allows customers to order food from Pizza Hut without ever having to leave Facebook (see Exhibit 10.2). Knowing that Facebook

Exhibit 10.2 Pizza Hut Facebook Ordering Application
Source: Reprinted with permission of Pizza Hut.

had become a preferred method of communication among its customers, the company wanted to create a presence that enabled it to become part of the conversation. Pizza Hut had long prided itself as an innovator in its industry and wanted to lead in the use of social media as well.

The company's Facebook Wall is filled with accolades from its fans, along with the occasional customer service issues. Although fairly infrequent, the company's posts represent a blend of entertaining comments about its latest marketing campaign and those that address such corporate responsibility initiatives as stories from the Pizza Hut BOOK IT!® reading incentive program or its participation in the World Hunger Relief effort. The Pizza Hut Facebook page also includes a link to its iPhone application, an active discussion forum, polls reflecting customer preferences, videos, and upcoming events.

Twintern to Tweetologist

Similar to most companies, Pizza Hut's use of Twitter got off to a slow start. As it did in its other digital venues, however, the company won the attention of the masses by figuring out an innovative and entertaining strategy. It was looking for someone who could relate to college students and young families and who understood how to socialize effectively on Twitter. Consequently, in the spring of 2009, Pizza Hut placed a job posting in the *New York Times* for the world's first "Twintern" (Twintern equals "Twitter" + "Summer intern"). The job description portrayed the position as that of "our social media journalist, chronicling in 140 characters or less what's going on at Pizza Hut."

The Twintern also would be responsible for tracking all mentions of the brand and alerting superiors whenever anything negative or requiring action was said. The salary was described as "competitive with [that of] other Twitterers," and job requirements included being a college student, demonstrating social-media skills, and being "happy to instill their thoughts into short and frequent bursts of text." The job posting garnered Pizza Hut an enormous amount of publicity from both traditional and digital social media, including stories written by

Exhibit 10.3 Pizza Hut Twitter Page
Source: Reprinted with permission of Pizza Hut.

bloggers who expounded upon the innovative idea of entrusting a well-known brand to an inexperienced college student as being either a good move or a risky one.

Alexa Robinson, 22, made national headlines when she became Pizza Hut's first official Twintern in June 2009. When she tweeted her first official message—"Luv my new job!"—under the Twitter ID @pizzahut, the company had 3,000 Twitter followers. In just a few short months, Pizza Hut drove that number up tenfold. In reading her tweets (see Exhibit 10.3), one knows for sure that she gets how to communicate on Twitter. Alexa has tweeted about giveaways, promotions, new products, the Pizza Hut iPhone app, menu changes, customer service issues, philanthropic efforts, and more. Authentic and engaging, she frequently invites followers to send tweets about their favorite foods, vacation photos, and celebrities.

Chris Fuller had a strong hand in developing the Twintern program. "In spring of 2009, we realized that we needed to dedicate someone full-time to Twitter," says Fuller. "Not someone to govern strategy, but more of someone who could act as a journalist of what was happening inside the corporate office. People wanted a peek inside the tent of Pizza Hut. She writes about it. She is the voice and the ear of the customer."

The initial Twinternship was a huge success, so much so that the program continues for other students; Robinson has become a permanent hire, having been promoted to the role of "Tweetologist," which now includes monitoring all the online chatter about Pizza Hut. At the time it hired Robinson to assume this full-time position, Pizza Hut again managed to garner positive, entertaining publicity: It asked customers to make suggestions for her new job title as a full-time employee. Of the more than 200 suggestions submitted, "Tweetologist" proved to be the winning name.

Tweetologist (tweet-ol-uh-jist), noun; definition: A Twitter specialist. Orig: 2009, Pizza Hut.

The winner was awarded a year's worth of free pizza in the form of $599 in Pizza Hut gift cards.

Other Social Networks

Doing a YouTube search for "Pizza Hut" returns hundreds of videos viewed by millions of people. Pizza Hut's digital videos range from past commercials, campaigns, and human-interest stories, to entertaining and comical tales with Pizza Hut as the backdrop. Various social-media sites may gain and lose popularity, but Pizza Hut has maintained its leadership ascendancy by closely following the trend and ensuring its position as an early participant in that site's conversation. "We are at the beginning of all the social-network 'brands,' " says Chris Fuller. When MySpace got big, we were already there. When YouTube got big, we were there."

THE "KILLER APP FOR YOUR APPETITE"

When your mobile application is termed the "Killer App," it's clear that you have catapulted to the head of the pack as an industry leader in customer engagement. "Killer App" is the name given by many to Pizza Hut's iPhone application, which was named the #1 Branded Mobile Application of 2009 by *Forbes* magazine (see Exhibit 10.4). To

Exhibit 10.4 Pizza Hut iPhone Application
Source: Reprinted with permission of Pizza Hut.

understand this leadership position, all one has to do is recognize the multiple applications that have been brought to market in many industry segments since July 2009, when Pizza Hut introduced this application to the market.

A Pizza Hut YouTube video available on its Web site describes its iPhone applications as follows:

> Introducing the killer app for your appetite. Brought to you by Pizza Hut. We've taken the coolest iPhone functionality and used it to make ordering pizza, pasta, and wings easy, fast, and fun! You can drag it, tap it, pinch it, stretch it, tilt it, shake it, play it, order it, and enjoy it. The Pizza Hut app is a revolution in mobile ordering.
>
> - Zoom in on your virtual fridge for the hottest deals.
> - Find a location.
> - Save your favorite orders.
> - Demo mode helps you learn your way around.
>
> Now let's take a look at how you order pizza with the Pizza Hut app. Are you ready? Let's go. First, scroll through the crust options and tap to choose your favorite. Mmmm hand tossed. Next, pick a size. You can pinch it to make it smaller. Or stretch it to make it bigger. Now you're ready for toppings. Just scroll through and drag them to your pizza. How about pepperoni? And mushrooms? Only want pepperoni on half? Just tap it and tilt it. Your pizza is ready to go.

Hey, are you hungry for some wings? Wing Street is just around the corner. First, tap to choose a wing style. Traditional? Crispy bone in or bone out? Let's try traditional. Now scroll through the sauces and choose your favorite. Decisions! Decisions! There we go. Now it's time to shake things up. Literally. Shake your phone to sauce your wings. There you go. Looking good. Want more wings? No problem. Just tap the quantity you want and you're ready to place your order.

Want to have some fun while your order is being delivered? Play The Hut Racer game. Your mission: avoid the obstacles in the road and navigate the course to get the best time. Tilt and turn your iPhone to speed up and slow down and maneuver your Hut Racer. And that's just a little taste of what the Pizza Hut app has to offer. You can also order your favorite Tuscani Pastas and zoom in on your virtual fridge to find the hottest Pizza Hut deals.

"People today are using their phones all the time to call and order pizzas," says Armando Garza. "How do you get people with a phone in their hand to become engaged in an ordering process, but make it simpler than just picking up the phone and calling someone? We wanted to be first. With the introduction of the iPhone app, we were able to make the experience very exciting." Besides the fact that it's been downloaded more times than any other brand's iPhone application, why is this one rightly called a "Killer App"? "[Because] most apps are accessed only on occasion. Pizza Hut's app provides something of benefit. You get a physical, tangible order on the back end," says Garza. "People love food. There's an emotional connection with food that creates a unique bond with the app. It's very relevant."

The Pizza Hut iPhone application has been enormously successful, not only in selling pizzas and building customer affinity, but also in extending Pizza Hut's brand equity. In its first year on the market, it surpassed one million downloads. The Pizza Hut iPhone App has won two Mobile Marketing Association awards: one for Best Mobile Display Campaign and one for Best Emerging Technology Campaign. The company also has won several other awards, as well as recognition by a number of media, marketing, social-media, and mobility groups.

Exhibit 10.5 Pizza Hut iPhone Augmented-Reality Application
Source: Reprinted with permission of Pizza Hut.

These important awards are only as strong as the customers' views and responses, which have been overwhelmingly positive.

"Ordering Pizza Has Never Been So Deliciously Fun!"

As of March 2010, Pizza Hut was already experimenting with mobile-augmented reality in an application used to direct customers to its physical stores (see Exhibit 10.5). This application, currently targeted at the Australian local market, includes an augmented-reality mobile platform using the iPhone camera, GPS, and compass to display annotations overlaid on the real-world view. Customers can choose to order a pizza for pick-up and then use the real-world, augmented-reality view to select the store they'd like to use for their pick-up order. Moving the phone around shows all Pizza Hut stores in the area in their actual physical locations, as well as the distance from the customer to the store. Not only is the camera used to show what lies in front of the user, but small tabs also highlight the direction and distance of nearby Pizza Hut locations.

Could this be the second "Killer App"? Pizza Hut hopes so. "It's been successful in Australia and is getting ready to launch in Europe," says Garza. "Competitors are hot and heavy on our heels, so our job is to win in the second set and win round two as well." A demonstration of the application can be found at www.youtube.com/watch?v= qsD_tDSgM6U.

Fast and Easy Ordering from Any Phone

While smart phones clearly provide a more compelling and entertaining experience, Pizza Hut has been an early innovator in mobile ordering for traditional feature phones as well. It promotes its two fast and easy ways to order from any mobile phone:

- **Fast: Text Message Ordering.** Using saved favorites from the Pizza Hut Web site, you can text in the order with one simple code.

- **Flexible: Pizza Hut Mobile.** Using the mobile version of pizzahut.com, you can browse the complete menu from your phone and place the order right from your phone.

BRANDED! THROUGH SOCIAL AND MOBILE CHANNELS

In response to its customers' sentiment that Pizza Hut needed better value, the company began in 2010 a major marketing campaign called "Any Pizza, Any Size, Any Crust, Any Toppings. Just $10." The campaign has been highly successful: The chain has managed to promote itself out of a slump and arrest same-store sales declines. In accomplishing this feat, Pizza Hut took its strategy to traditional media, as well as to digital media, including social and mobile networks and its own Web site.

Through its social networks, Pizza Hut received a lot of feedback suggesting that customers wanted the campaign to stay in effect after the stated promotional period. Always ready to create another positive public relations opportunity, especially at a time when state primary elections were heating up around the United States, Pizza Hut decided to put the $10 Pizza Deal in the hands of the American voters. Recognizing that this strategy might well draw millions of people to the Pizza Hut Facebook page to cast their votes, the company appointed Tweetologist Alexa Robinson as the campaign manager. She spread

Exhibit 10.6 Facebook Vote for the $10 Pizza Campaign
Source: Reprinted with permission of Pizza Hut.

Exhibit 10.7 Facebook Post and Responses to the $10 Pizza Campaign
Source: Reprinted with permission of Pizza Hut.

the word virally through Facebook, Twitter, and YouTube, even physically touring various cities, accompanied by a team of aides, to hand out campaign stickers and buttons and post "election" signs that read, "Vote Yes to Keep the $10 Pizza." Votes were cast through Facebook, and Robinson tweeted and posted information about her campaign stops, complete with photos (see Exhibits 10.6 and 10.7). On Facebook, hundreds of people responded to the posts with "Like" or actual comments as word spread through Twitter with each stop. (Note: the final outcome of the vote was "yes," resulting in Pizza Hut keeping the $10 Pizza.)

A Company with a Huge Heart Spreads Its Love Socially

Pizza Hut also has figured out how to gain large numbers of online supporters for corporate responsibility initiatives. Two recent examples of how the company has utilized social media to promote worthy causes include its use of Twitter to increase Pizza Hut's donation to World Hunger Relief and its use of social media to feature its BOOK IT! National Reading Incentive Program.

Feeding the World Through Twitter

Pizza Hut effectively uses social media to combine marketing with philanthropy, thereby carrying forward the Yum! Brands mission: "A Company with a Huge Heart." In September 2009, Pizza Hut launched a campaign to donate meals to Yum! Brands' World Hunger Relief, the world's largest private-sector, hunger-relief effort. The campaign raised awareness, volunteerism, and funds for the United Nations World Food Programme (WFP) and other hunger relief agencies. For every Twitter user who re-tweeted the link to the Pizza Hut World Hunger Foundation donation page, Pizza Hut donated four meals. Tweeters simply had to help by posting a tweet on Twitter that included a link to the donation page and the hashtag #pizzahut—and the company would donate four meals to the hungry. Donations were made for the first 25,000 tweets, which meant 100,000 donated meals. This added to the nearly $60 million that Yum! Brands Pizza Hut, KFC, Taco Bell, Long John Silver's, and A&W Restaurants raised since 2007 for WFP and other hunger relief agencies. The company's World Hunger Relief global effort is helping to provide approximately 250 million meals, saving the lives of millions of people in remote corners of the world where hunger is most prevalent. (For more information about Yum! Brands World Hunger Relief effort, visit FromHungertoHope. com.)

The BOOK IT! National Reading Incentive Program

The BOOK IT! program is the Pizza Hut National Reading Incentive Program, designed to inspire children in grades kindergarten through 6 to develop a lifelong love of reading. Established in 1985, its goal is to help children become better readers. The BOOK IT! program rewards children for their reading accomplishments with praise, recognition, and pizza. The initiative, which runs every school year from October through March, reaches over 10 million students annually.

This is how the program works: The teacher sets a reading goal for each child in the class. As soon as a child meets the monthly reading goal, the teacher presents him or her with a Reading Award Certificate redeemable at a participating Pizza Hut location. The company's restaurant managers and teams congratulate every participant who meets the monthly reading goal, rewarding him or her with a free one-topping Personal Pan Pizza®, BOOK IT! card, and backpack clip. BOOK IT! now has its own Facebook and Twitter pages, where students, teachers, and parents comment on their favorite books, favorite former teachers, and other relevant topics (see Exhibit 10.8).

LISTENING, ENGAGING, EXCITING!

Pizza Hut's social-media and mobile strategies focus on the three fundamental premises of listening, engaging, and exciting its customers. "On any day, we can get as many as 25 to 50,000 mentions of our brand," says Fuller. "They come across chats, forums, blogs, communities, and social networks. Our first step is listening. Then we go to the areas that are most fertile for engaging with our customers. If someone is mentioning our brand or a competitor's brand, we want to convert them to [become] a fan of Pizza Hut. And on customer service, we want to remedy problems. The third tent pole is 'Exciting.' We have a leadership halo through our iPhone initiative with new ways to order online and do other innovative things."

Pizza Hut may be the leader, but a good leader is always learning, and—according to Fuller—Pizza Hut's Tweetologist has taught the company a lot from her listening: "As we have evaluated what our

Exhibit 10.8 BOOK IT! Facebook Page
Source: Reprinted with permission of Pizza Hut.

followers and consumers want to see, it's not always about getting exclusive deals and special discounts. More often than not, they want information first. It may be that they want to be the first to know that you have a new ad debuting on Sunday or that you have a new topping coming out. It's actually much better. We don't always need special discounts when they really would rather hear what's new—or be in the know about the company."

When it comes to proving return on its investment, Garza admits, "A lot of things that we've done haven't been proven out. You have to be willing to make a bet, but not bet the entire farm every time. Technology changes so fast that you have to be able to place multiple bets across the table. We know that this space is continuing to change quickly. As a leader in the industry, we're listening to our consumers, and we want to be ahead of them in terms of where they're going. The underlying thread in our culture is leadership and being first."

NOTES

1. "The World's Most Valuable Brands. Who's Most Engaged?" ENGAGEMENTdb, Ranking the Top 100 Global Brands, Wetpaint/Altimeter Group, available at http://www.engagementdb.com (accessed August 10, 2010).
2. Interview with Armando Garza, conducted via phone, May 10, 2010. All subsequent quotes from Garza are from this interview.
3. Interview with Chris Fuller, conducted via phone, May 10, 2010. All subsequent quotes from Fuller are from this interview.

11

Best Buy: The Connected World

Your smart phone. Your television. Your GPS device. Your game console. Your digital camera. Your digital camcorder. Your home computer. Your printer. Your iPad. Your DVD player. Your home theatre. Omnipresent digital technology has become an integral part of people's everyday lives, and its promise has never been greater. Best Buy CEO Brian Dunn paints his company's vision by describing technology as a "constant backdrop in people's lives, at home, at work, on the road, and literally in the palms of their hands."[1] The more technology's complexity increases, the more difficult it becomes to keep pace with it. He calls it "The Connected World" and sees Best Buy's job as showing customers the art of what's possible with digital technology: "We believe that the promise of technology has never been greater to help people realize their dreams."[2]

At 21% of market share,[3] Best Buy is the largest consumer electronics specialty retailer in the United States. While the company continues to expand internationally, Best Buy's total global revenue for fiscal 2010 was $49.7 billion, with the United States representing approximately 80% of the company's business.[4] The total number of stores operating in the United States at the end of fiscal year (FY) 2010 was just under 1,100. Best Buy is supported by 180,000 employees worldwide, tied together by great communication and commitment to the company's success. The company holds an important position in the business world, having been recognized as one of the World's Most Admired Companies for 2010 by *Fortune* magazine.[5] In addition, Best Buy was listed as one of the World's Most Ethical Companies in 2010.[6]

Although Best Buy competes in one of retail's most challenging and competitive segments—selling technology-based, short-life-cycle merchandise—the company has produced continued growth. From 2003 to 2008, Best Buy doubled its revenue, and it continues to increase its position as a leading brand. In the mid-1990s, a number of consumer electronics retailers began to drop out of the market, culminated by the closing of Circuit City in early 2009. Despite this change in dynamics and Best Buy's growth during this period, competitive pricing continues to be aggressive. Price comparisons have always been important in this retail sector and that has only been magnified by online shopping comparison engines. Also, competition continues to grow, with discounters, wholesale clubs, and new Web-only retailers entering the market.

The powerhouses Wal-Mart, Amazon, and Costco are the company's direct competitors, but Best Buy uniquely positions itself as a market leader with a strategy that is consistent with the desires of today's consumer. There is no question that value remains in the consumer's mind, yet an enormous market exists for a consumer electronics retailer that provides information, solutions, and service. Best Buy has developed and is executing compelling strategies in merchandise assortments, technology leadership, a powerful information platform, transparency, service, and integration of marketing and social-media communities. Additionally, the company is a leader in the rapidly growing mobility field.

GROWTH STRATEGY

Best Buy, ever mindful of the incredibly competitive market, continues to grow its business. For FY 2010, a difficult period for all retailers, the company set the following objectives:

- **Grow market share.** Best Buy's domestic market share grew 2.6 percentage points in FY2010. Although the company benefited from the loss of Circuit City during this period, it was also a year when the consumer electronics industry suffered sales declines. Enhanced merchandise assortments, service strategies, and new store openings contributed to Best Buy's revenue improvement. The company's commitment to expanding the communication channels of social media and mobility continues to increase Best Buy's brand equity.

- **Connected world.** Best Buy is committed to helping customers lead a digital lifestyle, where they can seamlessly create, access, and share content over mobile phones, computers, and television. By providing access to a wide selection of hardware, digital content, and software applications, it can offer customers end-to-end solutions. Claims of this magnitude have been made for many years by commission-based retailers, but Best Buy's 2010 performance demonstrates that its strategy is working.

- **International growth.** Best Buy continues to grow globally, employing specific strategies in various countries based on market opportunity. Over half of the total company revenue increase in 2010 came from its international operations. This expansion, which began in 2002, is now gaining significant momentum and becoming a meaningful element of the company's business.

- **Efficient and effective enterprise.** Recognizing the continuing need to be both competitive and efficient, Best Buy made strategic cost reductions in 2010 through re-engineering and acting on recommendations from its valued employees.

In this ever-changing, fast-paced world of technology, consumers often are left confused about what and when to buy the variety of digital products available to them. Barry Judge, Best Buy's Chief Marketing Officer, describes the company's response in a direct, easy-to-understand way: "Best Buy's strategy is about trying to ensure [that] people get out of technology what they want. Technology is getting so much more complicated, as competitors like Wal-Mart and Amazon got involved in the market, more focused on price, so we became more focused on how our people [can] make a difference."[7] It is the aggregate of these strategies and initiatives that makes Best Buy an industry leader.

Building the Brand

Offering broad selections of name-brand products is essential to sat-isfying consumers' needs for product features and confidence in quality brands. To ensure high quality and a predictable source of supply, Best Buy determines which suppliers best support its strategy. In FY 2010 the company's 20 largest suppliers represented almost 60% of the total merchandise purchased. Five suppliers—Apple, Hewlett-Packard, Samsung, Sony, and Toshiba—represented 35% of the total merchandise purchased. This supplier partnership provides a significant opportunity for Best Buy, and Brian Dunn, who became CEO of Best Buy in June 2009, plans to take the quality brand strat-egy to another level by becoming a partner in leading technology and the timing of its introduction to the market. Dunn's merchandis-ing team is working early in the product cycle with the company's quality manufacturing partners to influence product design and features.

Best Buy has its own venture capital fund and invests in technol-ogy startups around the world. "We are talking to players deep into engineering the future,"[8] says Dunn. "It leads us nicely to a space where we can make a difference to consumers." Dunn further states, "We want to become a digital playground where people come in, experience it, and find out how all these things can work together around their life."

Because Best Buy is such a respected brand, the company is able to source and sell its own private-label products. It operates a global sourcing office in China to design, develop, product-test, and purchase product in concert with manufacturers in Asia. This strategy benefits the company in terms of gross margin, reliability of shipments, and overall quality, and the customer enjoys value pricing, quality mer-chandise, and in-stock position.

Partnering Brings Sales-Product Knowledge

Think of how many times you have shopped for electronics or big-ticket merchandise and been disappointed by the store personnel's lack of product knowledge. Best Buy is at a significant advantage because it limits the number of major suppliers it partners with and is able to work closely with them to understand product features and relationships. Best Buy then takes this product knowledge and develops it into clear, extensive product training for its sales team, known internally as "The Blue Shirts" (referring to the uniform worn by store employees). This provides the Best Buy customer with an enormous advantage, as the sales team's objective is to recommend products and software that the particular customer wants and needs. Because the sales team is noncommissioned, it can focus solely on helping the customer make an informed purchasing decision.

Barry Judge sums it up this way: "Really, it's about how our channels work together to let customers get the solutions they want. [We provide] broader assortments, better product, Blue Shirts, better training, and service. We are providing a holistic experience for the customer, not just price. Our people make a difference by building trust in the long run. It's all about 'brand promises,' sharing all we know, transparency, giving customers information, ratings, and reviews and letting them make their decisions."

Geek Squad

The constant changes in technology, software upgrades, and new features lead to plenty of consumer challenges and frustrations. Best Buy strives to educate its customers to avoid problems during the sales process; nevertheless, there is a need for high-quality customer service after the sale. The 15,000-person Geek Squad tech support service is extremely important to customer confidence and loyalty. Many customers have purchased a technical product from a retailer that does not provide this important service so they appreciate the professional support from Best Buy. Geek Squad technical support builds trust and loyalty in the brand.

CROSS-CHANNEL: MEETING CUSTOMERS WHERE THEY ARE

Best Buy has built an excellent e-commerce business that is the core of a compelling cross-channel strategy, which is built on synergy that best satisfies customers where they want to shop, and in doing so builds sales and Best Buy brand equity. There are no individual silos. It's about Best Buy delivering on the promise, and the results demonstrate that achievement. John Thompson, Senior Vice President and General Manager of bestbuy.com, describes the strategy as having three key components: accessibility, localization, and personalization.

Accessibility

"Accessibility is how we mobilize the brand and bring it to where people are—meet them on their own terms, so to speak,"[9] says Thompson. It's no longer enough to expect customers to find your Web site or go to your stores. Retailers need to bring their brand to customers. "You used to create a Web presence and people found you either via search or shopping comparison or logging onto your Web site. While tons of people are getting to your brand that way, that's not enough."

One example of accessibility is Best Buy's new Twitter-based customer service organization called Twelpforce (Twitter + help force = Twelpforce). "It's a way to empower and mobilize our employees and customers to help each other. You now have to go where people are spending their time. We are also taking our brands with widgets and Facebook pages and other properties on the Web where it makes sense to have our presence. We have significantly increased our points of contact with consumers who not only want to find our brand, but also want to find our technology and services."

Localization

Localization is about integrating offline and online. Best Buy recognizes significant opportunity in better servicing its customer at the critical point of purchase, the local store. Thompson mentions that there are opportunities that the company's merchant team cannot possibly see and that may not make sense for a large group of stores, but may be perfect for a particular local area. Thompson related the example of a store employee in Wilmer, Minnesota, who figured out

Best Buy - Westbury

1100 Old Country Rd
Westbury, NY 11590
Phone: 516-357-9025
GEO: 40.744160, -73.600525

Customer Reviews:

★★★★★ 5 of 5

Read reviews (1) or Write a Review

Send a comment:
STMgrs000454@bestbuy.com

Maps & Directions | Weekly Ad

Store Hours
Mon: 10-9:30; Tue: 10-9:30; Wed: 10-9:30; Thurs: 10-9:30; Fri: 10-10; Sat: 10-10; Sun: 11-8;

Exhibit 11.1 Best Buy Store Level Web Page and Review
Source: Reprinted with permission of Best Buy.

how to install GPS devices on farmers' tractors to help them plow more land—something very practical in that community, but not very practical as a corporate-wide program. The Blue Shirts provide the best insights on these kinds of strategies because they are involved in the local community. The key is knowing what unique products should be carried at a particular local store. And if it doesn't make sense to carry the product in the store, it would always be available on the Best Buy Web site. Best Buy now provides each store with its own Web site, accessible from bestbuy.com, including the store manager's cell phone number. The store's performance is measured by customer-generated ratings and reviews prominently displayed on its Web site (see Exhibit 11.1). Localization allows Best Buy to be viewed as a problem solver in the local community.

Personalization

Personalization is about looking at individual customers and giving them a richer, more "personalized" experience with the company. "This is the ability to customize our interaction with customers based on our relationship with them," says Judge. While this is a very difficult thing to do in retail, Best Buy has cracked the code. "We are sitting on a mountain of data," continues Judge. "We have 120 million people in our Reward Zone® loyalty program and we can identify 80% of the transactions. We have a pretty good picture of people through looking at the data and we're able to develop specific purchase profiles of our best customers." Judge gives the example that Best Buy sends out 15 million promotional emails each week, and that there are five million separate versions based on customers' individual preferences.

Judge gets more passionate when talking about taking personalization into the store to better serve customers: "Mobile is big for a variety of reasons, not just for consumer buying but mobile as a platform in the store to help consumers find what they want, but also to help Blue Shirts become 'human search engines.' Imagine you walk in a store and we hand you a mobile device. On that device are specific apps to help you shop the store, such as buyers' guides, customer reviews, and more. Then imagine Blue Shirts walking around with mobile pad devices. The customer gives her Reward Zone number and the Blue Shirt instantly sees what she's purchased in the past and can help make additional purchase and service recommendations."

A WIKI CULTURE

Twelpforce. Blue Shirt Nation. Geek Squad. A video entitled *The Company as Wiki*. Go onto YouTube and you'll find numerous videos showing Best Buy's transparent, innovative, tech savvy, energized culture. This is not a startup Web 2.0 company, but rather a $50 billion specialty electronics market retail leader, with an understanding of the enormous human assets within the company, and an advanced comprehension of the new world of technology. Best Buy recognizes the importance of communicating in a Web 2.0 world, but how did it make the transition? It was a watershed decision for Best Buy's management to take a company founded nearly 50 years ago and turn it upside down, empowering its employees. Their first step was to recognize the talent within the company, talent coming from a technologically savvy employee pool whose average age is 22.

The idea was to leverage and empower employees to communicate within the Web 2.0 world they're comfortable with. "Best Buy's open culture has been a benefit to its growth. We're not top down. We encourage people from all over the business to be innovative," says Barry Judge. This philosophy created a culture where everyone in Best Buy is listened to, participates, and makes things happen within the company.

Judge describes how out of a groundswell for an internal social network the "Blue Shirt Nation" (or BSN for short) was born. BSN is an employee-built social network that connects Best Buy workers across the company. "About two years ago, those individuals who grew BSN told me that I could be a better CMO if I was more transparent and became a Blue Shirt Nation CMO. So, I learned Twitter. Soon after, I was at a meeting and a person asked me a question. I didn't know the person but realized from the question that we had met on Twitter. Through this interaction I realized that I could actually help the brand through [participating in] social media and that would make it OK for others to participate in the company if I did." At that point, Judge engaged on Twitter (@bestbuycmo) and that gave other employees permission to do the same. "Our strategy is people talking to people so why wouldn't we do it on social media?" says Judge. "Our CEO is on Twitter and Facebook and he's the biggest leader of the brand and our cheerleader!"

SOCIAL MEDIA: FROM THE INSIDE OUT!

Best Buy is one of the most advanced companies in terms of integrating social media into its brand and culture. There have been hundreds of videos, blogs, interviews, and stories written about Best Buy's Web 2.0 journey, not only in terms of how it communicates with its customers, but also internally. "We think social media is a great way to demonstrate our culture and servicing our customers that goes beyond the store," says Judge.

In concert with its transparent culture, Best Buy has uploaded several videos to its YouTube channel about how it transformed its culture. One video, *The Company as Wiki*, posted in August 2008, describes what Best Buy is doing internally with social media (www.youtube.com/watch?v=H_jhLGxH-m4).   Several employees discuss the journey, its tangible benefits, and the social-media tools they use for internal communication. In the video, Jennifer Rock, Director of Internal Communications, discusses how Best Buy recognized it needed to embrace employees' desire to communicate through social networks. "Most companies traditionally communicate *at* employees . . . but that's not the way the world works anymore," she said. "We're moving from a role of owning the messages and delivering those messages to a role where we are facilitators—encouraging and enabling. . . . It allows us to use those insights and feedback to do better at serving our customers."

It Began with a "Nation of Blue Shirts"

Back in 2006, a group of employees got together to make a difference and change the way internal communications within Best Buy worked. They began this journey by first creating the internal social network Blue Shirt Nation, which was like Facebook inside the enterprise. One of the greatest assets Best Buy has is the collective knowledge of all of its store associates, and the BSN was born to help capture and share that knowledge. "We have a very young employee base very comfortable with technology," says John Thompson. "This is more of an evolution of how they live their lives so they came up with an internal social network because that's how they connect with the outside world."

Gary Koelling and Steve Bendt, the original developers of BSN, persuaded senior management to fund an internal social network for employees. The target audience was primarily Best Buy's tens of thousands of store associates, many of whom are in their late teens. The objective was simple: Create a network that provides a platform for promoting an exchange of ideas among employees at all levels. The concept was to have employees "live and breathe the same air as customers do." The sooner accurate information about Best Buy products and services could be communicated to the Blue Shirts, the more responsive the company could be to customers' needs.

BSN let employees post videos and blogs, start groups, and basically get to know one another. Employees were free to talk about anything, although the majority of the discussions centered on work, for instance, problem solving about customer issues and operational challenges in the stores. BSN let employees collaborate, share information, and be social. It ultimately gave way to a variety of other internal social-networking tools as well as an external Facebook page for Best Buy employees, but whose content is open to the public.

A WEB 2.0 TOOL KIT IS BORN

Today, Best Buy's team is connected through a variety of Web 2.0 tools, all built internally by Net Generation associates who felt empowered to make positive change. These include:

- **Watercooler.** A mass-communication and dialogue tool for employees at all levels; one employee describes it as "Best Buy's message board on steroids." Watercooler is made up of online discussion forums that provide a direct line between employees in-store and at other locations to talk about business topics directly with corporate leaders, their own teams, and one another. In the first three months the program gained 85,000 users (see Exhibit 11.2).

Exhibit 11.2 Best Buy Watercooler Employee Forum
Source: Reprinted with permission of Best Buy.

- **Best Buy WIKI.** A place where employees can share what they know, edit information, and search for knowledge. Best Buy employees feel empowered because they are able to use and modify the content of the Wiki.

- **The Loop Marketplace.** A Web 2.0 version of the employee suggestion box that actually works more like an idea incubator. Employees post an idea that they believe would be good for the company. Other employees can then provide feedback, offer to help, or recommend the idea. Budget owners can fund a portion or all of the money required to execute the idea. The video *The Company as Wiki* explains the Loop Marketplace by using the real-life example of Robb Erickson, a store employee who wanted to create Geek Squad Gaming Services. Erickson wasn't sure how to communicate his idea, so he went to his manager, who suggested he post it on the Loop Marketplace. Within four hours of posting, Erickson received feedback and the idea was funded.

- **Tag Trade.** A prediction market game. Barry Judge best describes it as "an internal stock market for ideas and internal programs." Stocks represent future outcomes, and people trade in the market based on what they think will happen in the future. Employees receive fictitious money, and the tool allows them to "trade" on the future outcome of existing projects or new ideas being surfaced within Best Buy. For example, if a project manager found out that his project was trading 20% below where it was yesterday, he'd immediately begin checking all of his stakeholders and resources to find out what went wrong and correct the problem. Tag Trade takes internal transparency to its limits by involving and allowing all employees to influence the success of company initiatives. The game has been so well received internally that Judge believes Best Buy may one day take it to the public by rewarding customers with Reward Zone points if they submit good ideas.

Other examples of internally developed Web 2.0 tools, which are accessible to the public, include:

- **GIFTAG** (giftag.com). Allows people to select an item from any Web site, add it to a list, and then share that list with family and friends.

- **Spy** (spy.appspot.com). Allows people to "listen in" and monitor social-media conversations through keyword searches.

- **Connect** (bby.com/connect). Allows people both inside and outside of Best Buy to access employee blogs and Tweets, including those of senior executives who are active Twitter participants.

- **Best Buy Remix** (remix.bestbuy.com). Best Buy's open application programming interface for its product catalog, which includes full product information such as pricing, availability, specifications, descriptions, and images for nearly a million current and historical products. Any developer can use Remix free of charge to develop applications, and an affiliate program is available if the software enables commerce.

Best Buy employees are constantly inventing new social-media tools, so many that—in doing research—it was nearly impossible to keep an accurate count. But as Bethany Kinsella, Director of Connected Digital Solutions for Best Buy, describes it: "It's not about the tool. The magic is in the culture it enables—patience, openness, honesty, trust, learning, and iteration."[10]

Best Buy's culture is all about openness, honesty, trust, learning, and allowing ideas to develop and continually improve. Social media empowers people to express themselves, listen to others, collaborate, solve problems, and find opportunities. The company, through its innovative and passionate employees, is trying a lot of new ideas. Some will work. Some will continue to evolve. Some will fail. The company encourages taking calculated risks as long as employees continue to learn and improve.

THE HUB FOR ALL THINGS BEST BUY

Best Buy is a retailer executing a cross-channel strategy in every sense. With $2 billion in e-commerce revenue—a year-over-year growth

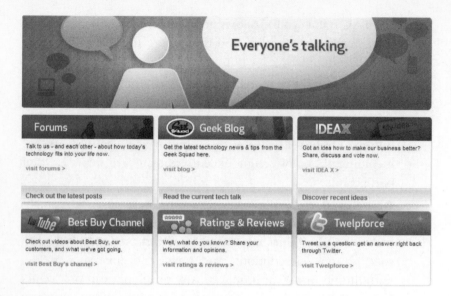

Exhibit 11.3 www.bestbuy.com: Stay Connected
Source: Reprinted with permission of Best Buy.

spike of 20% in 2009—its Web site is an enormous virtual store. But the site is also the hub for all customer interaction, as 70% of its customers come to view items before going into the store for pick-up or purchase, so online is having a substantial positive impact on offline revenue, according to John Thompson. The Best Buy Web site has a host of 2.0 tools, including social-media and mobile access points (see Exhibit 11.3):

- **Best Buy On (www.bestbuyon.com).** Best Buy On is an online magazine that includes a wide variety of "how to" videos and stories on topics such as streaming movies and music; playing online games and accessing social networks from your TV; and a digital photo tutorial. Products sold at Best Buy are demonstrated in the videos, and customers can comment online about what they've learned.

- **Ratings and Reviews.** Each product has a detailed listing of customer ratings and reviews. Best Buy encourages its customers to rate products by making it a simple three-step process (see Exhibit 11.4). Customers can share product reviews and

Exhibit 11.4 Customer Reviews and Ratings
Source: Reprinted with permission of Best Buy.

overall aggregated ratings directly from the Best Buy site by
linking to Facebook, Twitter, Digg, MySpace, Redd it, Stumble-
Upon, and delicious.

- **Online Chat.** The Web site includes the ability for customers
  to chat with a live customer service representative.

- **Geek Squad Online.** Online technical support is also available from Geek Squad. Several Geek Squad agents are listed as
  currently being on duty. The customer has the ability to select
  a specific agent, read his or her review, connect directly with
  that agent online, and then provide a satisfaction rating.

- **Idea X (bestbuyideax.com).** Idea X is a forum for Best Buy
  customers to share, vote on, and discuss suggestions on how to
  make Best Buy better.

- **Best Buy Unboxed (www.forums.bestbuy.com/bb).** Best
  Buy's Web site includes a customer community forum where

customers can converse with other customers and Best Buy associates about "technology and life integration." It's a place to ask questions and to exchange ideas, information, opinions, and tips with other technology users.

- **Blogs.** The Web site has blogs ranging from topics such as mobile, Geek Squad, and Napster, to personal blogs by Best Buy executives.

- **Social Networks.** Customers can link directly to Best Buy's Twelpforce Twitter customer support page, Facebook page, and YouTube channel.

- **Mobile.** Customers can link to Best Buy Mobile, the company's iPhone application.

Facebook

Best Buy rapidly rose to being one of the most successful brands on Facebook, ranking third among retailers with a current fan base of over 1.1 million and growing. The Best Buy corporate Facebook page was launched in early Fall 2009. Shortly afterward, the fan base was at 27,000. Best Buy ran only one ad on Facebook for 24 hours, encouraging its customers to connect with the brand. It was so effective that it drove the fan count to 163,000. The company then let the referral effect of Facebook take over and the fan count jumped from 163,000 to 900,000 in only nine days.

Best Buy's Facebook page includes several impressive and innovative features, some of which are described here.

- The **Shop + Share** Facebook storefront allows customers to browse the entire catalog of Best Buy products, complete with customer reviews and pricing. Clicking on the "Advice" button allows the customer to post an item of interest to his or her Facebook wall as well as to the walls of all Best Buy fans (see Exhibit 11.5). The viral benefit of this feature is largely responsible for the steep and steady climb of Best Buy fans. The "Buy Now" tab takes the user to that product page on the Best Buy Web site, where he or she can purchase the item.

Exhibit 11.5 Facebook Shop + Share
Source: Reprinted with permission of Best Buy.

- The **Idea Gift Center** looks at your Facebook friends and recommends top-rated gift ideas by gender or age, for you or your friends, and then adds them to your news feed with a comment such as, "I want this new digital camera," or "Would you like this new game?"
- **Recycle It On** provides details on where to drop off retired electronic items for recycling. Regardless of where the item was purchased, Best Buy will recycle it.
- **My Store** allows customers to connect directly with their favorite Best Buy store through store-specific Facebook pages.
- **The Wall** is mostly filled with posts from consumers with technical or service questions. Best Buy typically responds within several hours of the original post.

Additional Best Buy Fan pages exist for Best Buy Gaming, Best Buy Music, Best Buy Mobile, Best Buy Employees, and even Best Buy Racing.

Best Buy is uniquely carrying out its accessibility, personalization, and localization strategies through Facebook. First, from an accessibility standpoint, it is bringing its brand, products, store, support, and applications directly to where a large portion of its customers spend their time—on Facebook. For the average customer, there isn't much they can do on the Best Buy Web site that they can't do from its Facebook page. Personalization is woven throughout by allowing customers to share Best Buy products, ask questions of their fan bases, and get gift ideas. And Best Buy has a creative approach to localization. Customers can click on the "My Store" tab and either type in a zip code or save a particular store as a favorite. Every Best Buy store has its own Facebook page, complete with the store manager's email address, store hours, driving directions, relevant services, announcements, and store specific promotions.

Best Buy's presence on Facebook is relatively new, and the company is clear that it is still learning how to best use the site to determine what works, what doesn't work, and what it needs to do more of or do differently. In an October 2009 interview with *eMarketer*, Tracy Benson, Senior Director of Interactive Marketing and Emerging Media, describes its key goal in using Facebook as "generating brand awareness in a social space, driving a strong and solid reputation and generating fans and leads that help us enable other people to interact and engage with our brand."[11]

Crowd-Sourcing a Brand through Twelpforce

Nothing is more frustrating than calling a technology helpline and punching through a series of numbers, only to be put on hold for what can seem like an eternity. Twelpforce should interest any consumer who has ever had to call a technical support help desk and any retailer who wants to improve its own customer service. A typical Twelpforce commercial goes something like this: A consumer walks up to a microphone in the middle of a football field and asks a question like, "I'm going to college. What kind of laptop should I buy?" He looks up into a sea of thousands of Blue Shirt Best Buy employees in the stands. One by one, the Blue Shirts shout out practical advice. It ends with the Best Buy logo but no mention of its Web site; only the words Twitter.com/twelpforce are included—just enough to arouse consumers' curiosity.

In July 2009 Best Buy launched Twelpforce, which uses the power of Twitter for customer service (see Exhibit 11.6). Twelpforce enlists

Exhibit 11.6 Twelpforce
Source: Reprinted with permission of Best Buy.

the passion and knowledge of Best Buy's vast employee base to respond to customer service and technical service issues. Unlike most other customer support groups, what makes Twelpforce so unique is that it taps into Best Buy's existing talent pool and gives them a chance to contribute and share their knowledge.

Although only 600 were expected, so far more than 2,600 Best Buy employees have signed up to be Twelpforce agents. Best Buy employees register to be Twelpforce agents, and their tweets are displayed on the Twelpforce Twitter page in a single stream. Staffed by employees across all operations, including Blue Shirts and Geek Squad, the Twelpforce sends messages from the @twelpforce account. If they add the hashtag #twelpforce, their messages will surface under the Twelpforce handle. Because Twelpforce attributes the answer to the individual employee's Twitter ID and photo, employees feel an extra sense of pride and ownership. Twitter users send their service issues and technology questions to @twelpforce to get real-time responses.

In less than a year, Twelpforce has responded to nearly 28,000 customer Twitter inquiries and paid for itself many times over through improved customer satisfaction, brand perception, and viral positive public relations that continues to grow.

In a July 2009 blog post following the launch of Twelpforce, CMO Barry Judge was transparent in his description, calling Twelpforce "an experiment. A very public one." But he described it as a risk worth taking for a number of reasons, including its potential to become a resource for Best Buy customers to help them effectively use technology and that also builds trust. Judge also talks openly about what Twelpforce can do for Best Buy in terms of how the company views customer service. "Twelpforce can be a catalyst to think very differently across our company about customer service. No longer do we need to passively wait in our channels for people to come to us. . . . We can actively seek out the conversations that increasingly are happening outside our channels. I also think this initiative can change our definition of customer service. No longer is customer service a department, but something that all of us can do." And even outside of Twelpforce, a number of Best Buy employees and executives such as Judge and Best Buy's CEO, Brian Dunn, are on Twitter and answering service questions posed to them.

The Real Power Yet to Be Unleashed

In addition to the early successes of Twelpforce, another side of the coin exists in terms of added benefits—a side that is just beginning to be explored: the value hidden within the data. Think about it. Twelpforce offers a real-time view of trending topics and customers' needs. By analyzing these data, Best Buy can better forecast its call center staffing needs, identify the categories and products that garner more than their fair share of technical support, ramp up certain product inventory, and promote specific items. Well aware of the potential, Best Buy is already working on a more sophisticated open source social-media analysis tool (www.bbyfeed.com).

Twelpforce leverages all of Best Buy's assets. It listens to the customer, and the trust that the company places in its employees in a transparent public venue is powerful. There is no screening process. Just a steady stream of solutions to problems from the company's concerned and focused employees. Through its strategy of communicating openly and engaging directly with its customers without trying to control the conversation, Best Buy has remained ahead of its major competition. Twelpforce is a powerful model that eventually may be adopted by other retailers. Best Buy's deep engagement with customers deputizes thousands of employees, enhances responsibility, and improves customers' loyalty and engagement.

Twitter Beyond Twelpforce

While its @twelpforce customer hotline is clearly a model for the effective use of Twitter, Best Buy also maintains several other corporate Twitter accounts:

- @bestbuy provides "the latest and greatest from Best Buy, including updates from employees, deals, event notices, and more."
- @bestbuy_deals lists the latest promotions.

Some Best Buy store managers have already begun setting up store-level Twitter accounts to engage with their customers (see Exhibit 11.7), and many Best Buy employees and executives such as

Exhibit 11.7 Best Buy Westbury Store Twitter Page
Source: Reprinted with permission of Best Buy.

Judge and CEO Brian Dunn are also active on Twitter. To display a running stream of Best Buy-related tweets, the hash tag #bbytweets often is attached to company tweets from employees, stores, and the corporate office.

YouTube

Best Buy got an early start with YouTube, setting up its own YouTube channel in March 2006. Doing a search for "Best Buy" yields hundreds of videos, some of which have been viewed several million times. Most of these videos were uploaded by people outside the company, which shows the power of the brand. Separately, Best Buy uses its YouTube channel to share videos of employees, customers, and activities in which it is involved. Best Buy has uploaded more than 500 videos to its channel, resulting in more than 774,000 upload views. Best Buy encourages "employees, customers, friends, and foes" to submit their own videos to Best Buy to be considered for inclusion on its official channel (see Exhibit 11.8).

Exhibit 11.8 Twelpforce YouTube Video
Source: Reprinted with permission of Best Buy.

HELPING MOBILE CUSTOMERS "SHOP, LEARN, AND BUY"

"It's so personal"—"It's changed the way that I share my feelings and my memories"—"I think I'm kind of addicted to it"—"I hate to admit this, but I sleep with my phone"—"The first thing I do when I wake up is I look for that phone, and when I can't find it, I freak out!"— "This is the most important device that I've got!"—"It's basically my lifeline between my friends, my family, and my business"—"Young people want to be connected all the time, 24/7"—"You've got a computer in your hand and that unlocks all kinds of opportunities." If you ever want to access a vision of how mobile technology can affect the consumer market, take just five minutes to listen to these comments and others from this video:

> *Why Best Buy Loves Mobile*
> (www.youtube.com/watch?v=UpcODCSTx3w)

As with cross-channel retailing and social media, Best Buy again is taking a leadership role in bringing its brand into customers' hands through their mobile devices. The company is in a unique position as one of the largest sellers of smart phones and has firsthand knowledge of customer dynamics in this rapidly growing market. Best Buy has the ability to understand who is buying the phones, what features are most important, how the phones are being used, as well as adoption rates. Customers have high expectations of Best Buy's ability to deliver strong mobile solutions around its own brand.

In 2009, Best Buy began offering mobile commerce for shopping its products and other customer-friendly mobile solutions such as a GPS-based store locator, weekly ads, and customer product reviews. The company readily admits that it's learning along the way, yet it's making major investments in mobile. Consumer appetite for smart phones is experiencing enormous growth. "The growth of mobile Internet usage is far outpacing traditional Internet saturation and I think that it's a place where many of our consumers are going to interact with us," says John Thompson. There are an estimated 500 million mobile subscribers worldwide, and approximately 54 million in United States use mobile Internet. Thompson continues, "36% of all smart phone users and 62% of iPhone users access the Internet daily so if your brand is available to consumers and you're trying to meet them where they are, you have to have a mobile capability."

While many retailers focus on mobile marketing, location-based marketing, and mobile commerce, Best Buy looks at those as "nice to haves"; although they are part of good marketing communications, "it is not where the company sees the most value," says Judge. He articulates Best Buy's strategy concisely: "Help customers shop, learn and buy." Best Buy is in the solution-selling business, often marketing complex hardware and software to its customers. The better Best Buy can educate its customers, the more loyal they will be. Best Buy's strategy is based on the premise that mobile affects every customer interaction, from browsing, learning, asking, and sharing to eventually buying. Best Buy wants to solve its customers' problems through mobile platforms that connect their physical and digital worlds.

Judge sees the use of mobile in the stores as a way to facilitate a better customer experience. "It's about helping our Blue Shirts help our customers," he says. "Imagine Best Buy employees having mobile devices in their hands and, when customers have questions employees can't answer, they can network with colleagues in any Best Buy store for on-the-spot help."

"The glue between physical and virtual worlds" is how Thompson describes mobile. "It will be the likely place where many customers will interact with your brand and get the first interaction prior to going into stores and maybe even prior to going on from a home-based Internet connection. Mobile will play a huge role in cross-channel integration across all the other channels, our Geek Squad agents, our Blue Shirts, our in-store environment, Twelpforce, call centers, etc. We know that customers want access wherever they are. They need instant gratification so we need to allow them to order that special item on the mobile device and actually pick it up in store or to find out key information about where inventory is in a given store."

Mobile Initiatives

Best Buy currently offers both a mobile Web site as well as applications for both the iPhone and Android. The company promotes its current mobile functionality (see Exhibit 11.9) as:

Exhibit 11.9 Browse and Buy—Anywhere
Source: Reprinted with permission of Best Buy.

MOBILE WEB
DO IT ALL FROM YOUR PHONE.

* Browse all of BestBuy.com from your mobile device
* Check out ratings and reviews
* Securely purchase on your phone
* Text WEB to 332211 to send link to your phone*

MOBILE APP
ALL THE FEATURES. ONE APP.

* Buy, browse & save with one app
* Search & check inventory
* Manage favorites and your cart
* Text APP to 332211 to send link to your phone*

Download mobile app now ›

TEXT ALERT
REVIEWS & DEALS DELIVERED.

* Text any product SKU # to 332211 for reviews and ratings*
* Sign up for weekly special offers when you text DEALS to 332211*
* Text your ZIP Code to 332211 for information on your closest Best Buy location*

Exhibit 11.10 Mobile Options
Source: Reprinted with permission of Best Buy.

■ **SHOP ON THE GO**—With Our Mobile Web Site and App.

■ **SEE CUSTOMER REVIEWS**—Anywhere. Anytime.

■ **FIND YOUR STORE**—Get Store Hours and Locations.

■ **GET WEEKLY DEALS**—Sent to Your Phone.

Through its "Text or Dial" program, Best Buy provides mobile access to product details and customer product ratings. Best Buy distributes a call-to-action, offering product information on demand in weekly print ads and in-store signage. Simply text the item's SKU number to a Best Buy text number, or dial a toll-free number (see Exhibit 11.10).

Best Buy's three mobile platforms—its mobile Web site, its iPhone app, and its Android app—are all commerce enabled. Customers also can search for products, inventory, or stores. And let's not forget Twitter (in the form of Twelpforce) and Facebook as well as other social-media programs that consumers have come to use so frequently from their phones. Best Buy is in a partnership with Google testing the ability for customers to search an item from their phone and determine whether it is in stock in their favorite store.

Best Buy's iPhone application allows customers to do pretty much anything that they can do in the online store. Features include searching by product description or SKU; sorting by price or popularity; viewing product pictures, specifications, and customer reviews; and adding items to the shopping cart and then purchasing them. Promotions are highlighted, and the app also includes links to the Reward Zone (as described earlier) and Idea X (also as earlier) pages as well as the IdeaGiftr which provides gift ideas from across the web, by gender and by age group. The GPS-based store locator functionality is built in but allows an override of the user's current location with a zip code. Its newest feature is the ability to scan Quick Response (QR) codes from Best Buy flyers (QR codes are 2D bar codes that can be scanned with a mobile device). Taking a picture of the code with the phone's camera alleviates the need to type in an item number. Best Buy plans to have mobile bar codes on all products in the store, which consumers would then be able to scan with their mobile phones to get product information and customer reviews right in the aisle.

Judge and Thompson both clearly described the enormous growth potential of Best Buy's mobile channel. Says Thompson, "When you're in the product categories that we're in where we're trying to help customers get the most out of their technology purchase—the ability to interact with us from a mobility standpoint, the ability to call our call center agents, to log onto our Web site, to go into the store and engage with some of the most technology enthusiastic individuals on the planet that wear our Blue shirts . . . we think that those are all things that are going to bode well as this consumer becomes more and more mobile in the future."

THE CONNECTED WORLD, TAKE TWO

Best Buy's plans to continue to meet customers wherever they are to help them get the most out of their technology purchases. As with social media and mobility, Best Buy's initiatives into these new channels are in their infancy. But it's clear that these two channels are already proving to be compelling points of differentiation for Best Buy. In describing its future direction, Brian Dunn, Best Buy's CEO, refers to the "connected world." Thompson says, "In the connected world, the hypothesis is that we as consumers are always connected. We're connected with our friends on Facebook. We're connected to professionals through LinkedIn. We're trying to connect with content and whether that's digital content or physical content, we use the devices that we buy as a way of an entry point. All of these connections of people to people, from a networking standpoint, from a device standpoint, and from a content standpoint, are areas where we think that we are uniquely positioned as a brand to actually get at the customer pain points and get customers the information that they are looking for in a very relevant manner."

Best Buy's "connected world" begins with its culture. We find it remarkable that a company over 50 years old has made such a rapid and dramatic transition into the 2.0 world. It has a transparent culture of openness, sharing, and empowering its young employee base—something rarely seen in any other large corporation. The leadership has moved beyond telling employees what to do, to being facilitators who empower, encourage, and enable them to be innovative, creative, and enthusiastic. That is what has allowed Best Buy to embrace social media and mobility as an early industry leader. With a leadership team that has an intellectual curiosity, a keen awareness of technology and its enormous cultural impact, and a willingness to make heroes of its employees, Best Buy has found a wonderful combination for success.

NOTES

1. "Brian J. Dunn, President and COO of Best Buy, to Assume Role of CEO," Best Buy Press Release, January 21, 2009, available at www.bby.com/ 2009/01/21/brian-j-dunn-president-and-coo-of-best-buy-to-assume-role-of-ceo/. (accessed July 15, 2010).

2. Ibid.

3. Mary Ellen Lloyd, "Best Buy Gaining Market-Share Following Circuit City Demise," Dow Jones Newswires, September 15, 2009, available at www.nasdaq.com/aspx/company-news-story.aspx?storyid=20090915 1728dowjonesdjonline000592#ixzz0qz1su4B9, (accessed July 15, 2010)

4. Best Buy Company, Inc., Annual Report 2010, April 28, 2010.

5. "Best Buy Selected for 2010 *Fortune* List of 50 Most Admired Companies," Best Buy Company News, March 3, 2010.

6. "2010 World's Most Ethical Companies," *Ethisphere*, March 2010.

7. Interview with Barry Judge, conducted via phone, May 7, 2010. All subsequent quotes from Judge are from this interview.

8. Cliff Edwards, "Why Tech Bows to Best Buy," *Bloomberg BusinessWeek*, December 10, 2009, available at www.businessweek.com/magazine/content/09_51/b4160050951315.htm, (accessed July 15, 2010).

9. Interview with John Thompson, conducted via phone, May 7, 2010. All subsequent quotes from Thompson are from this interview.

10. Best Buy's Web 2.0 Journey, Beth Kinsella, Director, Connected Digital Solutions, Best Buy, available at www.slideshare.net/LeeAase/best-buy-web-20, (accessed July 15, 2010).

11. "Best Buy Talks Social Commerce on Facebook," *eMarketer*, Clark Fredricksen, October 21, 2009, available at www.emarketer.com/blog/index.php/buy-talks-social-commerce-facebook/ (accessed August 10, 2010).

12
Analyzing Value: Social Media

Retailers always have focused on better understanding their customers. Now, because of social media and mobility, retailers can build an interactive connection with thousands of consumers, listening, engaging with them, and taking action around their needs. The individual company initiatives highlighted in previous chapters review a variety of ways in which retailers are building customer loyalty and *brand equity* through digital channels. Other potential applications of social media are being developed constantly and that is why this interactive customer channel has so much potential.

GETTING STARTED

Social-media and mobile initiatives are large undertakings and to be successful they require internal commitment. The good news is that the initial investment in developing a social-media program is relatively low compared with other types of customer-interfacing expenditures, such as traditional media. Most of the initial expense is represented by the human capital required to proactively monitor and maintain social Web sites. Retailers of any size can tailor a social-media program to fit within their budget. In fact, because of the large number of consumers following their brands through these new channels, many retailers are redeploying expense from traditional media such as newspaper circulars and investing in social and mobile efforts with little to no incremental expense. While the initial financial cost of these programs is low, they require ongoing commitment in order to succeed. Because social media exposes an organization to the world, a company should be certain of its willingness to commit for the long term.

We encourage any retailer just getting started in social media to listen and learn as much as possible—especially in the beginning. The good news is that this new world stands for transparency, and companies with digital teams dedicated to this effort are usually open to sharing and helping one another more than in the past. Industry organizations like the National Retail Federation, with its Shop.org digital division, and the Retail Advertising and Marketing Association,[1] Retail Industry Leaders Association,[2] Retail Connections,[3] Internet Retailer®,[4] National Restaurant Association®,[5] and Food Marketing Institute®[6] offer online and live seminars, sharing groups, and social-media forums focused on these areas. Plenty of cross-industry social-media and mobile-sharing groups also exist.

WHAT'S THE RETURN?

You probably are asking what sort of return on investment (ROI) you can expect from a social-media program and how to measure returns quantitatively. We continually probed many retailers about ROI. Given the newness of social media and retailers' chosen initiatives, the companies highlighted were positive about their results, but not yet at the point of definitive financial returns. All were impressed with the number of customers with whom they were now engaging digitally and aware that they were at the beginning of a long journey. In fact, regardless of the industry, when it comes to measuring the ROI of a social-media initiative, very little quantitative data currently exist.

According to a 2009 study undertaken by Mzinga and Babson Executive Education, 84% of professionals in a variety of industries reported that they do not yet measure the ROI of their social-media programs.[7] While qualitative data exist about the value of these initiatives, results are difficult to quantify as the initiatives are new, many less than a year old. Consequently, the software needed to monitor, extract content, and measure the impact from the mountains of unstructured data produced, is just now coming to market. With use of this software, retailers' ability to quantify social-media value will be reality. When it comes to how to measure ROI in these new channels, no one right answer exists. For measurements to be effective, they must align with previously set specific, actionable, and realistic objectives.

The metrics of a social-media initiative depend, of course, on its application. Defining a clear social-media strategy helps companies attain goals such as increased conversion, sales, links (the currency of the social Web), votes, and customer-satisfaction scores. Marketers are interested in measuring awareness, attention, reach, and conversions. Public relations wants to gauge sentiment about a brand, whereas customer support is focused on customer satisfaction and the number of issues resolved. A merchant would be keenly interested in customer sentiment about a new trend, a new outfit, or a particular product, as well as conversion rates on promotions and incentives. The ultimate measurement is whether company sales increase as a result of utilizing social-media channels; however, sophisticated analytics are required to understand all of the individual elements that affect sales.

MINING THE GOLD

The years 2009 and 2010 were about customer engagement for retailers. Brands often secured pages on Facebook, Twitter, and other social-media channels to amass as many "fans" as possible in hope of creating brand advocates spreading the message virally to online friends. Many companies achieved that goal, but recognized that there was much more value to social media. We are now entering a new era of social-media usage—one based not only on qualitative data, but also on quantitative insights and rationalization. The lack of ROI standards and the scarcity of tools to measure these standards have many executives hesitant to move their social-media initiatives beyond the first phase. Many executives want established metrics in order to measure social-media success against established business goals.

Despite the many potential benefits of social media, the pot of gold at the end of the rainbow is the ability to mine all data about customers, brand, products, and stores. In the cases of Starbucks' My Starbucks Idea and Wet Seal's Fashion Community, these retailers have developed their own private social networks, therefore owning the valuable customer data and making the analysis easier than that from public sites such as Facebook and Twitter. "We can get a read on where our customer is headed faster than ever before," says Wet Seal's CEO Ed Thomas. "It gives us unbiased, immediate feedback on what the customer is doing with the merchandise. She's voting on it. So we get a lot of information about trend." As for Starbucks, it has been able to gather more than 100,000 potential customer suggestions about how to improve its stores, and the company has acted upon many of those suggestions.

These new communications channels produce enormous amounts of data to be analyzed, understood, and acted on to better serve the consumer and improve the overall business. When it comes to analyzing the data generated by customers chattering over many external social channels, the challenge becomes far greater over a period of months and eventually years. Gathering data from a personal Facebook page, Twitter stream, and YouTube channel is challenging enough, but much of the chatter that retailers will want to analyze is taking place outside company-sponsored sites. The key is to "listen" and engage customers—and analyze their sentiments on a multitude of cyberspace social channels that are not directed to company-sponsored pages. The remainder of this chapter focuses on tools now available to effectively capture and analyze this data.

SOCIAL-MEDIA ANALYTICS

Retailers need to understand how customers feel about their brands, products, service, employees, and stores, and social media provides an excellent unfiltered source for gathering this information. The challenge lies in knowing where to look and then sifting through thousands of streams of conversation over a broad enough sample size and a significant enough time to give meaningful results. Social-media analysis—the term describing the software and services used to gain insight from social media—is designed to meet this challenge. Specifically, social-media analysis incorporates monitoring, measuring, and analyzing Internet-based social media, combining automated systems and human insight, and turning raw data into useful information. Mark Chaves, Director of Media Intelligence Solutions for SAS Institute, says, "Without the aid of intelligent software, it is impossible for humans to access, collect, and analyze data, gain insight, and then be able to act on this new information."[8]

Social-media analytical software solutions help companies discover conversations that are happening out in the social space that pertain to a retailer's brand, or perhaps to competitive brands that are also of interest. Social-media analytics software resembles Web site analytics software from a few years ago, but is designed specifically for the social-media space. These solutions are used to measure conversation, engagement, sentiment, influence, and other social-media-specific attributes, and are used specifically to monitor conversations on blogs, social networks, video views, ratings, and favorites on video-sharing networks, as well as an array of other activities on other social-media destinations. They can provide a wealth of information about such variables as the reach of a current message or which influencers to target. Most recently, social-media customer relationship management (CRM) systems also have entered this category; such software is used in blogger outreach and community outreach to manage relationships with key influencers.

In recent months, social-media analysis has evolved rapidly to provide retailers with timely, relevant, and actionable information about customer sentiment and other valuable data as expressed through social media. In fact, similar to what happened with Web analytics software in the early dot-com revolution, an entirely new technology industry has sprouted around social-media analytics. Various free online tools attempt to measure followers and influencers of particular topics, but these usually are geared to a particular social network such as Facebook or Twitter and lack the sophistication that most companies require. The past several years have seen the emergence of dozens of startup software and services companies designed to monitor and analyze online social media. Furthermore, in recent months, analytical leaders such as SAS[9] and IBM[10] have announced their entry into this market, both validating its legitimacy and offering their own robust, enterprise-ready, highly scalable solution offerings for analyzing social-media data.

Social-Media Analytics Go Mainstream

Retailers often began social-media programs by initially outsourcing them to marketing agencies that also performed monitoring services. While this is always an option, a number of companies are now looking to bring these efforts in-house for more control. When choosing social-media monitoring and analytics software and/or services, retailers now have a variety of choices. These include free online tools such as those offered by Google, as well as pay-for-play software and services from companies such as Attensity, Attentio, Buzzient, Clarabridge, Nielsen, Radian6, Scoutlabs, and Socialmention.

For larger retailers, with several thousand or more mentions per month, which need an enterprise-ready, highly scalable solution, offerings from mainstay analytical software leaders such as SAS and IBM also should be considered. These solutions are designed for companies to scale from smaller, entry-level analysis up to having the ability to collect, archive, and analyze vast amounts of social-media data over a period of several years; provide multilanguage support; and even quantify influence, forecast future volume of social-media conversations, and predict their impact on business results.[11] Retailers can then correlate key marketing metrics such as brand preference, Web traffic, online campaign effectiveness, and media mix.

The more sophisticated social-media analytics solutions integrate, analyze, and enable organizations to act on intelligence gleaned from online conversations occurring across professional and consumer-generated media sites (see Exhibit 12.1). This process enables organizations to attribute online conversations to specific parts of their business, allowing an accelerated response to shifts in the marketplace. The benefits of using social-media analytics are that they allow companies to:

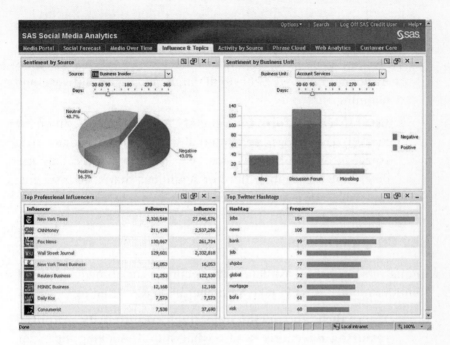

Exhibit 12.1 SAS® Social Media Analytics
Source: SAS Institute. Used with permission.

- **Analyze conversation data.** By continuously monitoring online and social conversation data, the software enables companies to identify important, relevant topics and content categories.

- **Identify advocates of, and threats to, corporate reputation and brand.** By analyzing professionally generated media (e.g., articles) and consumer-generated media (e.g., blogs), the software can serve as an early-warning system to identify influencers (good or bad) on a company and its brands.

- **Proactively make decisions by predicting future growth of conversations about their brand(s) on various social-media sites.** By identifying key conversations and forecasting future growth, companies can resolve issues before they snowball out of control.

- **Quantify interaction among traditional media/campaigns and social-media activity.** By analyzing online social-media sources, marketers can understand how to reach consumers through improved behavioral targeting, media buying, and planning.

- **Establish a platform for a social CRM strategy.** By merging market data (blogs) and internally generated customer data (surveys or Web forms), market research professionals can determine a consumer need or sentiment shared across a customer base or market.[12]

Key Considerations

In analyzing social-media data and selecting a social-media analytics solution, retailers should take a number of steps, including:

- **Tie analysis to specific objectives and identify potential resulting decisions.** Know what you are looking for in the data. For example, running a promotion on Facebook or Twitter, points to measuring the number of responses to that specific promotion code. Tracking customer sentiment about brand positioning, a new product launch, or a new fashion style, is more challenging. First, identify what key words or phrases constitute negative or positive sentiment. It's always important to gather enough data to make the results statistically significant. Announcing a new line of clothing, for example, posting sample outfits on Facebook, and asking customers what they think will elicit a host of comments, many of which will be anecdotal. The key is to determine the amount of data necessary to identify a trend in sentiment and what action, if any, needs to be taken as a result of that sentiment (e.g., for a new fashion line, if sentiment is overwhelmingly positive, a retailer may choose to expand orders; if negative, to discount the merchandise and no longer feature the line).

- **Make analysis an ongoing process, not a project.** For social-media analysis to be effective in identifying trends and possibly changing business processes as a result of those trends, data must be monitored not just at a particular point in time, but rather over a long enough period to capture trends.

■ **Categorize data accurately.** This process often is referred to in the world of social-media analytics as establishing a taxonomy that designates how to classify data that will be analyzed over time. For a retailer, often the best way to think of this categorization is through its merchandise, location, and customer hierarchies. For example, sometimes a retailer will receive overall customer feedback about the company ("I love Best Buy"). At other times, the feedback will be more specific to a brand or type of product ("I love that I can buy an iPad or an iPhone at Best Buy," or "Model number xyz is not a product that I would recommend because . . ."). Sometimes, the feedback may be about a particular store ("The Best Buy store at St. Johns Town Center gives outstanding service") or, in the service world, about a particular person ("Best Buy Geek Squad agent John Doe gave me outstanding service. I would highly recommend him!"). The point is to be able to automatically classify the data collected over time.

■ **Understand customer sentiment.** While there are other ways to measure the value of social media, important "sentiment" data often are contained within a stream of online conversations, or what is referred to as "unstructured text." Retailers need to be able to understand how customers feel about their brand and products, as well as about competitive offerings. Social-media analysis often includes sentiment-analysis software that helps measure customer response in online conversations. Sentiment analysis involves understanding the emotion, the tone, and the underlying message— positive, neutral, or negative—that is being conveyed in written text. The software allows retailers to analyze the words used in conversation on social media so that they can turn conversations into actionable information.

Sentiment-analysis software applications are being deployed by companies in all industries to monitor changes in customer attitudes as expressed in surveys, news feeds, and internal CRM systems, as well as online social networks, blogs, and customer forums. To identify overall sentiment about a brand, a product, or a service offering, a company must analyze abundant online streams of conversational data, retrieve relevant data, and gain practical insight that can be applied to real-world decisions. Because much online traffic about a particular brand may be expressed in multiple languages (a customer complaint written in Spanish or French is still a customer complaint), sentiment-analysis software also should be multilingual, enabling a company to identify sentiment, regardless of the native language.

■ **Determine the level of influence.** People become upset when someone attacks them and appreciate it when they are praised, but not all sentiments are created equal. In order to focus its efforts, it's most important for a retailer to determine the actual impact or "influence" of the individuals, blogs, or media sources that are spreading either positive or negative sentiment, and whether they are changing how others are talking about its brand, its products, and its service in the marketplace.

Sophisticated social-media analytics solutions can apply data-mining techniques and arrive at an "influencer score" to help detect the actual influence of people talking about a brand online. For example, in analyzing a user on Twitter, a retailer may want to look at what percentage of tweets that person sends on a particular topic and how often they are retweeted. Or, in the blogging world, a company needs to understand how many followers particular bloggers have and also whether they are influential.

■ **Understand sentiment over time.** A general view of the sentiment about a brand, product, or store at a particular point may be helpful in making a quick decision, such as fixing the lighting in a store when customers are complaining about its dull appearance; but to have sustainable value, accurately monitoring sentiment over time is vital. Take, for example, a retailer that makes proactive changes in response to negative sentiment about customer service. It is important for the retailer to then measure the impact that change has on customer sentiment.

The idea is to be able to look at customer sentiment on a particular topic over a long enough time to identify trends, causes, and effects of business decisions pertinent to that sentiment.

- **Predict future trends.** Over time, a retailer may detect significant growth in the level of conversation about its business on social channels. Applying predictive analytics to forecast the future volume of social-media conversations and help predict their impact can be valuable to a business. Predictive software allows a retailer to become proactive and make decisions before small issues spread across the digital airwaves and become much bigger ones. According to an April 2010 *InformationWeek* article, "This helps companies allocate resources, create 'what-if' scenarios and correlate marketing metrics such as brand preference, Web traffic, online campaign effectiveness and media mix."[13] Exhibit 12.2 depicts a sample screenshot of

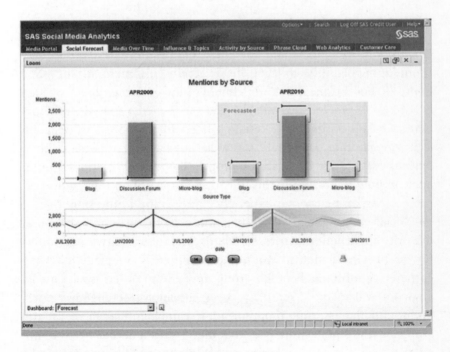

Exhibit 12.2 SAS® Social Media Analytics: Social Forecast
Source: SAS Institute. Used with permission.

social-media analytics, showing both current and forecasted future volume of topic mentions on various social forums.

- **Institute scalability.** Thanks to the social-media phenomenon, the amount of data that companies have to process has grown exponentially. Cyberspace sites can generate tens of thousands of comments per day about a retailer's business, and these comments should be analyzed. Furthermore, in addition to the sheer volume of social conversation, the amount of related data is further increased because a conversation consists of "unstructured text," meaning that the entire conversation frequently needs to be collected and analyzed to determine the context or sentiment being conveyed. To make sense of the data, companies must first process the data, filtering out a lot of noise, in a period as close to real time as possible. This requirement means that processor speed and data storage must be highly scalable.

INSIGHTS TO ACTION

Because of social media and analytics, retailers now have an unprecedented opportunity to "get inside their customers' heads" and improve their businesses. The richness of the customer data provided is unlike any previously available, and social-media analytics are now here. Chaves comments: "Retailers need to develop a strategy for capturing, storing, and analyzing social-media data to enhance their businesses. At SAS, we're seeing progressive retailers asking for guidance on how to best apply this new insight toward improving pricing, promotions, and customer experience online and in the store."

Social-media analytics are beginning to mature, and with that maturity come better metrics, standards, and robust software solutions for quantifying benefits. Much like other areas of retail that have garnered enormous benefits from applied analytics, social-media analytics will follow a maturity curve similar to merchandise price, promotion and assortment optimization, campaign management, and Web analytics—all technologies that didn't exist a decade ago, but are now critical competitive weapons for many retailers. Social-media analysis and the accompanying technology are gaining wide acceptance, and certain software and service providers with retail-specific expertise can assist a company in embarking on such a program.

No book can possibly cover all the elements that should be analyzed, or identify all the various software and service providers, along with their specific areas of expertise. The key is for retailers to recognize that experts *are* available to help with this process, and that thanks to social-media analytics, companies now possess the ability to properly analyze vast amounts of social-media data and make the data part of their ongoing business processes. Doing so will allow the company not only to listen to customers and engage with them, but also to use relevant feedback in turning insights into action.

NOTES

1. www.nrf.com (accessed June 17, 2010).
2. www.rila.org (accessed June 17, 2010).
3. www.retailconnections.biz (accessed June 17, 2010).
4. www.internetretailer.com (accessed June 17, 2010).
5. www.restaurant.org (accessed June 17, 2010).
6. www.fmi.org (accessed June 17, 2010).
7. Survey: Social Software in Business, conducted by Mzinga and Babson Executive Education, September 2009, available at www.mzinga.com/d_l/pdf/mzingababson-socialsoftwaresurvey.pdf, page 6 (accessed June 16, 2010).
8. Interview with Mark Chaves, conducted at SAS Global Forum Conference, April 12, 2010. All subsequent quotes from Chaves are from this interview.
9. Very Official Blog, "Social Media Integration Means Business," Shannon Paul, April 12, 2010, available at http://veryofficialblog.com/2010/04/12/sas-social-media-analytics-product-launch-initial-thoughts/ (accessed June 16, 2010).
10. "IBM Debuts New Social Media Analytics Tool," Mashable Social Media, May 11, 2010, available at http://mashable.com/2010/05/11/ibm-social-media-analytics-tool/ (accessed June 16, 2010).
11. "Conversations and Connections. Social Media at SAS," David Thomas, April 12, 2010, available at http://blogs.sas.com/socialmedia/index.php?/archives/90-SAS-Global-Forum-SAS-Social-Media-Analytics-launch.html (accessed June 16, 2010).

12. "SAS® Social Media Analytics, Integrate, Analyze and Act on Online Conversations," available at www.sas.com/software/customer-intelligence/social-media-analytics/#section=1 (accessed June 16, 2010).

13. "SAS Offers Social Media Analytics Service," *InformationWeek*, Doug Henschen, April 13, 2010, available at www.informationweek.com/news/hardware/utility_ondemand/showArticle.jhtml?articleID=224400121 (accessed June 16, 2010).

13

Conclusion:
Take the Lead

I nnovative leadership. Open culture. Digital customer engagement—
all are attributes of the eight companies we've highlighted in this
book. These retailers differ greatly in size, age, geographical presence, and industry segment, but their strategies consistently capture
the new world of bringing the store to the customer. We thoroughly
enjoyed interacting with these companies and offering our perspectives on how social media and mobility are affecting retailers' customer engagement and brand equity. These two new channels are
forever changing the way retailers and consumer products companies
interact with their customers. Because of this reality, we will continue
to keep abreast of this rapidly changing technology, closely following
and interacting with these and other leading retailers as they advance
in this new world.

The digital transformation occurring since the arrival of Web 2.0
and smart phones is moving at lightning speed, and the storm has just
begun. Technology companies that didn't even exist a few years ago
are now market leaders. Facebook, which now seems omnipresent,
just celebrated its sixth birthday and is so young that Microsoft Word's

spell checker doesn't even recognize it as a real word—and Microsoft is an investor in Facebook! If Facebook were a country, it would already be the world's third largest, with a population of approximately 500 million and growing.[1] The iPhone, in a matter of months, has ushered in a whole new generation of smart phones that customers have enthusiastically embraced. When the iPhone 4 went on sale for preordering in June 2010, the massive surge in demand from more than 13 million consumers caused Apple's Web site to crash, creating a "high-grade problem."[2] The Google Android is further fueling the smart phone market. While feature phones are still in the hands of hundreds of millions of consumers, we predict that—following a typical technology pattern—the smart phone eventually will become available at lower prices, and connectivity between retailers and consumers will grow even faster.

This intersection of retailers, technology, and customers has created vast opportunities for all. The confluence of the consumer and the retailer embracing technology will forever change the way commerce is conducted. Equally important, social media brings with it sentiment, behavioral, and other valuable customer data not previously available. Through the use of social-media analytics tools, retailers can now sift through volumes of unstructured data to listen to ongoing conversations, identify trends, quantify results, and determine appropriate actions. Enterprise-ready social-media analytical tools now exist.

Many of you may think: "I have heard the revolution or transformation message before." It was the message of the World Wide Web in the 1990s, which took longer than predicted to affect retail. The important point, however, is that social media and mobility have profoundly changed how retailers and consumers communicate and do business. Consider the developments that have occurred since the first days of the Web, and think about what they mean to us now. The current digital transformation differs from the characteristics of the initial Web. Customers are leading this time. The technology is here, progressive retailers are utilizing it, and customers are tangibly benefiting from it. We are not talking about an extension of the Web, but about bringing the store to the customer, wherever the customer may be, and that development is unprecedented.

As authors, we have different primary business experiences, career timeframes, and points of view, yet we have arrived at the same conclusion about this digital transformation. We know that you, our readers, represent varying backgrounds and experiences, and that diversity can create objective dialogue. We also understand that a transformation of this magnitude cannot occur without an open culture. We believe that it is critically important to foster an open culture within retailers, and to invite associates to play a role in driving this customer-focused digital transformation. Regardless of your role in retail or consumer products, you have an opportunity to lead this transformation and to gain market share through the intelligent use of digital communication. An open culture has enabled several retailers to take the lead in this historic advancement in the retail industry—and that is very exciting! In a sense, it is ironic that we discuss this new world of technological interaction in a traditional, printed book, and we contemplate a future publication in the form of a digitally interactive Wiki. In the interim, we welcome the opportunity to interact with you through Twitter, Facebook, and email. We invite you to engage with us in discussing the retail industry and the digital world, for we all can benefit from a continuing dialogue. In a fast-moving world, everything is subject to rapid change—and it will never move back, only forward—so continuing dialogue is critical. Thank you, and please let us hear from you.

Bernie Brennan
Twitter: @bfbrennan
Facebook: Bernie Brennan
Email: bfbrennan@comcast.net

Lori Schafer
Twitter: @ljschafer
Facebook: Lori.j.schafer
Email: lorischafer@comcast.net

NOTES

1. "Facebook: 3rd Largest Country in the World and Still Growing," A New Decade, a New FP, Mike Sottak, February 12, 2010, available at www.tcfreepress.com/index.php?option=com_content&view=article&id=

1226:facebook–3rd-largest-country-in-the-world-and-still-growing&
catid=15:business-news&Itemid=32 (accessed June 16, 2010).

2. "Apple Website Crashes as New iPhone 4 Goes on Sale for Pre-orders,"
   Daily Mail Reporter, June 15, 2010, available at www.dailymail.co.uk/
   sciencetech/article-1286756/Apple-iPhone-4-pre-order-Website-crashes-
   new-iPhone-goes-sale.html#ixzz0rKw1Duqz (accessed June 19, 2010).

Index